D1557092

THE KURDISH QUESTION
AND TURKEY

THE KURDISH QUESTION AND TURKEY:

An Example of a Trans-state Ethnic Conflict

KEMAL KİRİŞCİ

and

GARETH M. WINROW

Department of Political Science and International Relations,
Boğaziçi University, Istanbul, Turkey

FRANK CASS

LONDON • PORTLAND, OR

First Published in 1997 in Great Britain by
FRANK CASS & CO. LTD.
Newbury House, 900 Eastern Avenue
London IG2 7HH

and in the United States of America by
FRANK CASS
c/o ISBS, 5804 N.E. Hassalo Street
Portland, Oregon 97213-3644

British Library Cataloguing in Publication Data:

A catalogue record for this book is available from the British Library

ISBN 0-7146-4746-2 (cloth)
ISBN 0-7146-4304-1 (paper)

Library of Congress Cataloging-in-Publication Data:

A catalog record for this book is available from the Library of Congress

Typeset by Vitaset, Paddock Wood, Kent
Printed in Great Britain by
Bookcraft (Bath) Ltd, Midsomer Norton, Avon

Contents

List of Tables

Preface

As always with books dealing with current issues, since the completion of the original text a number of significant developments have occurred concerning Turkey and the Kurdish question. The failure of the ANAP–DYP coalition to form a stable government led to the formation in summer 1996 of another coalition of the RP and DYP. Necmettin Erbakan, the head of the RP, became the first Islamist Prime Minister of Turkey. Commentators speculated whether Erbakan would appeal to Islamic solidarity to attempt to reach a peaceful solution to the Kurdish question in Turkey.

The Erbakan government in July 1996 extended the mandate of Operation PROVIDE COMFORT – the allied air force based in Turkey which, in theory, aimed to protect the Kurds in northern Iraq from attack by the Baghdad regime – for another five months. Previously, RP deputies had voted against prolonging the mandate and, indeed, Erbakan had promised his constituency that he would disband the Operation. The Erbakan government endeavoured to justify this volte-face by arguing that various concessions had been wrung from the Americans, the British and the French. Most importantly, the US administration announced that it had no intention of violating Iraq's territorial integrity or of undermining Turkey's security. The new government in Ankara failed to secure the transfer of Operation PROVIDE COMFORT's Military Coordination Centre from Zakho in northern Iraq to Silopi in Turkey. Some Turkish officials believed that the presence of the Centre in northern Iraq was encouraging the formation of a Kurdish state. The US administration insisted that the Centre should remain in northern Iraq to demonstrate to Saddam Hussein that the US had a firm interest in the area. In August 1996 the Centre had to be relocated to Turkey after Saddam's forces supported Barzani's KDP in an assault against their northern Iraqi rivals, the PUK, led by Talabani.

In the face of opposition from the military, President Demirel and other political parties, including the RP's coalition partner the DYP, Erbakan appeared to backtrack from an initial interest in developing an indirect dialogue with the PKK. The RP had also prepared a package of measures for south-eastern Turkey. The package referred to the lifting of restrictions on Kurdish radio and television, and encouraged the development of Kurdish language and culture. Emergency rule would only continue in four border provinces until the area was fully pacified. The village guard system would be abolished and a partial amnesty would come into effect for those who had harboured terrorists. Public resources would be mobilized and private sector involvement encouraged to improve the economy of the region. Most significantly, according to the terms of the package, the problem of terrorism would be separated from the problems of south-eastern Turkey in general. The struggle against terrorism would continue unabated. However, under pressure from the DYP and from the National Security Council, most of these measures were eventually dropped from the government programme presented to Parliament. Only those measures concerned with tightening security remained.

Before the Erbakan government had assumed office the second General Congress of HADEP – the pro-Kurdish political party in Turkey – was convened, in late June 1996. A number of HADEP deputies were arrested, including the party's General Secretary Murat Bozlak, after the Turkish flag was torn down and a PKK flag unfurled together with a portrait of the PKK leader Öcalan when Bozlak was addressing the Congress. Some analysts argued that this was a deliberate provocation aimed at discrediting HADEP. The party faced the prospect of closure with the opening of a trial against Bozlak and his associates on the charge that HADEP was, in effect, a legal front for the PKK. In a nationwide outburst of patriotism, Turkish flags were displayed from offices, shops and homes for several days after the incident. The ex-DEP – the DEP is a previously banned pro-Kurdish political party in Turkey – deputy Sırrı Sakık was arrested for comments he made on a private television channel after the Congress, apparently declaring that people who ask for respect for their flag should show the same respect for the flag of others. This remark was interpreted as promoting separatism and thus against Article 8 of the Anti-terror Law.

Earlier, in April 1996, the State Security Court retried, on the basis of the amended Anti-terror Law, the former Kurdish deputies Sakık, Ahmet Türk and Sedat Yurttaş, and independent deputy Mahmut Alınak. They were each to be sentenced to one year and two months' imprisonment and fined. In September 1996 an appeal court would uphold these convictions. Earlier, in July 1996, the European Commission of Human Rights decided to pass the case of all of the imprisoned ex-DEP deputies against the Turkish government to the European Court of Human Rights. The Commission ruled that Turkey had violated certain provisions of the European Convention on Human Rights with regard to periods of detention. And in September 1996 the European Court of Human Rights, for the first time in a case involving Kurds in Turkey, condemned the government in Ankara for violating the Convention with regard to the destruction of a village in south-eastern Turkey. The Turkish Foreign Ministry complained that recourse should have first been made by the plaintiff to Turkish courts, according to the usual practice.

The authorities in Ankara are still being pressed to seek a peaceful, political solution to the Kurdish question in Turkey. In April 1996 the Hungarian Socialist Party deputy, Andreas Barsony, presented a report to the Council of Europe Parliamentary Assembly. This report advocated the repeal of Article 8 of the Anti-terror Law, called for a general amnesty in Turkey, and referred to a previous resolution which had urged the establishment of a 'watch process' to monitor human rights issues in Turkey. In June 1996, in a non-binding resolution, the European Parliament pressed Turkey to end its violent campaign against Kurdish separatists, clean up its human rights record, and open negotiations with all Kurdish organizations. The European Parliament recommended that the EU Council of Ministers should challenge Turkey's record on the Kurdish question by making use of the OSCE. Then, noting that little had been achieved with regard to human rights, in October 1996 the Parliament voted to freeze EU aid to Turkey which was to be used to implement the Turkey–EU Customs Union agreement. A review of the funding Turkey was to receive from the EU's Mediterranean Development Aid programme was also recommended. In July 1996 the fifth annual session of the OSCE Parliamentary Assembly in Stockholm endorsed an advisory resolution critical of the policies of the PKK and the Turkish government. Ankara was encouraged 'to establish consultative mechanisms with non-violent Kurdish-based organizations which recognize the territorial integrity of Turkey'.

In the wider regional context, by August 1996 the fragile ceasefire, brokered originally by the US between the rival northern Iraqi Kurdish parties, had collapsed. After accusing the PUK of obtaining support from Iran the KDP in a Baghdad-backed operation gained control over most of northern Iraq. In October the PUK regained control over territory traditionally under its influence. Turkey was able to re-establish some authority in northern Iraq when talks between the two warring Kurdish parties were held in Ankara with American and British participation. A ceasefire was announced in November. At the time of writing it was not clear whether the ceasefire would hold. The KDP and PUK tentatively agreed to crack down on the activities of the PKK in northern Iraq. It was envisaged that Turkey, the United States and Britain would play a prominent role in monitoring the ceasefire.

The Erbakan government is seeking to improve relations with Iran, Iraq and Syria. In August 1996 Erbakan himself visited Iran and concluded an important natural gas agreement. Ministerial contacts with Iraq have developed. Turkey is hoping to benefit from the so-called 'oil for food' deal. On 8 August 1996 the UN Sanctions Committee formally approved the procedure to implement this deal on the basis of UN Security Council resolution 986 of April 1995, allowing Iraq to sell two billion dollars worth of oil every six months on a renewable basis in order to finance the humanitarian needs of the Iraqi people, including the Kurds in northern Iraq. Here, Turkey hopes to buy oil and sell food and medicine. However, the implementation of this deal was placed on hold after Saddam Hussein's forces moved into northern Iraq in August 1996 to support the KDP.

The US administration has expressed its concern at Erbakan's policy in the region. The natural gas deal with Iran was concluded immediately after Clinton had approved an Act which stated that sanctions could be applied against any foreign company which invested substantial sums in the oil or gas industry of Iran and Libya. Concerning Libya, it should be noted that when Erbakan visited there in October 1996 Ghadafi had publicly remarked that the Kurds deserved a state of their own. Erbakan had not responded at the time. This precipitated a government crisis in Ankara. The opposition parties called for a motion of censure which was subsequently defeated.

It is not possible to predict future developments concerning the Kurdish question in Turkey and in the region as a whole. It remains to be seen whether an RP-led government will be able to tackle this question more effectively than previous Turkish governments.

November 1996

Acknowledgements

This book is the product of research that started in late 1993 and was made possible by a generous United States Institute of Peace (USIP) grant. This grant enabled us to do a content analysis of Turkish and Kurdish newspapers. The grant also made it possible to travel within and outside Turkey to interview various officials, academics, political activists and members of the public. We are grateful to Ismail Kaplan and Boğaç Erozan who worked for us as research assistants. Mete Tunçay and Zafer Toprak, two prominent historians, gave moral support and guidance, which enabled us to reconstruct the details of late Ottoman and early Turkish Republican history with regard to the Kurdish question. Ali Çarkoğlu, a friend and colleague from our Department, kindly allowed us to use his data set for the 1995 national elections.

Many others have helped and supported us during the last three years. Space precludes us from naming them all individually, but there are some to whom we must convey our special thanks. To Sencer Ayata (Middle East Technical University, Ankara) for discussing and sharing some of our arguments; to officials of the Anatolian Development Foundation and the Turkish branch of the Helsinki Citizens Assembly who made it possible for us to travel and talk freely to many people in the cities, towns and villages of the provinces of Hakkari and Van in eastern Turkey; to the Boğaziçi University Library for their help; to the personnel of the American Library in Istanbul for allowing us the generous and friendly use of their facilities; to our students for their patience and forbearance; to Andrew Mango and Sylvia Kedourie for the careful reading and assessment of the original manuscript; and finally to Candan, Nazan and Marc Sinan for their attention, moral support and understanding, without which this research could not have been completed. We dedicate this book to them.

List of Abbreviations

ANAP   (Anavatan Partisi) Motherland Party
AP   (Adalet Partisi) Justice Party
CHP   (Cumhuriyet Halk Partisi) Republican People's Party
CSCE   Conference on Security and Co-operation in Europe
CUP   Committee of Union and Progress
DDP   (Demokratik Değişim Partisi) Democracy and Change Party
DEP   (Demokrasi Partisi) Democracy Party
DIE   (Devlet İstatistik Enstitüsü) State Statistics Institute
DP   (Demokrat Parti) Democratic Party
DSP   (Demokratik Sol Parti) Democratic Left Party
DYP   (Doğru Yol Partisi) True Path Party
ECHR   European Convention for the Protection of Human Rights and
        Fundamental Freedoms
ETA   (Euskadi ta Askatasuna) Euskadi and Freedom
GAP   (Güney Doğu Anadolu Projesi) South-East Anatolia
        Development Project
GP   (Güven Partisi) Reliance Party
HADEP   (Halkın Demokrasi Partisi) People's Democracy Party
HCA   Helsinki Citizens Assembly
HEP   (Halkın Emek Partisi) People's Labour Party
IHD   (İnsan Hakları Derneği) Turkish Human Rights Association
IHV   (İnsan Hakları Vakfı) Turkish Human Rights Foundation
KDP   Kurdistan Democratic Party
KKP   (Kürdistan Komünist Partisi) Kurdistan Communist Party
KSP   (Kürdistan Sosyalist Partisi) Kurdistan Socialist Party
MHP   (Milliyetçi Hareket Partisi) Nationalist Action Party
NSC   National Security Council (of Turkey)
OSCE   Organization of Security and Co-operation in Europe
ÖZDEP   (Özgürlük ve Demokrasi Partisi) Freedom and Democracy Party
PKK   (Partia Karkaren Kürdistan) Kurdistan Workers' Party
PNV   (Partido Nacionalista Vasco) Basque Nationalist Party
PUK   Patriotic Union of Kurdistan
RP   (Refah Partisi) Welfare Party

SDRA-R	Society for the Defence of Rights of Anatolia and Rumelia
SHP	(Sosyal Demokrat Halkçı Parti) Social Democratic Populist Party
TBMM	(Türkiye Büyük Millet Meclisi) Turkish Grand National Assembly
TC	(Türkiye Cumhuriyeti) Turkish Republic
TİP	(Türkiye İşçi Partisi) Turkish Workers' Party
TOBB	(Türkiye Odalar ve Borsalar Birliği) Turkish Chamber of Commerce and Commodity Exchanges
UN	United Nations
YDH	(Yeni Demokrasi Hareketi) New Democracy Movement
YTP	(Yeni Türkiye Partisi) New Turkey Party

1

Introduction

THE TURKISH authorities have been engaged in a fierce struggle against insurgents of the PKK (Kurdistan Workers' Party) in south-eastern Turkey. Villages have been evacuated or destroyed as innocent Kurdish civilians are caught in the cross-fire between the assaults of the PKK and the Turkish security forces. Sporadic acts of terrorism have targeted urban centres and tourist sites in other parts of the country. The PKK has been able to operate out of bases located in neighbouring Iran and Iraq where large Kurdish communities also live. Seeking to destroy the PKK's network of bases in Iraq in March 1995, the Turkish armed forces launched the largest assault hitherto against the Kurdish insurgents in northern Iraq. This was followed up a few months later by a smaller scale Turkish operation in northern Iraq. The PKK's declaration of a unilateral ceasefire in December 1995 had little impact on the course of events.

The resolution of what one may call here a trans-state ethnic conflict between the Turkish government and Kurdish elements – the conflict is not confined within the borders of Turkey – will not be achieved without serious difficulties, given developments since the foundation of the Turkish Republic in 1923. Most Turkish officials are aware that a peaceful solution of the Kurdish question in Turkey would improve Turkey's image abroad and would, for example, improve prospects for Turkish admission into the EU as a full member.

The official line of Turkish governments has been to deny the existence of a Kurdish minority let alone a separate Kurdish nation in Turkey. Indeed, only in recent years have certain leading Turkish politicians acknowledged the existence of a Kurdish 'reality' in Turkey. The Treaty of Lausanne of 1923 had referred only to the presence of non-Moslem minorities – Armenians, Greeks and Jews – within Turkey. According to the *millet* system of the Ottoman Empire, non-Moslem communities were allowed a measure of self-government, but the Moslem inhabitants were considered to be united as members of the 'nation of Islam' and were thus subjects of the Sultan who was also their Caliph. The Kurds, along with the Albanians, Arabs, Bosnians, Circassians, Laz, Pomaks, Tatars and Turks, were grouped together within the single nation of Islam. Today, the Turkish authorities are prepared to acknowledge the existence of people of Kurdish origin who as citizens of Turkey enjoy, or should enjoy, the full rights of Turkish citizenship. Accordingly, it is argued in official circles that there is no need for the people of Kurdish origin to press for the recognition of a Kurdish minority and the granting of minority rights since full rights are already bestowed upon them as citizens of Turkey. In the opinion of some officials in Ankara, there is not a Kurdish issue or problem *per se*. Rather, the problem is solely one of PKK-sponsored terrorism.

In February 1995 a state security court in Ankara passed an important ruling in a lawsuit against Yavuz Önen, Chairman of the Turkish Human Rights Foundation (IHV), and Fevzi Argun, a member of the executive board of the foundation. Both were tried on charges of spreading separatist propaganda in a booklet entitled *Torture File*. The ruling noted that the phrase 'Kurdish people' did not come under the crime of spreading separatist propaganda and thus was not against Article 8 paragraph 1 of the Anti-terror Law of Turkey.[1] This article was revised in October 1995. The Turkish authorities were hence prepared to tolerate the expression and the notion of a 'Kurdish people'. An acknowledgement of the Kurdish 'reality' was clearly in evidence.

As well as addressing the question of what does it mean to be a Kurd, one should also attempt to come to terms with the related question of what does it mean to be a Turk. One of Mustafa Kemal 'Atatürk''s most famous phrases was '*Ne mutlu Türküm diyene*' – 'Happy is one who can say one is a Turk'. Schools throughout Turkey proudly carry an inscription of this phrase. The hillsides of south-eastern Turkey are also marked out with the words in bold letters. It was particularly interesting and striking, therefore, when in early January 1995 the Turkish Prime Minister Tansu Çiller in a speech at Karabük declared, 'Happy is one who can say one is a citizen of Turkey'.[2] The implication here was that the importance of common citizenship had not been adequately stressed in the past with reference to the designation 'Turk'. What did Mustafa Kemal exactly mean when he referred to a Turk? Was a specific ethnic group, an ethnic group of the Turks, actually implied? Or was the term 'Turk' meant to be an all-embracing and inclusive one where if someone said he/she was a Turk then that person was indeed a Turk? This, of course, left open the question of how to react when individuals in the new Turkish Republic did not perceive themselves as Turks. How have other officials in the Turkish Republic interpreted the term Turk?

Significantly, President Süleyman Demirel in his end of year press conference in late December 1994 stated that the constitutions of the Turkish Republic did not specify origin, belief or language as the basis for citizenship or 'national belonging'. Membership of the Turkish nation merely entailed that one must be a Turkish citizen.[3] Therefore a Turk was anyone who was a citizen of Turkey. Hence, in practice, the term 'Kurdish Turks' was permissible, i.e., referring to a people of a different origin who were currently citizens of Turkey. On the other hand, the term 'Turkish Kurd', with its emphasis on Kurdishness as opposed to Turkishness would be much more problematic for the authorities in Ankara.

The Kurdish question, and more specifically relations between the Turkish government and the Kurds in Turkey are topics which are increasingly attracting the interest of Western scholars and commentators. Many of these analyses develop a position sympathetic to the Kurds and hostile to the policies of the Turkish state. There is a tendency here though to examine the Turks, the Kurds and the Turkish state as monolithic entities. Often there is little attempt among analysts, including those within Turkey, to differentiate between the aims and objectives of Turkish and Kurdish elites in Turkey and the views and opinions of the Turkish and Kurdish masses. Indeed, identifying individuals within Turkey who perceive themselves as Kurds is no easy matter. Some people may identify themselves as being both Turk and Kurd. The views and opinions of individuals are also subject to change over time. Moreover, the lifestyle and values of a Kurd living in Istanbul may be in stark contrast to the attitudes and way of life of a Kurd working on the land in south-eastern Turkey. And in that area there are divisions between Kurdish groupings often along tribal lines.

The Kurds have been labelled a 'stateless nation', a 'people without a country', and are referred to as the largest national group in the Middle East without a state.[4] Along with the Basques, Sikhs and Tamils, for example, the Kurds have been listed as an example of an 'ethnonationalist movement' or 'proto-nation'. Proto-nations have been depicted as 'nations without a state' which are seeking to establish their own state.[5] But what is a nation in the first place? And do nations actually establish states? It would seem that the role of key individuals and elites within certain ethnic groups is in fact crucial.

Focusing on the specific case of Turkey and the Kurdish question, one should avoid the ambiguous use of such terms as 'proto-nation' and 'stateless nation'. The conceptual tools at our disposal, such as, for instance, 'nation' and 'ethnic group', do not adequately convey the sense of identity or multiple forms of identity that individuals and groups within a population may hold. The term 'nation' in particular is politically loaded. Liberal use of this term by scholars, journalists, commentators and the like may aggravate what may probably already be tense relations between the central authorities of a state and a section of the population which may perceive themselves as having a separate identity. Tensions could further escalate if politicians elsewhere are thereby encouraged to take up the cause of the supposed nation or ethnic group in question.

In the case of Turkey and the Kurds, it will also be seen that single-factor or mono-causal explanations do not enable one to comprehend fully what are in effect highly complex processes of state-building and nation-building. Taking into account the on-going and violent conflict between the Turkish state and elements of the Kurdish population, and given the seemingly intractable nature of this trans-state ethnic conflict, it is admittedly no easy task to avoid passing value judgements and to remain unaffected by deep-rooted and longstanding popular prejudices prevalent within Turkey and beyond.

Originally, modernization and social mobilization theories argued that improvements in communications and transportation and the development of mass education and literacy programmes together with increased urbanization within states would lead to more intense contacts between population groups whose separate ethnic identities would in effect wither away.[6] In practice, the reverse could take place. The processes involved in modernization may threaten the continued existence of separate ethnic groups which could no longer remain isolated and which may at the same time be made more aware of the differences between themselves and other ethnic groups within the same state.[7] Members of these threatened ethnic groups, particularly privileged elites, as in the case of the Shaikh Said rebellion in Turkey, could feel that their culture was under attack from the state. These groups may perceive the state as identifying itself with the interests of a majority/dominant ethnic group/nation.

Certainly, beginning in the 1960s groups such as the Bretons, Catalans, Basques and French Canadians have been striving for autonomy within their states and have even pushed for secession. With the crumbling of communism in eastern Europe and the disintegration of Yugoslavia and the former Soviet Union, the issues of nationalism and ethnicity are likely to remain a prominent feature of European politics for the foreseeable future. Many Marxists had believed that the advent of socialism would lead to the disappearance of ethnic consciousness and the tensions and conflict associated with it. The international community's heightened interest in recent years on the question of the right of self-determination as a basic one of all peoples, and the increased concerns of human rights organizations to monitor and attempt to prevent the discrimination and repression of ethnic groups by particular regimes, are also likely to encourage the ethnic mobilization of what were previously 'quiescent communities'.[8]

Problems associated with nationalism and ethnicity with reference to Turkey and the Kurdish question are not likely to disappear in the short to medium term. The future prospects for the Kurds within Turkey could be viewed in line with three possible options: 'exit', 'voice' or 'loyalty', to employ Gurr's use of Hirschman's original terms.[9] 'Exit' would entail ultimate secession. 'Voice' could consist of protests aimed at improving conditions for the Kurds within Turkey. With regard to 'loyalty', the Kurds would not question the political system within Turkey but would seek to improve their lot by making use of opportunities provided within the Turkish polity. However, different elements within the Kurdish population in Turkey, assuming that they were aware of their identity in the first place, could be pursuing each of these three options simultaneously. The three options are also not necessarily mutually exclusive. Certainly groups professing 'loyalty' could also be demanding a greater 'voice' in the running of affairs in the state. Within each option there are also various permutations possible.

What Is a Nation? What Is an Ethnic Group?

There has been a debate over whether more emphasis should be given to subjective or objective criteria in defining a nation. According to one argument, the members of a nation must feel bound by a sense of solidarity, common culture and national consciousness.[10] Self-awareness and self-perception are key determinants. If a particular identity means nothing to a particular population, then that population does not have that identity.[11] However, there is a problem of identifying which self-aware community should be regarded as a nation and which should be regarded as another form of grouping, club, association or whatever. It would seem that other criteria are required to help to instill a feeling of national consciousness. Furthermore, how many members of a particular community need to feel that they are a nation before this nation is said to exist? Do a majority of members need to be self-aware, or do only a small number of leaders within a particular community need to perceive themselves as a nation?

What objective criteria would be necessary for a nation? A certain territory, and shared language, religion, culture and a common descent are some characteristics which come to mind. Smith has defined a nation as '… a named human population sharing an historic territory, common myths and historical memories, a mass public culture, a common economy and common legal rights and duties for all members'.[12] A combination of objective and subjective elements may be employed to define a nation. For example, Gurr has noted: 'The key to identifying communal groups is not the presence of a particular trait or combination of traits, but rather the shared perception that the defining traits, whatever they are, set the group apart'.[13] Although he was referring to a much broader category, a 'communal group', Gurr's assertion is also relevant for the identification of a nation. Again, though, how many and which members of a nation should perceive these defining traits?

There is also a difference of opinion concerning the relative importance of a nation being self-defined or rather 'other-defined'. Clearly, any self-defined group needs to be self-aware.[14] A group is other-defined when it is perceived as a group by an authority. Tilly has stated: 'A connected set of people qualify as a nation when they receive (whether willingly or not) some authorities' certification of distinctiveness in origin and culture sufficient to justify separate treatment with respect to rights and obligations of citizen-

ship.'[15] However, even though a nation may have certain objective characteristics and may have a degree of self-awareness, according to Tilly recognition
and hence certification would come about only through a group providing a
convincing demonstration that it merits the title nation.[16]

The relevance of 'other-definition' must be taken into account in attempting to differentiate a nation from other groupings. One may argue that for a
nation to exist it should be other-defined by the government of the state
whose territory the nation inhabits, or by the governments of other states.
Recognition of a nation by scholars and journalists, for example, would mean
little in practice without this official sanctioning, although, of course, scholars
and journalists may encourage politicians to acknowledge new identities.
Indeed, in the case of the Ottoman Empire and the question of Turkish
identity, it was outside scholars and historians together with Pan-Turkic
thinkers who referred to the largest ethnic group within the Ottoman Empire
as Turks when the Turks themselves were only aware of a Moslem identity.
This 'other-labelling' as it were – although not an official other-definition –
did play a part in encouraging much of the elite of the newly-founded Turkish
Republic to call itself Turkish and appeal to a Turkish nation.

In short, self-definition is not enough for a nation to be said to exist,
although in almost all cases the national awareness of a group is required for
an official authority to recognize that group's nationhood. One relevant
exception to this rule discussed later appears to be the case of the Kurds with
reference to the provisions of the Treaty of Sèvres of 1920, although in this
specific instance the international politics of the immediate post-First World
War period must also be considered. Recognition of nations is much more
problematic than recognition of states. One could argue a case that recognition
of nationhood by the government of only one state – perhaps the host state
but not necessarily – would be enough to meet the requirements of other-
definition. However, the issue is clearly a controversial one as this line of
argument leads inexorably to the thorny issue of self-determination and the
recognition of 'peoples' and their possible right to statehood.

Other scholars, stressing the relevance of the self-definition of a nation,
have contended that a nation is imagined, invented or reconstructed. A nation
has been depicted as an 'imagined political community' that has emerged
with the development of print capitalism which hastened the spread of
vernacular languages.[17] Another related approach has conceived of the nation
as an 'invention of tradition' where there is normally an attempt to establish
continuity with a 'suitable historic past'.[18] And again, a nation is defined as
an artifact, a product of nationalism, which is itself the product of particular
economic and social circumstances connected with the emergence of
industrial societies. Industrialization provides conditions ripe for the creation
of a nation. And by providing a 'common high culture', linked with homo-
geneity in the education system, a nation is necessary for economic growth.[19]

Each of these views stresses that a nation is constructed by certain elites. The masses appear almost to accept passively the engineering of nations by these elites. But in one criticism of these approaches Smith has argued that the creation of a nation actually involves the reconstruction of a past with which the masses (or a large portion of them?) must be able to identify.[20] Elite manipulation has its limits.

Smith has differentiated a so-called Western 'civic' model of a nation from a non-Western 'ethnic' model. The former is based on historic territory, a legal-political community with legal-political equality of its members, a common civic culture and shared ideology. The last, according to Smith, stresses the significance of birth, common descent, genealogy, popular mobilization, vernacular languages, customs and traditions.[21] It has been suggested that civic nationalisms are normally features of well-institutionalized democracies, whereas ethnic nationalisms appear where there is an institutional vacuum, or when existing institutions are not satisfying basic needs and no alternative structures are readily available.[22] One should note, though, that Smith admitted that all nationalisms contain civic and ethnic elements in varying proportions.[23] He also contended that all nations, including civic nations, needed 'ethnic cores' to survive.[24]

Are other ethnic groups and even other nations able to flourish within the same state where a nation – which in the case of two or more nations within the same state would be the dominant nation – has as its ethnic core another distinct ethnic group? Will leading members of a nation or dominant nation insist on the assimilation or integration of these other ethnic groups or nations? Or is it the aim of a civic model of nationalism to create a 'political community' following the example of, for instance, Switzerland? It has been argued that in the case of ethnically-divided states, for a political community to form there must be a 'transcending bond of national unity'. This, in turn, suggests the existence of 'an inclusive code of political understanding, a shared political culture, common respected symbols of statehood, and, most critical, a shared view that the outcomes of the political processes (most notably, elections) are legitimate.'[25] The absence of a dominant nation or ethnic group within an ethnically-divided state could also perhaps facilitate the development of a 'transcending bond of national unity' within a 'political community'.

It would seem that other nations, usually enjoying cultural rights or a measure of home rule, could successfully co-exist within this transcending bond of national (or, rather, more accurately speaking supranational) unity. However, a nation could also co-exist with other nations within states which may be far from being replicas of the Swiss model. For example, a Turkish nation may be said to exist in western Thrace in Greece, although the Greek authorities are not even prepared to acknowledge the existence of a 'Turkish' minority within their territory. These nations must be other-defined though by an official authority. In the case of the Turks of western Thrace the Turkish government provides the recognition. It will be observed that the complete assimilation of the whole of a separate ethnic group or nation is not a simple task.

Certainly, it is not easy to emulate the Swiss model. In practice, in many instances the distinction between a so-called civic and an ethnic model of nationalism is not as obvious as seems at first sight. Unlike political communities, most states supposedly based on civic nationalism would have dominant ethnic cores which could seek to some extent at least to assimilate or integrate other nations or ethnic groups within the same state in order to shape a common civic culture and ideology. In reality, therefore, states may only be based on forms of declaratory civic nationalism. The leadership of a dominant ethnic core may seek to legitimize its authority by deliberately presenting its policies as consistent with those of civic nationalism, but the politically-active members of other ethnic groups within the same state may perceive their policies differently. This was certainly so in Turkey in the 1930s with regard to certain Kurdish groups and the policies of the Turkish state. In these cases, other ethnic groups could then feel compelled to appeal to their own form of ethnic nationalism in order to counter the perceived ethnic nationalism of the dominant ethnic core or risk being almost fully assimilated, as was the case of all other ethnic groups in Turkey apart from the Kurds.

As noted above, within a state more than one nation may exist. This runs contrary to the opinion that to warrant the label 'nation' a community should have its own state. For example, Gellner has stressed that political and national units should be 'congruent', where 'ethnic boundaries should not cut across political ones'.[26] The implication here is that a state would fragment if two or more nations co-existed within its territory. Other scholars have played down the importance of the close nation–state linkage. According to Kedourie, 'any body of people associating together and deciding on a scheme for their own government, form a nation'.[27] At the time though, this 'body of people' need not have possessed a state of their own. Kedourie's stance was in line with Ernest Renan's classic assertion that fundamentally a nation was the matter of the will of individuals who could choose to bring a nation into existence. However, as noted earlier, for a nation to exist in practice there should also be an element of other-definition.

The term 'nationalism' is obviously closely connected with the concept of nation. Nationalism in its modern sense is commonly traced back to the late eighteenth century and the success of the American and the French Revolution. It was linked here with the doctrine of popular freedom and sovereignty and the need for a people to be united and have its own territory. Smith has referred to nationalism as 'an ideological movement for attaining and maintaining autonomy on behalf of a population deemed by some of its members to constitute an actual or potential nation'.[28] Note here that not all members of a population need share a belief in the existence of a nation or potential nation. Also, a nation may not seek to establish its own state, but it must aim to defend and protect its interests. It will be demonstrated later that the development and maintenance of nations may be tied in with the processes of both nation-building and state-building.

In his depiction of nationalism as a political movement Breuilly has emphasized much more than Smith the role of elites using nationalism as a form of power politics.[29] This line of argument has been disputed by Connor: 'The essence of nationalism is not to be sought in the motives of elites who may manipulate nationalism for some ulterior end, but rather in the mass sentiment to which elites appeal.'[30] The importance one places on either elite manipulation or mass sentiment in the formation of nations, and also states and ethnic groups is clearly an issue which must be addressed.

According to Smith, nationalism gives ethnicity a political direction.[31] The term 'ethnicity' is also defined as the state of being ethnic, concerned with identification with a particular group. A common language, religion and race are some of the important attributes of ethnicity and ethnic groups, although the group should also be conscious of being a distinct entity on the grounds of ethnicity. Objective and subjective criteria are again important. De Vos correctly noted that: 'An ethnic group is a self-perceived group of people who hold in common a set of traditions not shared by the others with whom they are in contact.'[32] These traditions could include in addition to religion and language, a sense of historical continuity, common ancestry and place of origin. In the opinion of Horowitz, a subjective belief in common descent seems to be particularly crucial, whether or not an objective blood relationship exists. He has emphasized that an ethnic group is perceived as a 'form of greatly extended kinship'.[33] As in the case of nations, therefore, the self-awareness of ethnic groups is important. In the formation and preservation of ethnic groups it will be seen that the drawing and maintenance of boundaries between different groups is a crucial factor. The role of elites in this process must also be taken into account as will be seen in the case of the Turks and the Kurds.

How should one distinguish between a nation and an ethnic group? The distinction is not obvious bearing in mind that all nations have at their centre a dominant ethnic core – i.e., a dominant ethnic group. Some ethnic groups, therefore, are able to become nations. To qualify as a nation usually – but by no means always as will be seen – a group should exhibit, *inter alia*, a common division of labour or economic unity, have common legal codes with equal rights and duties for all, and have a territorial base. These are features not associated with ethnic groups *per se*, although an ethnic group may have an association with a particular territory.[34] An ethnic group may also have its own traditions and 'rules' that almost amount to 'legal codes' although they would not apply to other ethnic groups.

The term ethnic group is not as politically significant as that of nation. An ethnic group may still exist when a self-aware elite of a particular ethnic community is pressing for the recognition of cultural rights from the authorities constituting a state but has been hitherto unsuccessful due to the state's refusing to recognize its existence as a separate ethnic group. However, for an ethnic group to enjoy the possible rights of an ethnic minority it must be recognized – other-defined – by the authority of the state in which the ethnic group resides. Unlike the term ethnic group, but like that of nation, the term ethnic minority is of political and legal importance and thus requires other-definition.

Ethnic groups are usually depicted as more exclusive and nations as more inclusive entities. In order to qualify for membership in the former it is argued that one should share certain 'exclusive', inborn attributes. The importance of birth and common ancestry are emphasized.[35] However, it will be seen in the case of the Basques, for instance, that the significance of some notion of ascription is not necessarily crucial. Moreover, ethnic groups which have become the dominant ethnic cores of a nation may still pursue a policy of forced inclusiveness through assimilation and integration. In the case of Turkey, the dominant Turkish ethnic core would invent an argument that the Kurds were also Turks who had forgotten their Turkishness.

A nation may thus be defined as a politicized ethnic group which quite often – though by no means always – has acquired its own state. This nation must be other-defined. In some cases, as indicated above, a nation may co-exist with another dominant nation within the same state. In these instances, the nation will enjoy or seek to enjoy the preservation of its cultural rights or autonomy in some form. It may, though, aim to unite with another state or create its own independent state. Nations co-existing with another dominant nation in State A may be recognized – other-defined – as nations by State B, where the non-dominant nation of State A provides the dominant ethnic core of the nation (or dominant nation) in State B. This would be the case, for instance, of the Turks of western Thrace. Most Turks there probably feel that they are part of a Turkish nation although they would also acknowledge themselves to be Greek citizens living in the state of Greece – controlled by a nation composed of a separate and dominant Greek ethnic group. The feeling of a distinct national identity on the part of the western Thrace Turks is able to survive because of the recognition of their Turkish nationhood by the Turkish state – it is self-defined and other-defined.

There may be different types of ethnic group. The leaders of some may be aspiring for nationhood, thereby hoping to acquire independent statehood or at least a considerable degree of autonomy. In other ethnic groups the leadership may be aiming to ensure the respect of its cultural rights. All ethnic groups are politicized to the extent that their leaders will wish to maintain what they perceive to be a separate group identity. They must be self-defined. In order to at least enjoy the possible rights of an ethnic minority, they would also need to be other-defined by the government of the state in which the ethnic group resides. If the demands of the leaders of an ethnic group for nationhood are recognized by a government or governments, the ethnic group may then be regarded as a nation.

The Formation of Nations and Ethnic Groups

How was the Turkish nation created? Nation-building had to run parallel with state-building following the demise of the Ottoman Empire and moves toward the establishment of a modern Turkish Republic. How was a Turkish ethnic core for the Turkish nation shaped? Although key elites projected the line that they were working for the development of a Turkish civic national-ism, how did other groups within the Turkish state perceive this policy? What of the role of the elites and masses within these various groups? What impact did the previous *millet* system of the Ottoman Empire have on these developments, bearing in mind that, according to this system, a measure of autonomy had been allowed for non-Moslem minorities within the Empire, while all Moslems irrespective of their ethnic background were grouped as one category?

Undoubtedly, elites perform important roles in the nation-building and state-building process. Hroch has referred to three separate structural phases of a national movement. In Phase A intellectual elites inquire into the linguistic, cultural, social and possibly historical attributes of a group of people. In a later Phase B more politicized activists, the professional intelligentsia, pick up on these initial intellectual forays and seek to awaken the national consciousness of the masses. By Phase C a mass national movement would be formed. Progress through each phase would apparently occur through a series of crises and external developments.[36]

How relevant is Hroch's model for the formation of a Turkish nation? Certainly, both intellectual elites and a professional intelligentsia consisting mainly of military officers and leading bureaucratic officials did play an important role in the replacement of the Ottoman ruling class with a new leadership which would aim to foster the image of a Turkish national identity. They were able to make use of the arguments of earlier, outside historians, scholars and Pan-Turkic thinkers who had originally defined a Turk on an ethnic basis. This was at a time when within the Ottoman Empire identity was defined on grounds of religion rather than ethnicity. Arguably, therefore, using Hroch's terminology, intellectual elites played a key role in what could be termed Phases A and B. It appears that, initially at least, Mustafa Kemal and his close associates intended that this Turkish national identity should be endowed with the features of a civic nation. Nevertheless, the ethnic core of this nation would be based on Turkish ethnicity with its language and culture. In this simultaneous nation-building and state-building exercise several intellectuals were called upon to construct (or reconstruct as Smith would argue) and mould a Turkish nation by making use of history, myths and symbols. Outside recognition of the establishment of the Turkish state and external approval of the formation of the Turkish nation were also important factors.

A state consists of a territory with well-defined borders. Its institutions have a monopoly of political power and the legitimate use of force within this territory. A state is generally recognized by other, similarly constituted states as being an independent and sovereign entity. In state-building, elites create new structures and organizations to 'penetrate' a society and regulate its behaviour by drawing more resources from it. A bureaucracy develops in this process, and at the same time an attitude of obedience among the population in general takes shape. State-building may occur due to the threat of the survival of a political system from the international environment, or because of a revolutionary process within the society itself, or states may emerge as a result of elites pursuing expansionist goals.[37] Initially, at least, it would seem that state-building in the case of the Turkish Republic was prompted by external and also internal (in the form of Greek and Armenian secessionist groups and Kurdish uprisings) threats against the Ottoman Empire. One should note, in addition, that an important but often overlooked part of state-building concerns the need to give the new state a name. This could be particularly significant if a new state wishes to dissociate itself from a previous empire. However, the names of states 'usually reflect some image out of the remote or recent past of a people, a place, an idea'.[38]

It has been argued that nation-building deals with questions of loyalty and commitment. Nation-building stresses the cultural aspects of political development. It involves a process where a population transfers its commitment and loyalty from smaller units such as a tribe and village to a larger, centralized political system. Nation-building is thus closely related to but separate from state-building. State-building could be successfully accomplished without having fully completed nation-building, i.e., without having created a common national culture of loyalty and commitment.[39] Recognition of the nation by an official authority though would be sufficient for a nation to come into existence as mentioned above. Note, however, that in the case of a transition from empire to state, the nation-building process involves to an extent the transfer of commitment and loyalty from a larger unit to a smaller one, although within an empire a population may also have demonstrated a loyalty to a village, tribe or *millet*. Nation-building may never be fully completed – in spite of outside recognition and other-definition – if ethnic, racial, class and other cleavages continue to threaten the unity, legitimacy and existence of a state.[40]

Nation-building could be especially problematic when within the same state distinct ethnic groups or nations continued to exist. These distinct groups could object to what they regard as policies of assimilation or discrimination instigated by the central authorities of the state which they perceive is controlled by another, and in this case dominant ethnic group. The connections between assimilation and modernization and nation-building and state-building may lead to a complicated picture. A dominant ethnic group within a newly established state may be able to win over the support of peoples from other ethnic groups by making modernization a key plank of the new state's ideology. In the case of Turkey, the Albanians, Bosnians, Circassians and other groups including also some Kurds, were assimilated rapidly along these lines. Other Kurdish groups though consciously resisted assimilation or remained largely untouched by the modernization of the state.

The term 'assimilation' is notoriously difficult to define. Its meaning is not always clear, although the term is often considered in a pejorative sense. Assimilation usually denotes a power relationship between two groups, a dominant and non-dominant one. However, this is not always so. A dominated community may seek assimilation in order to secure a more advantageous position in society, but be denied it. The case of the blacks in the American South is one such example. Discrimination is, after all, another negative expression. On the other hand, a non-dominant ethnic group may feel that its cultural distinctiveness is under threat when a state stresses the importance of equal rights and duties for all its citizens.[41]

A UN study on racial discrimination in the political, economic, social and cultural spheres noted that assimilation was based on the idea of the supremacy of a dominant group which aimed to produce an homogeneous society by getting other groups to discard their cultures in favour of the dominant one. The dominant group would then be willing to accept the members of other groups on these conditions. According to the same study, 'integration' was defined as 'a process by which diverse elements are combined into a unity while retaining their basic identity. There is no insistence upon uniformity or elimination of all differences, other than the difference of each component group which would disturb or inhibit the total unity.' The final phrase rings particularly ominously and separates clearly integration from 'pluralism'. The latter, in the words of the same study, involved a policy 'which aims at uniting different ethnic groups in a relationship of mutual interdependence, respect and equality, while permitting them to maintain and cultivate their distinctive ways.'[42]

Assimilation has been linked with the much more odious expressions 'ethnocide' and even 'genocide'. Both refer to the destruction of a culture, with the latter involving the physical destruction of the members of a society bearing this culture. Ethnocide also refers to a conscious policy which seeks to destroy an ethnic group, although the process is much slower and violence is usually avoided. It is based 'on the conviction among members of an ethnic group of the superiority of their culture in relation to all others and thus the rejection of otherness'.[43]

An attempt has been made to separate so-called 'ethnic assimilation' from 'civic integration'. In the latter case, the objective is to establish a common civic, national or patriotic identity where ethnicity is ostensibly to be barred from the public arena. The focus is on equal rights for individuals rather than communities. Ethnic assimilation, on the other hand, apparently aims to create a common ethnic identity through the merging of differences into one established or new identity.[44] Parallels may be drawn here with the attempt to differentiate civic and ethnic forms of nationalism. Again, the same obstacle hindering the possible formation of a political community is encountered. Other non-dominant ethnic groups may perceive – perhaps justifiably – that so-called civic integration is being used to cloak an official policy which resembles more one of ethnic nationalism. The picture is made more complicated, for instance, by the fact that in nation-building and state-building the central authorities will inevitably attempt to standardize education and promote the development of a common, official language. Other ethnic groups may perceive this as a policy of attempted ethnic assimilation, although the central authorities might argue that their actions are based on civic integration.

Forced assimilation by the authorities of a state representing a dominant ethnic group is likely to provoke a reaction by at least some members of non-dominant ethnic groups. It has been suggested that an individual or entire group could be culturally assimilated but not psychologically assimilated. In spite of shedding their 'overt cultural manifestations', individuals could still maintain their 'fundamental identity'.[45] The Laz in Turkey, for example, are a case in point here. Individuals may hold a number of identities as noted previously. To be successful, assimilation must proceed gradually and almost imperceptibly. More and intense contacts between the centre and peripheral regions of a state, which would tend to occur as a consequence of modernization and improved social communications, would thus prove counterproductive to the goal of assimilation.[46]

When attempting to analyse whether assimilation is taking place, it is important to examine the feelings, perceptions and reactions of the groups involved. This is no simple task. How may one accurately ascertain the genuine feelings of a population group which may be reluctant to express itself openly through fear of possible persecution? And how may one then distinguish and relate the views of prominent individuals of particular groups from those of the rank and file of that group? A dominant ethnic group will not usually admit that it is pursuing an official policy of assimilation, given the negative publicity that would then ensue. Assimilation, though, may perform an invaluable role in state-building and nation-building, especially in those instances where the two processes run parallel. The central authorities of a state need not declare that they are conducting a policy of assimilation. Denying the existence of other cultures, building certain myths, making use of a centralized state education and employing other tools of modernization may in practice be attempts at *de facto* assimilation, although these may by no means be successful as already indicated.

One proposed solution to the problem of assimilation is to encourage the development of 'multiculturalism', where citizenship and full civil rights need not imply a particular cultural identity.[47] A genuine 'political community' would be based on multiculturalism. The circumstances and conditions conducive to the establishment of such a political community will be discussed later.

The pressures of modernization in general and a conscious policy of assimilation by the elites of a dominant ethnic core within a state, as well as contributing to the politicization of other ethnic groups, may also encourage the formation of ethnic groups themselves. For example, ethnic groups could emerge from loose coalitions of tribes.

A 'tribe' is usually depicted as an 'ethnically, homogeneous socio-political unit ... which forms only part of a larger interrelated grouping'.[48] In addition to this notion of 'sub-ethnic status', a tribe is often regarded as a pre-modern, primitive and evolutionary stage in human organization.[49] Common history, language, territory and culture are all important features of a tribe which must also be self-defined. The implication would seem to be that in modern societies tribes will disappear or at least lose any political relevance. They may attempt to resist the processes of state-building and nation-building but it is generally assumed that the pressures of modernization and assimilation will lead to the declining importance of tribal divisions. Tribal groupings would thus be totally assimilated into the dominant ethnic group. Alternatively in these circumstances tribes could become more aware of their common identity separate from the dominant ethnic core of the state. They could then coalesce and form larger politically-active ethnic groups while perhaps simultaneously maintaining their tribal identities.[50] In times of crisis, when tribal identities are endangered, charismatic religious figures may play a critical role in uniting tribes into larger groups to resist centralization.[51]

Ethnic groups may also emerge through the original politicization of what was previously an 'ethnic category'. Unlike a tribe, a population referred to as an ethnic category has little self-consciousness. Only some outsiders would consider that the population of an ethnic category constituted a separate cultural and historical group. According to Smith, the Turks of Anatolia before 1900 constituted an ethnic category.[52] Such a population is dissimilar from other people in terms of objective cultural criteria but it lacks a subjective self-consciousness.[53] Ethnic categories are other-defined (not necessarily by an official authority though) but not self-defined entities. Ethnic identity formation – the shift from an ethnic category to an ethnic group for a particular population – requires a population to be more self-aware and conscious of its differences in relation to other groupings. This may result from policies of attempted assimilation or discrimination, or could be the product of modernization or even war. The development of ethnic groups from both tribes and ethnic categories requires the support of key elites who are able to mobilize the masses.

Ethnic groups are not rigid nor monolithic entities. In time, individual members of an ethnic group may no longer wish to identify themselves with it but rather opt out and align themselves totally with another ethnic group or national identity. An individual may choose to opt out in order to advance socially within a society and escape from what he or she may perceive to be a negative, social self-identity. Pressures toward assimilation and integration may also be contributory factors. Thus ethnic groups are only to some extent exclusive and ascriptive. In order to survive and adapt to changing circumstances ethnic groups must also be flexible enough to embrace other individuals who may not obviously meet certain objective criteria. As Horowitz noted: 'Ethnic groups differ in the fluidity they are prepared to tolerate at the margin and in the alacrity with which they adapt their identity to changing conditions.'[54] Ethnic groups are formed and preserved by establishing and maintaining boundaries which separate them from other ethnic groups. Certain objective criteria and shared traits help to form and solidify these boundaries. However, these boundaries are largely psychological. They are in the minds of the individuals who identify themselves with a particular ethnic group.[55] Dominant ethnic cores of nations which seek to assimilate within their ranks individuals of another ethnic group aim to break down these boundaries. However, it has been previously noted that individuals may hold a number of different identities, e.g., regard themselves as both Turk and Kurd. In these instances identity becomes contextual. An individual may choose to stress his or her Turkish or Kurdish background dependent on particular circumstances.

Ethnic identity formation may also entail a struggle between prominent individuals and sub-groupings within an ethnic group itself for the control of the group's 'material and symbolic resources'. This in turn would have an impact on the definition of the group's boundaries and on its rules, as it were, of inclusion and exclusion. One may not assume then that ethnic groups are fixed and unitary entities.[56]

Key leaders within an ethnic group may aim to secure nationhood for their group not only because of the pressures of assimilation or modernization which would threaten to eradicate their boundaries. A rising intelligentsia within an ethnic group may believe that career advancement is blocked by the entrenched presence of old bureaucrats from the dominant ethnic group within the state. This frustrated intelligentsia, instead of choosing to opt out and seeking to join the ranks of the dominant ethnic group – if such an option were possible – may then, in reaction, campaign for autonomy or separate statehood for its own ethnic group.[57] In the case of Turkey, one may examine whether politically conscious Kurds are able to advance within the state bureaucracy.

Economic factors may also help to explain why the elites of certain ethnic groups may pursue autonomy or separate statehood. An ethnic group may be concentrated in an economically-backward region of a state. Leaders of this group may blame the policies of the central authorities for their current impoverishment. These leaders could perceive themselves to be the victims of the 'internal colonialism', of a 'metropolitan "nation state"' exploited for their cheap labour and large markets. They may regard themselves as being discriminated against in a cultural division of labour, where individuals are assigned certain social roles on the basis of their cultural backgrounds. Certain Kurdish elements in Turkey argued along these lines in the 1960s. Similarly, the elites of some ethnic groups may perceive their populations, often living on the periphery of a state, to be relatively backward – although not necessarily impoverished – compared with the higher standard of living enjoyed by inhabitants at the centre.[58]

Theories based on 'internal colonialism' and 'relative deprivation' may offer partial explanations with regard to nation formation. In the case of the Basques, an ethnic group has become politicized to the extent that some of its members are determined to secede from Spain. However, in this century the Basque territory has flourished as one of the most prosperous regions of Spain. A further criticism is that ethnic groups are not necessarily concentrated in a particular territory of a state. Another product of modernization has been the increase of internal migration from rural to urban areas within the same state. This has certainly been the case with the Kurds in Turkey. More generally speaking, other historical, social and cultural variables also need to be taken into account, in addition to economic factors, to understand the formation of ethnic groups and nations. However, the importance of economic factors should not be underestimated.

Trans-state Ethnic Conflicts

Conflict involves a form of interaction between two or more individuals or groups. This interaction is usually purposeful and takes the form of a struggle which may be non-violent (for example, protest action) or violent (for example, a rebellion). The leaders of a group perceiving themselves to be disadvantaged may seek to improve their status through resort to conflict. Likewise, those heading an advantaged group may turn to conflict in an endeavour to consolidate their position. Conflict between groups may help to establish and maintain their identities and boundaries. It may also, though, result in the disintegration of groups or lead to the emergence of despotism in those cases where group cohesion was weak before the outset of the conflict.[59]

According to Brown: 'An "ethnic conflict" is a dispute about important political, economic, social, cultural or territorial issues between two or more ethnic communities.'[60] This would often involve a conflict between two or more ethnic groups, where one of these would form the dominant ethnic core of the nation controlling the state. Non-dominant ethnic groups could be resisting attempts at assimilation or domination by the dominant ethnic group. However, one should also bear in mind that ethnic groups are not unitary bodies. Conflict could thus occur within an ethnic group itself between individuals who may be aiming to pursue different objectives for their group.

Ethnic conflicts between two or more ethnic groups are invariably 'intractable' partly because they tend to lead toward zero-sum outcomes.[61] In extreme cases, a group may secede or may be a victim of ethnocide or genocide. Compromise is difficult to achieve. The ascriptive character of many forms of ethnic identification makes ethnic conflict 'intense' and 'permeative'.[62] The longer a conflict persists, the more intense it usually becomes and group identities often become firmer and more exclusive.

The resolution of an ethnic conflict is a difficult task. Such conflicts are ontological in that they deal with questions of identity and essential human needs. Conflicts should be differentiated from disputes. A 'dispute' involves negotiable interests which may be dealt with by a settlement through negotiation or arbitration. On the other hand, a 'conflict' requires a resolution where the interest needs of all involved in the conflict must be satisfied. Conflicts are concerned with non-negotiable issues which relate to human needs. In these cases it is considerably more difficult to reach a solution which could satisfy the needs of all concerned.[63] Possible means to reach a resolution of the Kurdish issue in Turkey will be discussed later.

Ethnic conflicts are usually internationalized. They are often not confined within the borders of one state. The leaders of an ethnic group perceiving that they are disadvantaged, may search for support from the governments of neighbouring states, hoping thereby to make the conflict an international or, more precisely, 'inter-state' one, i.e., between two or more states. Strictly speaking, a trans-state ethnic conflict, though, as opposed to an inter-state conflict, requires the presence and involvement in some form – if only by offering refuge – of members of the same disadvantaged ethnic group in other neighbouring or nearby states. For example, the Kurds are widely distributed throughout Turkey, Iran, Iraq, Syria, Armenia and Azerbaijan. In none of these do the Kurds form the dominant ethnic core.

The term trans-state is preferred here rather than the expression 'trans-national'. Transnational relations were originally depicted as 'the transfer of tangible or intangible items across state boundaries when at least one actor is not an agent of government or an intergovernmental organization'.[64] This definition was correct to indicate that states were not the only actors involved in transnational relations. However, with regard to issues involving self-determination and thus invariably ethnic conflict, the term 'trans-state' is more appropriate than 'transnational'. This is because of the general confusion in the use of the term nation, which is employed by many to designate an ethnic and cultural community and is also used as an alternative word for state.[65] Furthermore, with regard to ethnic groups, for instance the Kurds, the use of the term transnational with reference to an ethnic conflict would seem to be misleading, implying that the Kurds were indeed a fully-fledged and recognized nation.

A trans-state ethnic conflict thus occurs 'across' states and is bound to have some regional impact. Out of 233 groups examined in his study of 'minorities at risk' Gurr has identified 159 cases where the same 'kindred' (i.e., population belonging to the same ethnic group) inhabited adjacent states.[66] Many trans-state ethnic conflicts are thus possible. In such instances the processes of 'diffusion' and 'contagion' may have an impact. Diffusion in this context involves a 'spillover' process where conflict in one state directly affects political organization and behaviour in adjacent states. One example would be where an ethnic group could find sanctuary and acquire support from kindred in another state. Contagion operates more indirectly. It 'refers to the processes by which one group's actions provide inspiration and strategic and tactical guidance for groups elsewhere'.[67] Contagion is thus more likely to occur with reference to different formations of the same ethnic group or community in other states. Both of these terms have relevance to the case of the Kurds in Turkey.

The importance of the so-called 'ethnic affinity link', however, should not be overlooked with regard to the same ethnic group straddling the borders between two or more states (nor, indeed, with regard to the same ethnic group being widely dispersed and inhabiting non-contiguous areas and thus possibly forming even diasporas).[68] These different formations of the same ethnic group may not share a number of key ethnic affinities. It has been previously observed that there are several criteria which may help to establish ethnic identity, such as religion, kinship and language. Moreover, it has also been indicated that ethnic identity is variable. One may thus not assume that kindred people understand one another. For different formations of the same ethnic group to co-operate across state borders these formations should feel that they share a number of affinities. Affinity in one area may be at odds though with an affinity elsewhere. Horowitz has argued that this is one problem of irredentism, which is concerned with an attempt to retrieve kindred groups and their territories across state boundaries.[69] Trans-state ethnic co-operation therefore may not always run smoothly. In addition to the concerns of the governments of the states in the region in question and possible complications caused by extra-regional actors and the international community, the elites and rank and file of the kindred formations of the same ethnic group may be at odds with one another in part because of the possible lack of firm ethnic affinity links. This could have a major bearing on the means of resolving a trans-state ethnic conflict.

The Case of the Basques in Spain

In the autumn of 1993 Prime Minister Çiller briefly referred to the possible relevance of the 'Basque model' of regional autonomy in regard to the case of the Kurds in Turkey.[70] Others have examined the relevance or otherwise of the example of the Basques for the possible resolution of the Kurdish question. In May 1995 a Spanish official recommended in a report prepared for the Western European Union that Turkey should follow the example of Spain and the Basques and grant the Kurds rights of cultural self-expression and forms of political and administrative autonomy that should not impinge on the territorial integrity of the Turkish state.[71] One should note immediately though that the Basque issue in Spain at the time of writing was far from being resolved with ETA [Euskadi and Freedom] Militar still engaged in sporadic acts of violence and terror.

At one time a trans-state ethnic conflict was clearly evident when the Basques in Spain were able to find refuge in neighbouring southern France, where another Basque community resided. However, the ethnic affinity link was never firm. The Basques in France (so-called northern Euskadi) had a different history and lacked the same sense of injustice and oppression which the Basques in Spain had lately experienced in the Franco era.[72] With the Spanish Basques in recent years no longer able to operate easily from France, what was once a trans-state ethnic conflict has assumed more of the form of conflict within Spain.

Within Spain the Basques are far from united. ETA-Militar aims to secede and establish an independent and sovereign Basque state and has not been loath to use violence and terroristic methods to secure this objective. It is supported by a parliamentary party, Herri Batasuna, which participates in both regional and national elections. Herri Batasuna usually obtains around 18 per cent of the vote in the Basque region but has been unable to take part in regional coalition governments owing to the opposition of other political parties. Several moderate Basque groups have splintered off from what was originally a united ETA. There is also a moderate Basque Nationalist Party (PNV), which was the original party of Basque nationalism formed toward the end of the nineteenth century. The PNV, which usually secures around 30 per cent of the regional vote, has co-operated with socialist governments based in Madrid. In recent years the PNV has been advocating a Europe of regions, with the Basque region forming one of the 40 to 50 regional components.[73] The Basque population in Spain has a range of nationalist parties to vote for although there are also Basques who vote for other, non-nationalist parties too, such as the Socialist Party.

If the Basques were to achieve independence the territorial limits of their state, 'Euskadi', would be open to question. According to ETA-Militar, in addition to the Basque provinces of Vizcaya, Guipuzcoa and Alava, Euskadi also includes Navarre and the Basque provinces in France. There are provisions in the current Spanish constitution for the Navarrese to hold a referendum to decide whether to integrate Navarre with the three Basque provinces in Spain. Kurdish nationalists also appear to be uncertain about the territorial boundaries of a would-be 'Kurdistan'.

Are the Basques in Spain a nation or an ethnic group? In spite of the divisions within the Basque leadership and rank and file it appears that the Basques are indeed a nation, both self-defined and other-defined. The other-defining authority is actually the central government in Madrid. It would seem that the Basques as a nation are able to reside within the same state with other nations including the Castillian, which is the dominant ethnic group in Spain. The Basque followers of ETA-Militar may not be content with this arrangement, but in recent years Spain has to all intents developed into another example of a political community, albeit not a peaceful one, in contrast to the Swiss model. Historical factors and the role of recent Spanish central governments have facilitated the formation of this political community. One should note here that the term *'nación'* in Spain may also refer to the 'historic nations' of Catalonia, Galicia and the 'Basque Country'.

The Basques in Spain enjoyed relative independence until as late as 1876 when their municipal, military and fiscal rights were finally abolished. In the late nineteenth century a Basque movement for autonomy developed. Here, initially a small circle of Basque intellectuals feared assimilation as a result of large numbers of migrant workers who moved to the Basque territories from other parts of Spain in order to work in new and expanding industries. This early Basque national movement was rural, catholic and conservative and stressed the importance of the Basques as a separate, historic race whose language and culture needed to be preserved. The Basque masses would be gradually mobilized over the next decades, but it was the repressive policies of centralization of the Franco regime which reawakened national consciousness among the Basque population. Different forms of nationalism would emerge including the more radical, secular, urban and socialist variant of nationalism of ETA.[74]

Theories based on internal colonialism and relative deprivation are not applicable in the case of the Basques in Spain. The Basque region is not a peripheral, backward economy in a Castillian-dominated country. As mentioned above, many industrial workers in Spain have migrated to the more prosperous Basque region in search of employment. The economic factor though has played a role in the formation of Basque extremist national-ism. One of the grievances of ETA-Militar is their claim that much of the wealth produced in the Basque region is diverted to Madrid and therefore not made use of by the Basques themselves.

Following the death of General Franco, the Spanish authorities decided upon a policy of decentralization throughout the whole of Spain by agreeing to allow regional autonomy for all of the country's 17 regions. Article Two of the 1978 Constitution formally recognizes the principle of autonomy for Spain's regions and 'nationalities', although it also refers to the 'indissoluble unity of the Spanish nation, the common and indivisible homeland of all Spaniards'. In reality, it would seem here that the distinction between 'nation' and 'nationality' is in part an artificial one. In return for agreeing to a common Spanish citizenship and remaining a part of the Spanish state, what are in effect different nations such as the Basques and Catalans are able to enjoy nationhood through a regional autonomy arrangement. The powers of regional governments are quite considerable. A regional parliament is empowered to approve a regional budget. In the case of the Basque region, self-government in fiscal and educational affairs is allowed, a regional police force works alongside the national police, a television channel broadcasts programmes in Euskera (the Basque language) which is recognized as the offical language of 'Euskadi' together with Spanish. In spite of this regional devolution of power, ETA-Militar is still prepared to resort to violent conflict to secure full independence. Clearly, given the failure to end violence in the case of the Basques in Spain, it is difficult to obtain the resolution of an ethnic conflict which would satisfy the interests and needs of all parties involved.

Significantly, ETA-Militar stresses the significance of class in developing its variant of Basque nationalism. The relative decline in Basque prosperity in recent years on account of ageing and declining industries has contributed to this class consciousness. The followers of ETA-Militar play down the importance of race and do not conceptualize the Basques as a totally homogeneous people. Nevertheless, ETA-Militar is keen to distance itself from the migrant industrial workers from other parts of Spain who have settled in the Basque region. Evidently, in this instance class is unable to act as a cross-cutting cleavage. It appears that according to ETA-Militar, Basque culture and socialism together form an overarching Basque identity. A person does not need to be of Basque descent or know Euskera to be regarded as a Basque. In fact, only 40 per cent of all 'Basques' are able to speak Euskera. It has been argued that 'for political purposes a person is not born Basque. To be Basque is a political option.'[75] The boundaries of Basque identity are thus quite flexible.

The earlier general discussion on nationalism and ethnicity did not focus on the possible importance of class on nation and ethnic identity formation. The internal colonialism argument is, of course, a Marxist-based one. Often ostensibly class-based nationalisms, especially in developing states, are in reality movements controlled by autocratic leaders. Many developing states lack the necessary levels of urbanization and industrialization to foster the creation of a genuine socialist-based nationalism. Usually in these states, in what are largely agricultural-based societies, traditional clan and tribal divisions are difficult to break down. The purportedly Marxist leanings of the PKK are of interest, but, as in the case of the Basques in Spain, this does not appear to be a cross-cutting cleavage uniting non-Kurdish elements. Moreover, again in line with the Basque example and the popularity of ETA-Militar and its ideology, many nationalists within the Kurdish ethnic group do not sympathize with the PKK leadership's avowed interest in Marxism-Leninism. It will be seen that in the December 1995 national elections in Turkey the largely Kurdish-based People's Democracy Party (HADEP), in an alliance with a number of small left-wing parties, was unable to capture enough votes although it had proposed what was in effect a socialist programme of action.

The Kurds and Turks in Turkey

Concerning the development of a Turkish identity, Smith has referred to the presence of an original ethnic category – that of the 'Turks' – which later crystallized into an ethnic group, and then eventually pursued a policy of ethnic nationalism within the Republic of Turkey.[76] As suggested earlier, civic nationalisms usually only emerge in well-institutionalized democracies. In the transition from Ottoman Empire to the Turkish state it would seem difficult therefore for a civic nationalism to be fostered in tandem with the complex process of state-building. In the case of Turkey, key elites from the professional intelligentsia and military officer class co-operating with leading intellectuals were certainly involved in a well-organized and orchestrated campaign to cultivate a Turkish nation – and obtain outside recognition of this nation for other-definition purposes – which would have as its dominant core the Turkish ethnic group. Given the previous emphasis on religious identity within the Ottoman Empire, clearly it was no simple task to promote a new form of Turkish identity and consciousness, And how would other originally Moslem groups of different ethnic backgrounds within the former Empire react to the state-building and nation-building programmes of the new elites of the Turkish Republic?

It is still far from clear what the term 'Turk' actually signifies. Different parties and individuals within and outside the Turkish ethnic group in the

Turkish Republic have perceived this term from time to time in a civic or ethnic sense. However, as previously emphasized, all nations, whether based on civic or ethnic lines, in practice have at their core a dominant ethnic group. The so-called Turkish nation is no exception. This nation is both self-defined and other-defined. It was reconstructed by Mustafa Kemal 'Atatürk' and his associates, making use of myths, symbols and interpretations of Turkish history, tracing the origins of the nation to a historic territory in Central Asia. These are important ingredients for a Turkish nation. The objective criteria of this nation are a well-defined state, a single economy, common legal rights and duties, and a shared language.

What of the Kurds within Turkey? Is one able to make a firm categorization of such a population group which is scattered throughout the region and has had no tradition of independent statehood? Even within Turkey the Kurds are a divided population. The boundaries of this ethnic group are not well-defined. What does it mean to be a Kurd? The question of self-perception is crucial. It would seem that some Kurds have become assimilated into Turkish society to the extent that they are no longer aware of a separate ethnic consciousness. Other Kurds in Turkey apparently recognize themselves as a separate ethnic group. Yet others appear to regard themselves as both Kurds and Turks. Some Kurdish groupings in Turkey and in other states have become more politicized and aspire to autonomy or independent statehood. In the case of northern Iraq some Kurds are aiming to preserve their autonomy, while in Iran Kurds have been struggling to obtain autonomy. Within the Kurdish ethnic community in Turkey a wide spectrum of differing views and opinions are expressed. Given these complexities it is not easy to assess whether a Kurdish national movement has fully entered Phase C of development, according to Hroch's model of analysis. Further confusion results from differing perceptions among officials in Ankara, in recent years especially. However, outside governments are not prepared in practice to assist the Kurds in Turkey, Iraq or elsewhere to establish their own state, largely because this could have grave consequences for regional security. Syria, though, appears to be offering some support to the PKK in order to wrest concessions from Turkey on other issues such as the dispute over water. In the light of the earlier discussion it would seem inappropriate to allocate to 'the Kurds' a particular label. But clearly some Kurds in Turkey do perceive themselves and behave as a politicized ethnic group.

The historical background of the Kurds has been extensively discussed in other works and it is therefore not the purpose here to recapitulate their arguments.[77] Briefly, some Kurds believe that they are descended from the Medes, a people incorporated into the Persian Empire in the sixth century BC. However, it would seem that the Kurds are an amalgam of Turkic, Armenian and Assyrian tribes and more dominant Indo-European groupings. The origins of the Kurds are hence somewhat obscure. Their history is one of tribal divisions and of a population scattered largely across what came to be the Persian and the Ottoman Empire. Local 'aghas' and chieftains, and in more recent times religious leaders or 'shaikhs' provided, in effect, Kurdish elites. This was especially after Ottoman and Persian pressure led to the dismantling in the mid-nineteenth century of a number of Kurdish principalities ruled by prominent families. By the early twentieth century some Kurdish communities within Turkey migrated to urban areas where they could come under the influence of Kurdish intellectuals and the professional intelligentsia. From time to time charismatic individuals would emerge who aimed to mobilize the Kurdish masses to pursue political objectives.

Divisions within the Kurds both in Turkey and in the region in general have impaired political mobilization. It will be seen that religious, tribal and perhaps to some extent linguistic differences (although, ironically, the common use of Turkish among Kurds in Turkey may be a unifying factor) have contributed to these divisions within Turkey. With reference to religion, the Sunni–Alevi divide among the Kurds has led to conflict between Kurdish groups which the central authorities in Turkey have been able to exploit.

Tribal identity remains important today for many Kurds, especially for those still living in rural areas. In spite of modernization, tribal identities have not disappeared nor lost their relevance in Turkey. Indeed, the authorities have been able to secure the loyalty of the leaders of certain tribes. Tribalism and Kurdish nationalism may thus clash. Some Kurdish tribal identities in rural areas may oppose Kurdish nationalism out of concern that their traditional ways of life could be threatened. Tribal chiefs may also look upon self-proclaimed Kurdish nationalists as political opportunists. Certain tribes may be wary of embracing nationalism out of fear of incurring the wrath of the Turkish state. However, some Kurdish tribal and religious leaders could use nationalism to reinforce their traditional roles and broaden their base of support.[78]

The picture is a complex one. As Van Bruinessen has argued, the Kurds within Turkey may feel that they have a multiple identity. Whichever identity a Kurd may choose to emphasize would be dependent on the situation. Thus a Sunni Zaza speaker may be a Zaza, a Kurd, a Sunni Moslem, a citizen of Turkey ('a Turk' – authors' addition), the member of a certain social class, tribe or village, depending on the particular context.[79]

The Kurds throughout the region, however, do appear to share an affinity with a territory known as 'Kurdistan', an imprecisely defined, broad swathe of land covering large areas of Turkey, Syria, Iran, Iraq and parts of Armenia and Azerbaijan. According to one Kurdish commentator the boundaries of 'Kurdistan' within Turkey may be demarcated as follows: 'It stretches from the Gulf of Alexandria and the Anti-Taurus mountains in the west, to the frontiers of Iran and the [former – authors' addition] USSR in the east. To the north it is bounded by the Pontic mountains, and to the south by the Turkish–Syrian and Turkish–Iraqi frontiers.'[80]

Have the official policies of successive Turkish governments unwittingly contributed to the formation of a separate Kurdish ethnic identity within the country in the twentieth century? As examined above, assimilation is a difficult concept to pin down and explain largely because of its association with perceptions and identity. It has been suggested, for example, that Kurds have been able to reach high office in Turkey only by suppressing their Kurdish identity.[81] On the other hand, one should recall that a group may be culturally but not psychologically assimilated. Individuals may simultaneously hold dual or multiple identities. In practice, it would seem that assimilation, discrimination, centralization and modernization in Turkey have all had an impact on the formation of an ethnic Kurdish identity.

One should note in passing here that some scholars have based their analysis of the Kurdish question in Turkey along the lines of the argument of the 'internal colonialism' model.[82] This argument is oversimplified and mono-causal and fails to take into account the fact that the Kurds are now widely scattered throughout Turkey and that the largest Kurdish city in the world is, in effect, Istanbul, the major business centre of Turkey.

At the time of writing there is an on-going, trans-state ethnic conflict in which the Turkish government and the PKK are heavily involved. There are also conflicts between different Kurdish groupings in the region and especially in northern Iraq. The extent of the ethnic affinity link among the Kurds in the region as a whole must be seriously questioned and this must have an impact on the amount of support the PKK, for instance, may receive from other Kurdish groupings outside Turkey. Many Kurds within Turkey itself are opposed to the policies and objectives of the PKK. A resolution of this particular trans-state ethnic conflict is bound to be exceedingly difficult. Hardliners within the Turkish state establishment may argue that the lessons of the Basque example in Spain are that democratization, decentralization and autonomy arrangements do not necessarily work. The central authorities in Madrid have also not had to deal with the security concerns that Turkish officials have had to encounter in what is after all a highly turbulent region.

One scholar has contended that Mustafa Kemal and his associates should have opted to name the successor state to the Ottoman Empire 'Anatolia' rather than 'Turkey'. The term 'Anatolian' is supposedly more neutral and all-embracing than the terms 'Turk' and 'Turkish'.[83] One could perhaps then argue that the Welsh and the Scots within Britain are more willing to regard themselves as British and not English citizens living in 'Britain' and not 'England', although it is the English which provide the dominant ethnic core in the United Kingdom of Great Britain and Northern Ireland. Even in this example of a political community there are Welsh and Scottish nationalists aiming to secure more autonomy if not independence for what they regard as separate Welsh and Scottish nations. Developing this argument further, would not the concept of a common Anatolian citizenship also have assisted in the peaceful co-existence and, perhaps, to some extent the voluntary integration of separate Turkish and Kurdish ethnic groups or nations within a state known as Anatolia?

Notes

1. *Turkish Daily News* (*TDN*), 9 Feb. 1995. The first sentence of the first paragraph of Article Eight of the original version of the Anti-terror Law (12 April 1991) reads: 'All propaganda, whether written or verbal, all meetings, demonstrations, or other acts which adversely affect the indivisible integrity of the territory and the nation of the State of the Turkish Republic, shall be forbidden, whatever the methods, goals and ideas thereof' (unofficial translation). For the full text of the original Anti-terror Law in Turkish see, *Yürürlükteki Kanunlar Külliyatı*, Başbakanlık Mevzuatı Geliştirme ve Yayın Genel Müdürlüğü (Ankara: Başbakanlık Basımevi) (1988, EK-15; [Feb.] 1993), 6, pp.7215–17.
2. *TDN*, 4 Jan. 1995.
3. Ibid., 30 Dec. 1994. In May 1994 President Demirel had similarly stressed the importance of the term 'constitutional citizenship' ('*anayasal vatandaşlık*') for Turkey.
4. C.G. MacDonald, 'The Kurds', in B. Schechterman and M. Slann (eds.), *The Ethnic Dimension in International Relations* (Westport CT and London: Praeger, 1993) p.124.
5. See for example, E.J. Hobsbawm, *Nations and Nationalism since 1780: Programme, Myth, Reality* (Cambridge: Cambridge University Press, 1990) p.65; and T.H. Eriksen, *Ethnicity and Nationalism: Anthropological Perspectives* (Boulder CO and London: Pluto, 1993) p.14.
6. See for example, K.W. Deutsch, *Nationalism and Social Communication: an Inquiry into the Foundations of Nationality* (Cambridge MA and London: MIT Press, 2nd ed., 1966).
7. W. Connor, 'Nation-Building or Nation-Destroying', in W.Connor, *Ethnonationalism: the Quest for Understanding* (Princeton NJ: Princeton University Press, 1994) pp.29–66.
8. R. Jalali and S.M. Lipset, 'Racial and Ethnic Conflicts: a Global Perspective', *Political Science Quarterly*, 107, 4, (1992–93) p.605.
9. T.R. Gurr, *Minorities at Risk: a Global View of Ethnopolitical Conflicts* (Washington DC: US Institute of Peace, 1993) p.87. For the original use of the terms see A.O. Hirschman, *Exit, Voice and Loyalty: Responses to Decline in Firms, Organizations and States* (Cambridge MA: Harvard University Press, 1970).
10. H. Seton-Watson, *Nations and States: an Enquiry into the Origins of Nations and the Politics of Nationalism* (Boulder CO: Westview, 1977) pp.1 and 5.
11. L. Greenfield, *Nationalism: Five Roads to Modernity* (Cambridge MA and London: Harvard University Press, 1992) p.13.
12. A.D. Smith, *National Identity* (Harmondsworth, Middlesex: Penguin, 1991) p.14.
13. T.R. Gurr, op. cit., p.3.
14. For one forceful argument in support of the importance of a nation being self-defined see W. Connor, 'A Nation Is a Nation, Is a State, Is an Ethnic Group, Is a ...', in W. Connor, op.cit., p.94.
15. C. Tilly, 'A Bridge Halfway: Responding to Brubaker', *Contention*, 4, 1, (Fall 1994) p.16.
16. Ibid., p.17.
17. B. Anderson, *Imagined Communities* (New York and London: Verso, 1991).

18. E.J. Hobsbawm and T. Ranger (eds.), *The Invention of Tradition* (Cambridge: Cambridge University Press, 1983).
19. E. Gellner, *Nations and Nationalism* (Oxford: Blackwell, 1983).
20. A.D. Smith, 'The Nation: Invented, Imagined, Reconstructed?', *Millenium: Journal of International Studies*, 20, 3, (Winter 1991) pp.353–68.
21. A.D. Smith (note 12) pp.9–12.
22. J. Snyder, 'Nationalism and the Crisis of the Post-Soviet State', in M.E. Brown (ed.), *Ethnic Conflict and International Security* (Princeton NJ: Princeton University Press, 1993) p.86.
23. A.D. Smith (note 12) p.13.
24. A.D. Smith, *The Ethnic Origins of Nations* (New York and Oxford: Blackwell, 1986) pp.212 and 216.
25. D. Welsh, 'Domestic Politics and Ethnic Conflict', in M.E. Brown, op.cit., p.53.
26. E. Gellner, op. cit., p.1.
27. E. Kedourie, *Nationalism* (Oxford: Blackwell, 4th ed., 1993) p.7.
28. A.D. Smith (note 12) p.73.
29. J. Breuilly, *Nationalism and the State* (Chicago and Manchester: University of Chicago Press and Manchester University Press, 1982) p.3.
30. W. Connor, 'Eco- or Ethno-Nationalism', in W. Connor, op. cit., p.161.
31. A.D. Smith, *The Ethnic Revival in the Modern World* (Cambridge: Cambridge University Press, 1981) p.20.
32. G. De Vos, 'Ethnic Pluralism: Conflict and Accommodation', in G. De Vos and L. Romannucci-Rose (eds.), *Ethnic Identity: Cultural Continuities and Change* (Palo Alto CA: Mayfield, 1975) p.9.
33. D.L. Horowitz, *Ethnic Groups in Conflict* (Berkeley, Los Angeles and London: University of California Press, 1985) p.57.
34. A.D. Smith (note 12) p.40.
35. J.G. Kellas, *The Politics of Nationalism and Ethnicity* (Basingstoke, Hants.: Macmillan, 1991) p.4.
36. M. Hroch, 'From National Movement to the Fully-Formed Nation – the Nation-Building Process in Europe', *New Left Review*, 198 (March–April 1993) pp.6–7.
37. G.A. Almond and G.B. Powell, *Comparative Politics: a Developmental Approach* (Boston: Little, Brown, 1966) pp.35–6.
38. H.R. Isaacs, *Idols of the Tribe: Group Identity and Political Change* (New York and London: Harper & Row, 1975) p.73.
39. G.A. Almond and G.B. Powell, op. cit., pp.35–6.
40. W. Bell and W.E. Freeman, 'Introduction', in W. Bell and W.E. Freeman (eds.), *Ethnicity and Nation-Building: Comparative, International and Historical Perspectives* (Beverly Hills CA and London: Sage, 1974) pp.11–12.
41. T.H. Eriksen, op. cit., p.142.
42. P. Thornberry, *International Law and the Rights of Minorities* (Oxford: Clarendon, 1991) p.4.
43. F. Fonval, 'Ethnocide and Acculturation', in G. Chaliand (ed.), *Minority Peoples in the Age of Nation-States* (London: Pluto, 1989) pp.149–50.
44. J. McGarry and B. O'Leary, 'Introduction: the Macro-Political Regulation of Ethnic Conflict', in J. McGarry and B. O'Leary (eds.), *The Politics of Ethnic Conflict Regulation: Case Studies of Protracted Ethnic Conflicts* (New York and London: Routledge, 1993) pp.16–17.
45. Connor, in W. Connor (note 7) p.46.

46.   Ibid., pp.54–5.

47.   T.H. Eriksen, op. cit., p.122; and McGarry and O'Leary, in J. McGarry and B. O'Leary (eds.) op. cit., p.21.

48.   Connor, in W. Connor (note 14) p.107.

49.   Ibid., p.108.

50.   P.S. Khoury and J. Kostiner, 'Introduction: Tribes and the Complexes of State Formation in the Middle East', in P.S. Khoury and J. Kostiner (eds.), *Tribes and State Formation in the Middle East* (Berkeley, Los Angeles and Oxford: University of California Press, 1990) p.2.

51.   R. Tapper, 'Anthropologists, Historians and Tribespeople on Tribe and State Formation in the Middle East', in ibid., p.65; and S.C. Caton, 'Anthropological Theories of Tribe and State Formation in the Middle East: Ideology and Semiotics of Power', in ibid., pp.96–9.

52.   A.D. Smith (note 12) pp.20–1.

53.   P.R. Brass, 'Ethnic Groups and the State', in P.R. Brass (ed.), *Ethnic Groups and the State* (New York: Barnes & Noble, 1985) pp.19 and 49–50, n.1.

54.   D.L. Horowitz, op. cit., p.56.

55.   F. Barth (ed.), *Ethnic Groups and Boundaries. The Social Organization of Culture Difference* (Oslo: Universitetsforlaget, Scandinavian University Press, 1969).

56.   Brass, in P.R. Brass (ed.) op. cit., p.1.

57.   A.D. Smith (note 31) pp.108–33.

58.   For these arguments see, M. Hechter, *Internal Colonialism. the Celtic Fringe in British National Development 1536–1966* (London: Routledge, 1975); and T. Nairn, *The Break-up of Britain: Crisis and Neo-Nationalism* (London: New Left Books, 2nd ed. 1977).

59.   L.A. Coser, *The Functions of Social Conflict* (New York and London: Free Press and Collier Macmillan, 1956) pp.38 and 87–95.

60.   M.E. Brown, 'Causes and Implications of Ethnic Conflict', in M.E. Brown (ed.) op. cit., p.5.

61.   D.L. Horowitz, 'Ethnic Conflict Management for Policymakers', in J.V. Montville (ed.), *Conflict and Peacemaking in Multiethnic Societies* (Lexington MA and Toronto: Lexington Books and D.C. Heath, 1991) p.115.

62.   D.L. Horowitz (note 33) pp.53–4.

63.   J.W. Burton, 'Conflict Resolution as a Political Philosophy', in D.J.D. Sandole and H. van der Merwe (eds.), *Conflict Resolution Theory and Practice: Integration and Application* (New York and Manchester: Manchester University Press, 1993) p.55.

64.   R.O. Keohane and J.S. Nye, 'Transnational Relations and World Politics: an Introduction', in R.O. Keohane and J.S. Nye (eds.), *Transnational Relations and World Politics* (Cambridge MA: Harvard University Press, 1971).

65.   M.H. Halperin and D.J Scheffer with P. Small, *Self-Determination in the New World Order* (Washington DC: Carnegie Endowment for International Peace, 1992) p.50.

66.   T.R. Gurr, op. cit., p.133.

67.   Ibid.

68.   R.R. Premdas, 'The Internationalization of Ethnic Conflict: Some Theoretical Explanations', in K.M. de Silva and R.J. May (eds.), *Internationalization of Ethnic Conflict* (London: Pinter, 1991) pp.11–12.

69.   D.L. Horowitz, 'Irredentas and Secessions: Adjacent Phenomena, Neglected Connections', in N. Chazan (ed.), *Irredentism and International Politics* (Boulder CO: Lynne Rienner, 1991) pp.14–15.

70. *TDN*, 12 and 13 Oct. 1993. Çiller evidently told Turkish journalists of her interest in the 'Spanish model', where considerable powers were devolved to local administrations, after having held talks with Spanish Premier Felipe Gonzalez in Vienna. After holding a meeting with the then Turkish Chief of General Staff Doğan Güreş, Çiller flatly denied having made such remarks.

71. *Eastern Mediterranean*, Report submitted on behalf of the Defence Committee of the WEU, Doc.1465, 24 May 1995.

72. J. Grugel, 'The Basques', in M. Watson (ed.), *Contemporary Minority Nationalism* (New York and London: Routledge, 1992) p.111.

73. M. Keating, 'Spain: Peripheral Nationalism and State Response', in J. McGarry and B. O'Leary (eds.) op. cit., p.222.

74. For more details of this general historical background see, M. Heiberg, *The Making of the Basque Nation* (Cambridge: Cambridge University Press, 1989).

75. Ibid., p.119.

76. A.D. Smith, 'The Ethnic Sources of Nationalism', in M.E. Brown (ed.) op. cit., p.34.

77. For a comprehensive background discussion of the Kurds see, M. Izady, *A Concise Handbook: The Kurds* (Washington DC and London: Taylor & Francis, 1992).

78. G.R. Garthwaite, 'Reimagined Internal Frontiers: Tribes and Nationalism – Bakhtiyari and Kurds', in D.F. Eickelman (ed.), *Russia's Muslim Frontiers – New Directions in Cross-Cultural Analysis* (Bloomington and Indianopolis IN: Indiana University Press, 1993) pp.140–2. See also L. Yalçin-Heckmann, 'Kurdish Tribal Organization and Local Political Processes', in A. Finkel and N. Sırman (eds.), *Turkish State and Turkish Society* (New York and London: Routledge, 1990) pp.289–312.

79. M. Van Bruinessen, 'Kurdish Society, Ethnicity, Nationalism and Refugee Problems', in P.G. Kreyenbroek and S. Sperl (eds.), *The Kurds: a Contemporary Overview* (New York and London: Routledge, 1992) p.47. Zaza is one of the major Kurdish 'languages' as well as being the name of a particular group of Kurds.

80. N. Kendal, 'Kurdistan in Turkey', in G. Chaliand (ed.), *People Without a Country: The Kurds and Kurdistan* (London: Zed Press, 1980) p.47.

81. P. Robins, 'The Overlord State: Turkish Policy and the Kurdish Issue', *International Affairs*, 69, 4 (Oct. 1993) p.661.

82. O. Sheikhmous, 'The Kurdish Question in Regional Politics: Possible Peaceful Solutions', in K. Rupesinghe (ed.), *Internal Conflict and Governance* (New York and Basingstoke, Hants.: St. Martin's Press and Macmillan, 1992) p.134. See also the works of the Turkish writer İsmail Beşikçi.

83. M. Izady, op. cit., p.119.

2

Minority Rights and the Issue of
Self-Determination

I N RECENT years the traditional, prevailing, state-centric view of the world
with its emphasis on the importance of territorial integrity, state sovereignty
and non-interference in the domestic affairs of other states has been increasingly challenged. The activities of international organizations, non-
governmental organizations, and multinational corporations in the Cold War
era had already led analysts to question increasingly the validity of an
exclusively state centric approach. The end of the Cold War has resulted in
a much less rigid but at the same time more unstable and volatile international
environment. The communist multinational entities of the Soviet Union,
Yugoslavia and Czechoslovakia have fragmented. But the tragedy in the
former Yugoslavia, and the civil strife in Burundi, Rwanda, Somalia and Iraq
have led to heightened international concern over the fate of oppressed
minority groups. This has even resulted in outside intervention on humanitarian grounds – initially at least – in order to protect minority rights and
prevent the gross violation of human rights.

The principles of territorial integrity, state sovereignty and the primacy of
domestic jurisdiction in the internal affairs of states (UN Charter Article 2
[7]) have thus come into question in recent years. However, the UN Charter
also referred to the principle of the self-determination of peoples (Article 1
[2]; Article 55) with its implication that the indivisibility of states and nations
could be challenged. In practice, nonetheless, the UN Charter has been
interpreted until recently in such a way that the principle of territorial
integrity has prevailed over that of self-determination. Furthermore, the right
of humanitarian intervention to help oppressed groups or peoples is not
mentioned in the Charter.[1]

It may be argued that it is in the common interest of governments to ensure
the continued predominance of the principles of state sovereignty and
territorial integrity. To some officials, the alternative leads to possible chaos,
as it does not seem clear where minority rights would end and self-
determination begin, with the latter often associated with a possible right of
secession. Even in the case of a successful secessionist movement, violence

could be precipitated as state officials and other groups within a state could endeavour to preserve the unity of the country by using force. A process could also be set in motion leading, as it were, to the danger of almost never-ending secessions as new problems of minority rights could emerge in newly created states.

Even in the Cold War period the principles of state sovereignty and non-interference in the domestic affairs of other states were clearly breached. For example, Tanzania invaded Uganda in 1979 and the United States has periodically become involved in Central America. Bangladesh was able to secede from Pakistan in 1971, albeit by non-peaceful means. But recent developments have created a new set of circumstances as noted earlier. Eritrea succeeded in breaking away from Ethiopia in 1993, and Slovenia, Croatia, Bosnia-Hercegovina and Macedonia effectively seceded from Yugoslavia. The declarations of independence in most of the Soviet republics resulted in the acceleration of the disintegration of the USSR. The issues of minority rights and human rights in general are also now firmly on the international agenda. However, it is interesting to note that UN Security Council Resolution 688 of April 1991, which paved the way for the establishment of what became known as Operation PROVIDE COMFORT in northern Iraq, insisted that Iraq should allow immediate access for international humanitarian organizations to all those in need. This was because the situation there was judged to be a threat to international peace and security owing to refugee flows and cross-border incursions. Concern for minority or human rights was not used to justify this particular outside intervention.[2]

A great many problems are raised in connection with the issues of minority rights and self-determination. What is a minority? What is meant exactly by self-determination? What are the rights of minorities? How should one distinguish – if indeed one should – the rights of individuals and universal rights from the rights of groups (minorities)? Who has the right to self-determination? How may this right be exercised? Does the right of self-determination automatically lead to secession and the break-up of states? Are the Kurds in Turkey a minority entitled to a number of rights, including possibly the right of self-determination? If so, what forms of self-determination could they be entitled to?

Officials in Ankara stress the importance of the territorial integrity of Turkey, the indivisibility of state and nation, and the unitary character of the Turkish state. These officials also underline the need to ensure that Turkish should remain the only official language. Quite clearly, therefore, they are sensitive to the issues of minority rights and self-determination. Turkish officials are concerned that a situation should not develop in which extremist Turkish and Kurdish nationalist groups may become engaged in a bloodbath on Turkish territory.

What Is a Minority?

International treaties and conventions have failed to define what is meant by a 'minority'. Efforts to agree upon a definition have resulted in considerable delays in the presentation and adoption of certain conventions. The failure to reach a consensus on what is meant by a minority weakens substantially the workings of these conventions. The problem of definition here is closely related to the highly sensitive and political implications of the recognition of a minority. Certain minority rights could be regarded by officials in some states as an infringement of state sovereignty and a possible threat to the integrity of a state and nation. In such cases, therefore, officials may deny the existence of minorities, or certain types of minority within their territory. There are close links here with the previous discussion of what is meant by assimilation and with the recognition or non-recognition of other nations and ethnic groups.

A report of the UN Sub-Commission on the Prevention of Discrimination and the Protection of Minorities released in 1985 attempted to define a minority as:

> A group of citizens of a state, constituting a numerical minority and in a non-dominant position in that state, endowed with ethnic, religious or linguistic characteristics which differ from those of the majority of the population, having a sense of solidarity with one another, motivated, if only implicitly by a collective will to survive and whose aim is to achieve equality with the majority in fact and in law.[3]

This definition appears comprehensive, but in reality officials in some states have been unable to approve of it or similar such definitions. Of course, a group of citizens constituting a numerical majority may also be oppressed, such as the blacks in Apartheid South Africa. The definition above implies that there are ethnic, religious and linguistic minorities. One may add that another important category is that of a national minority.

A minority is thus a self-aware, self-defined group which is seeking to survive and preserve its identity. As discussed earlier with regard to nations and ethnic groups, some individuals sharing similar objective characteristics with others may, however, not perceive themselves to be part of a minority in need of preservation. Again, in line with earlier discussions, other-definition is also important in connection with minorities.

Just as there may be different types of ethnic group, there may also be several kinds of ethnic minority. One form of minority may be referred to as a non-dominant ethnic group within a state which does not regard itself as a nation and whose leaders are not striving for a considerable degree of autonomy or complete independence. Its leaders, however, are seeking from the authorities of the state in which they reside recognition of their existence as an ethnic minority in order to guarantee the protection of what may be loosely termed their cultural rights. Those more politicized ethnic groups whose elites are trying to establish their own state or acquire extensive autonomy within the state in which they live may be regarded as another type of minority. The leaders of these ethnic minorities are not likely to be satisfied in the longer term with guarantees only for the protection of cultural rights. An ethnic group does not need to be other-defined. But for an ethnic group to be entitled to the rights of an ethnic minority – whatever these might be – the recognition of its minority status at least tacitly (i.e., other-definition) by the authorities of the state in question is necessary.

In this study a national minority refers to a group which considers itself to be part of a nation; but this group lives within a territory controlled by officials of another nation. Unlike those ethnic minorities which are seeking extensive autonomy or even statehood, a national minority is regarded as a national entity at least by the authorities of the state which is controlled by the nation of which the national minority considers itself to be a part. The members of a national minority in general perceive themselves to be part of a nation which already has its own state. A national minority is thereby self-defined and other-defined. The authorities of the 'host state' may not recognize the existence of this national minority and so its cultural and other rights may not be respected. This could compel the national minority to push for more rights, such as varying degrees of autonomy and even possibly secession, perhaps attempting to unite with the state controlled by its own nation.

A key problem again, then, is one of other-definition. State authorities are not obliged to recognize the existence of minorities. By denying their existence state authorities would not need to respect their rights even though, in practice, minorities may exist. It has been suggested that the existence or not of a minority should be decided independently of recognition by the host state. According to one proposal, a group of authoritative, neutral experts should compile a list of minorities deserving international recognition and protection.[4] The establishment of such an authoritative body is not likely in the foreseeable future. The Copenhagen Document of the Human Dimension of the then Conference on Security and Co-operation in Europe (CSCE) noted in 1990 that: 'To belong to a national minority is a matter of person's individual choice and no disadvantage may arise from the existence of such choice'.[5] A person may therefore choose to belong to a minority and express his or her will to protect his or her minority identity but states are not obliged to recognize the existence of a minority.

The term 'ethnic minority' could be added to the quoted text of the Copenhagen Document. In practice, some state authorities are prepared to recognize the existence of religious minorities but not ethnic nor national minorities on their territory. This policy has been pursued by the Greek authorities with regard to their 'Turkish minority'. The recognition of a religious authority, one may argue, is less contentious. Limited cultural rights could be granted in such instances which would not seem to threaten state cohesion in the manner that the recognition of ethnic or national minorities might. The problem here, of course, is the case of an ethnic group which shares the same religion as the dominant ethnic group/nation within a state. This group could not be officially classified as a religious minority. And members of this ethnic group may be seeking to obtain the so-called rights of an ethnic or national minority.

What Are the Rights of a Minority?

One commentator has referred to minority rights as 'the rights of minorities to receive equal treatment, to practise their culture, religion and language, and to participate fully in the political and economic life of the state'.[6] It would seem that these rights would be compatible with a state based on genuine civic, democratic pluralism, i.e., a political community. If minority rights are not granted, a 'minority group' could in certain cases be threatened with total assimilation and thus the leaders of this endangered group might attempt to secede. This depiction of minority rights is a description rather than a strict definition which could have legal and political meaning. In addition to the problem of identifying a minority group, one also must be clear what minority rights are and how they may be respected and enforced.

The League of Nations did attempt to establish a form of minority-rights protection system for newly created states or for those states defeated in the First World War. These states in eastern and central Europe were compelled to conclude Minorities Treaties which would be 'guaranteed' by the League. By these treaties minorities within these states were accorded, *inter alia*, rights to establish their own schools, use their own language, practise their religion and enjoy equality before the law. However, they were not granted the right to autonomy, for instance. The Polish Minorities Treaty, upon which other minority treaties were based, referred to 'persons belonging to racial, religious or linguistic minorities'.[7] It has been argued that while using this terminology the framers of the treaty were really referring to 'national minorities'.[8] But what was meant by a minority was not made clear. The members of the League's Council had the right and duty to call attention to actual or threatened 'infraction' of minority obligations with regard to these minority treaties. States not members of the Council and the 'minorities' themselves could petition Council members to take up their cause in the event of a possible infraction. The League's Secretariat would decide whether to accept the petition. If so, the petition would be directed to an *ad hoc* Committee of Three of the Council to investigate and attempt to resolve the matter.

In practice, the petition procedure was cumbersome and drawn-out. Redress for a minority was by no means guaranteed. The system lacked powers of enforcement. It remained dependent on the force of persuasion. Minorities complained that they had no legal standing as participants in the League system. There had been talk of forming a Permanent Commission to handle minority issues but nothing was realized. Moreover, the minorities treaties applied to only a certain category of states. Thus, for example, minorities in territories under the control of the victorious Great Powers had no rights whatsoever. In reality, the framers of this so-called minority rights protection system were more concerned not to offend the sensitivities of state leaderships. The so-called rights of minorities were of secondary importance. A main priority was the concern to maintain peace in the inter-war period, although some politicians were aware of the connection between stability and the proper guaranteeing of minority rights.

Unlike the League of Nations, the UN Charter of 1945 and the UN Universal Declaration of Human Rights of 1948 did not refer specifically to the rights of minorities. The primary concern of the UN was with state sovereignty and also with the civil, political, economic, social and cultural rights of individuals (their human rights) which should apply universally. Concerning these rights, the emphasis was on equality and non-discrimination. The omission of all reference to minority rights appears to have been deliberate, and seems to have been at least in part a reaction to Hitler's skilful abuse of minority rights in the late 1930s.

However, Article 27 of the UN International Covenant on Civil and Political Rights (signed in December 1966; entered into force March 1976) states: 'In those states in which ethnic, religious or linguistic minorities exist, persons belonging to such minorities shall not be denied the right, in community with other members of their group, to enjoy their own culture, to profess and practice their own religion, or to use their own language.'[9] This Covenant also listed the rights of these 'minorities', such as the right to participate in government, the right to equality before the law, the right to freedom of association, and the right to freedom of thought and religion.

In the Covenant a distinction was made between ethnic, religious and linguistic minorities. This acknowledgement that religious and linguistic minorities could exist and be separate from ethnic minorities would have pleased the authorities in those states reluctant to concede the existence of ethnic minorities within their territory. Again, no attempt was made to define a minority. Nor was a body appointed to attempt to designate minorities. These omissions appear to explain why the wording of this covenant secured the unanimous approval of states.[10] It also employed the formula of referring to the rights of 'persons belonging to such minorities' rather than expressly mentioning the rights of a minority *per se*. Other international conventions would follow this procedure. This was, in effect, a compromise between individual rights, the group rights of a minority, and a concern to protect state sovereignty. State authorities were anxious that minorities should not be given an international personality and were determined to ensure that minorities would not be made subjects of law. However, the reference to 'persons belonging to such minorities' at the same time does presuppose a community of individuals endowed with similar rights.[11] One major drawback with regard to Article 27 of the Covenant is the fact that the opening phrase almost invites state authorities to claim that no ethnic, religious or linguistic minority exists. An authoritative General Comment on Article 27 adopted by the UN in 1994 failed to address satisfactorily this particular shortcoming.

The UN General Assembly Declaration on the Rights of Persons Belonging to National or Ethnic, Religious and Linguistic Minorities issued in December 1992 referred in Article 1 to the need of states to protect the 'existence' and promote the 'identity' of these minorities within their territories. However, Article 2 reverted to the formula of referring to 'persons belonging to' these minorities who should 'have the right to enjoy their own culture, to profess and practice their own religion, and to use their own language, in private and in public, freely and without interference or any form of discrimination'. Other sections of the Declaration referred to the rights of minorities to participate in decisions affecting them at national and regional level (2.3); the right to set up associations (2.4); the right to maintain contacts with kinship groups across frontiers (2.5); and the obligations of the state to promote education in the mother tongue and impart knowledge of minority cultures (4.3).[12]

One should note that 'national minorities' are included in the UN General Assembly Declaration of December 1992. However, the Declaration again avoids attempting to define a minority. Efforts to do so had apparently stalled work on preparing the Declaration throughout the 1980s. There had been suggestions to grant minorities the right to 'autonomy' and 'self-management', but a number of states, fearful of the possible repercussions for their sovereignty and integrity, had forcibly objected to these proposals. Nevertheless, Article 1 – unlike Article 2 – did refer specifically to 'minorities'. This was was an advance on the 1966 UN International Covenant on Civil and Political Rights (and the accompanying UN International Covenant on Economic, Social and Cultural Rights) as the Declaration did appear to recognize the existence of minorities as identifiable groups entitled to certain rights.[13] However, other commentators have contended that Article 1 strengthens the role of the state insofar as it is the state which is the legal 'person' responsible for protecting the rights of minorities.[14] More weight is thus placed on the host state authorities' recognizing in the first place the existence of minorities within their territories.

The rights of minorities may also be covered in part by the International Convention on the Elimination of All Forms of Racial Discrimination, which was announced in a UN General Assembly resolution as early as December 1965 and entered into force in January 1969. Article 1(1) spoke of 'racial discrimination' on the grounds of 'race, colour, descent, or national or ethnic origin' which would nullify or impair the 'recognition, enjoyment or exercise, on an equal footing of human rights and fundamental freedoms in the political, economic, social, cultural or any other field of public life'.[15] However, the term 'minority' would for the first time be employed in a UN agreement the following year in the International Covenants.

One major problem with the International Convention on the Elimination of All Forms of Racial Discrimination and with all other UN instruments is the lack of effective monitoring and enforcement mechanisms. Article 14 of the Convention does refer to an Optional Declaration whereby a state could allow the Committee on the Elimination of Racial Discrimination to consider individual petitions, but only a few states have subscribed to this Declaration. An Optional Protocol is attached to the 1966 UN International Covenant on Civil and Political Rights which allows individuals who claim to be the victims of human rights violations by a state party to communicate to a Human Rights Committee after having exhausted all available remedies. Only a small number of states are party to this Protocol and the Committee merely passes general comments and not legally-binding judgments. No state is required to respond to UN requests for information or comply with General Assembly resolutions. There have also been problems in co-ordinating the activities of the UN Commission on Human Rights elected by the UN Economic and Social Council and its subordinate body, the UN Sub-Commission on the Prevention of Discrimination and the Protection of Minorities. The latter, in effect, provides recommendations to the Commission on Human Rights and assists in the collecting of information and the preparation of fact-finding mandates in connection with minority issues. Both UN bodies lack real powers of enforcement.[16] In 1995, however, the Commission on Human Rights approved the formation of an expert Working Group whose task would be to review the implementation of the General Assembly Declaration of December 1992 and to consider solutions to problems concerning minorities. A year earlier a UN High Commissioner for Human Rights was established with a brief to monitor and report on human rights violations.

In most cases documents released by the CSCE/OSCE (Organization for Security and Co-operation in Europe, the successor body to the CSCE) also only refer to principles which are political commitments but not legally-binding instruments. In line with their UN counterparts, the major CSCE/OSCE texts do not attempt to define a minority. In the Helsinki Final Act of 1975, Principle VII in the Declaration on Principles Guiding Relations between Participating States has a clause on 'national minorities'. The text specifies the need to respect the right of persons belonging to such minorities to equality before the law and calls for participating states to give them the opportunity to enjoy their human rights and fundamental freedoms which should be respected.[17] Unlike the earlier UN International Covenant on Civil and Political Rights, the Helsinki Final Act was much less specific with regard to the rights of minorities. Moreover, only 'national minorities' were mentioned. Nevertheless, 17 years before the General Assembly Declaration of December 1992, the Final Act did recognize the existence of a minority as a group, in addition to persons belonging to a minority.

In recent years, with the end of the Cold War, the then CSCE was able to focus more attention on minorities and their rights within its so-called Human Dimension mechanism. The CSCE meeting of June 1990 in Copenhagen outlined in greater detail the rights of 'persons belonging to national minorities'. They should not be the victims of discrimination and should enjoy equality before the law (Article 3.1); they should 'have the right freely to express, preserve and develop their ethnic, cultural, linguistic or religious identity and to maintain and develop their culture in all its aspects, free of any attempts at assimilation against their will' (3.2); they should have the right to use their mother tongue in private and in public (3.2.1); maintain their own educational, cultural and religious institutions (3.2.2); keep contact across frontiers with citizens of other states sharing the same cultural heritage (3.2.4); disseminate and have access to and exchange information in their mother tongue (3.2.5); effectively participate in public affairs 'including participation in the affairs relating to the protection and promotion of the identity of such minorities'. Moreover, they should even here be allowed to establish 'local or autonomous administrations' (3.5).[18] This possible right of autonomy was a major landmark in minority rights. The rights listed in the Copenhagen Document would be reiterated or referred to in the CSCE Summit in November 1990 (the Charter of Paris) and in the follow-up CSCE Summit in Helsinki in July 1992.

The CSCE Meeting of Experts on National Minorities in Geneva in July 1991 stated that: 'Issues concerning national minorities, as well as compliance with international obligations and commitments concerning the rights of persons belonging to them, are matters of legitimate international concern and consequently do not constitute exclusively an internal affair of the respective state.'[19] This was in effect a major assault against state sovereignty in the interests of the rights of minorities. Note, however, that in line with what had become standard CSCE practice since the Helsinki Final Act, reference was made only to 'national minorities'.

The Moscow Mechanism of the CSCE/OSCE Human Dimension is potentially an important instrument with regard to the protection of minority rights. In January 1989, after a meeting at Vienna, the so-called CSCE Vienna Mechanism was established by which member states could seek information and investigate cases relating to human rights abuses including the violations of the rights of minorities among other member states. The Moscow Conference on the CSCE Human Dimension in October 1991 provided the Vienna Mechanism with more teeth. By the terms of the new Moscow Mechanism, a set of procedures was drafted whereby missions drawn from a pool of experts could be sent to participating states to investigate cases referring to the Human Dimension. There were in summary three possibilities: a participating state itself could invite a CSCE mission of three rapporteurs to its territory to make an investigation. Or a mission could be sent to a participating state upon the request of six CSCE states and in co-operation with what became known as the OSCE Permanent Council. Finally, in a case of emergency, any ten CSCE states on their own initiative could despatch a mission of three rapporteurs to the participating state in question to 'establish the facts, report on them and ... give advice on possible solutions to the question raised'.[20] It seems that if an OSCE state refused to accept a mission of three rapporteurs in this instance, then that state's membership of the OSCE could even be suspended.

Given the possible tough sanctions involved one wonders in practice how far OSCE states would be prepared to go to push a recalcitrant member state to accept a mission to investigate alleged cases of the abuse of minority rights on its territory. In general, a careful reading of many of the CSCE texts would lead one to realize that a number of 'escape clauses' have been added to ensure that member states would not feel too constrained. Thus there are references to member states pledging to 'endeavour' or 'consider' various actions 'wherever possible and necessary' or 'in conformity with applicable national legislation'.[21] The OSCE High Commissioner on National Minorities, a post established in 1992, has become a useful tool in conflict prevention. But the High Commissioner is not meant to become involved in situations of violent ethnic tension. Separate from the Human Dimension Mechanism, the OSCE also may despatch fact-finding and rapporteur missions to member states as instruments of conflict prevention and crisis management. In practice, member states are likely to be more willing to accept brief fact-finding visits rather than longer-term missions.

The Council of Europe has a long-established interest in minority rights. As early as November 1950 the Council of Europe's European Convention for the Protection of Human Rights and Fundamental Freedoms (ECHR) (entered into force in September 1953) referred to the rights of a 'national minority'. Several articles outlined, inter alia, the rights of all individuals to freedom of thought, religion, travel, peaceful assembly and association. Article 14 specifically noted that the enjoyment of these rights 'shall be secured without discrimination on any ground such as sex, race, colour, language, religion, political or other opinion, national or social origin, association with a national minority, property, birth or other status.'[22]

Significantly, the Council of Europe has at its disposal mechanisms such as the European Commission of Human Rights and the European Court of Human Rights. The rulings of the latter are binding. Alleged violations of the ECHR by contracting states are first heard by the European Commission of Human Rights upon an application from other contracting states, or individuals, groups of individuals (ie., possibly minorities) and non-governmental organizations. If no settlement can be reached in what is judged to be a violation of the ECHR, the case could be taken up by either the European Court of Human Rights or by a Committee of Ministers of the Council of Europe. The European Court may pronounce judgments and demand just satisfaction for the injured party. The Committee of Ministers may decide by a two-thirds majority whether a violation has occurred and may demand that the guilty state remedy the situation. Failure to abide by these rulings or decisions could result ultimately in a state's being expelled from the Council of Europe.

In October 1993 the Council of Europe Summit in Vienna released a declaration which called for the drafting of a framework convention which would specify principles with regard to the protection of national minorities. On 1 February 1995 a number of countries signed this new Framework Convention for the Protection of National Minorities. The Framework Convention aims to transform the political commitments adopted by the CSCE/OSCE to the greatest possible extent into legal obligations. In line with the Copenhagen Document of June 1990, therefore, the Framework Convention refers, *inter alia*, to the rights of minorities to use and be taught in their own language, to practise their own religion, to enjoy cultural freedom, to have minority language radio and television, and to be able to contact kin-groups across frontiers. This Framework Convention will come into force once it has been ratified by 12 states. It is intended to be the first legally-binding, multilateral, European instrument for the protection of national minorities, but its principles are not enforceable. The Framework Convention also fails again to define what is a minority.[23]

In spite of the difficulties of definition and the problems and abuses of the inter-war period, there has been gradually an increasing awareness of the existence of 'minorities' whose rights need to be respected. However, the formula 'persons belonging to national minorities' is still also employed. There has developed a realization that greater protection for minorities would probably prevent the dismemberment of multi-ethnic states which were in the past held together by communist ideology or Cold War fears and tensions.[24] There are moves afoot to codify the rights of minorities and improve mechanisms in order to monitor and enforce these rights. This trend runs counter to the argument that minority rights are not necessary as all persons should be covered by individual human rights applied universally.

The Problems of Minority Rights

In a democracy would not the rights of all citizens automatically be covered? Or do minorities need additional, special rights even in a democracy? It has been noted earlier that the authorities in certain states, wishing to deny the existence of minorities and seeking to assimilate all groups, could employ the argument that, as they had established (ostensibly?) a democracy, no extra rights were required for any of their citizens. An article in *The Economist* has asserted that at first sight the concept of minority rights does seem flawed as by definition it applies only to some whereas basic democratic rights should apply to all. The article adds that one solution is to deal on a case-by-case basis, where some minorities might need special rights to protect their language and culture where these were threatened and in danger of extinction.[25]

Eide has attempted to resolve this problem by distinguishing between a 'common domain' and a 'separate domain' with regard to the rights of individuals and groups. With reference to the 'common domain', the same rights should apply to all citizens and states should be obliged to uphold here all relevant international standards. Concerning the 'separate domain', however, special measures would be needed to protect the 'identity' of a minority, such as, for instance, guarantees of the continued development of cultural expression, education in a minority's language and provision for minority self-administration in policy areas affecting the minority's special interests.[26] The right of a minority to its identity is crucial here. It has been suggested that with national minorities this right can only be realized through various forms of autonomy.[27] The problem of other-definition cannot be avoided though. The authorities of the host state need to recognize first, openly or tacitly, the existence of a minority; but officials may deny recognition in order to crush the identity of what is in reality a minority group. Recognition may also be denied by the central authorities out of fear that disintegration of the state may then ensue.

Closely linked with the issue of whether minorities need special rights, there is also a debate concerning whether only 'prevention of discrimination' is required to protect minorities and their rights, or is 'positive action' also necessary. Prevention of discrimination entails equality of treatment of all individuals and groups. With positive action, however, even after general equality of treatment with the majority, minorities also seek differential treatment in order to protect their basic characteristics – such as special measures to protect their culture and language. Here the minorities are opposed to assimilation which could be equated with a policy concerned with the 'prevention of discrimination'.[28] In line with a gradual shift in thinking from the recognition of individual rights only to an acknowledgement that groups also have certain rights, in recent years there has also been a marked tendency to emphasize more 'positive action' in international conventions. As one commentator has pointed out, there is a considerable difference between the key phrase 'shall not be denied' in the International Covenant on Civil and Political Rights and the expression 'shall protect and encourage' in the 1992 UN General Assembly Declaration on Minorities.[29]

According to another suggestion, the best policy for a government to follow is not to avoid special rights for a minority but rather to pursue a policy of 'benign neglect' and 'ethnic *laissez-faire*' – 'The government is best which pays least official attention to ethnicity.' Governments should ignore but not be indifferent to differences of ethnicity among the population of its state. Regional autonomy may even be tolerated following this line. Thus 'the state implicitly admits the reality of differences but officially opposes making them'.[30] In practice, it is exceedingly difficult to imagine how such a policy or non-policy could work. The governments of states are not likely to allow regional autonomy without very good reason – such as openly recognizing the presence of ethnic or national minorities. It also seems highly unlikely that any government would pursue a policy of so-called 'benign neglect' on issues as potentially explosive as those of nationalism and ethnicity.

Other possible difficult issues concerning the rights of minorities are related to the so-called 'minorities of minorities' problem and the question of the loyalty of minority groups. It has been suggested that Article 27 of the International Covenant on Civil and Political Rights refers to the rights of 'persons belonging to' ethnic, religious or linguistic minorities partly in order to protect the rights of dissenting members of minority groups who need not therefore be forced to comply with the wishes of the majority of the minority group.[31] A minority, like a nation or an ethnic group, is not a monolithic entity. The voices of all members of a minority should be heard even though this could be a complicating factor for minority rights.

Writing about the League of Nations and its ostensible minority-rights protection system, Claude noted that it was unrealistic to expect the authorities of states to grant liberal treatment to 'disloyal' citizens and spoke of the need for both 'tolerant majorities' and 'loyal minorities'.[32] This line of argument appears to remain relevant today. But what would 'disloyalty' entail? Demands for independence most probably, but what of calls for autonomy? There are many possible objectives that a minority within a state may pursue short of secession and independence such as calls for various types of autonomy or the introduction of a federal system of government. A right of secession is not generally recognized. However, given what has happened in recent years in the Soviet Union and the former Yugoslavia, the leaderships of many states, particularly of those states in unstable and volatile regional environments such as the Middle East, are especially sensitive to any developments which may threaten, however indirectly, the territorial integrity and indivisibility of their state.

The Kurds and Minority Rights in Turkey

In the nineteenth century the Western powers had become increasingly interested in the rights of Christian minorities in the decaying Ottoman Empire. The *millet* system was no longer able to accommodate the nationalist demands of many of the Empire's Christian subjects. Endeavouring to preserve the integrity of the Empire, the Ottoman authorities from time to time resorted to excessive violence against certain groups. Point 12 of President Woodrow Wilson's famous 14 Points declared that the non-Turkish minorities of the Ottoman Empire should be granted the right of 'auto-nomous development'. It was far from clear which groups at that time constituted 'non-Turkish minorities' as many individuals perceived their identity primarily in terms of religion rather than ethnicity.

Article 22 of the League of Nations Covenant noted that 'certain com-munities' of the Ottoman Empire 'have reached a stage of development where their existence as independent nations can be provisionally recognized', subject to the temporary administrative advice and assistance of a mandatory power. And, as will be discussed later, in the Sèvres Treaty of August 1920 the Kurds were specifically mentioned. Article 62 referred to the need for 'local autonomy for the predominantly Kurdish areas', while Article 64 looked forward to the possibility that 'the Kurdish peoples' might be granted 'independence'.

Taking the Polish Minorities Treaty as a model, in 1923 the Treaty of Lausanne was concluded between the victorious Western powers and the officials of the new Turkish Republic. Article 39 of the Treaty read:

> No restriction shall be imposed on the free use by any Turkish national of any language in private intercourse, in commerce, religion, in the press, or in publication of any kind, or at public meetings. Notwithstanding the existence of the official language, adequate facilities shall be given to Turkish nationals of non-Turkish speech for the oral use of language before their own courts.

The emphasis here was on the need to respect the language rights for 'any Turkish national', including therefore those citizens who would not in practice be a part of what would become the dominant ethnic (i.e., Turkish) core. By Article 37 the authorities of the Turkish Republic agreed to respect Article 39 with others as fundamental laws which could not be overruled by other laws. In line with the other minorities treaties, Article 44 formed the so-called 'guarantee clause'. This noted that the League of Nations Council had the right to oversee possible infractions or the danger of infractions of these obligations.[33]

It is important to note here that the Turkish officials insisted that the rights agreed to at Lausanne should apply only to 'non-Moslem minorities', i.e., principally to the Armenians, Greeks and Jews. This was seen as significant bearing in mind the recent killings and deaths of a large part of the Armenian population and the defeat of the invading Greek forces.[34] No assurances were provided for any 'Moslem minority' within the new Turkish Republic. The motives of Mustafa Kemal and his associates at this time *vis-à-vis* Islam and the fostering of a Turkish national identity will be discussed in detail later. The enforcement of the Law on the Unification of Education of 3 March 1924 with its closure of religious schools may have led indirectly also to the closure of such schools where the language of instruction was Kurdish.

Officials in Ankara have consistently argued that the minorities policy of the Turkish government is strictly based on the provisions of the Treaty of Lausanne. Religious minorities therefore do exist in Turkey, but there are no ethnic or national minorities. All citizens in Turkey enjoy equal rights and hence there is no need for additional rights other than those enjoyed by religious minorities.

The paramount concern of the Turkish authorities is to protect the integrity and indivisibility of the state and 'nation'. It appears that there is a prevalent feeling among official circles in Turkey that the granting of certain rights to an acknowledged ethnic or national minority would inevitably lead to further demands, including ultimately calls for secession in the name of self-determination. Turkish officials fear that the granting of certain rights to one ethnic group such as the Kurds could reawaken the consciousness of other ethnic groups in Turkey such as the Laz and the Circassians – the crisis in Chechnya and the hijacking of a Turkish ferry on the Black Sea by Chechen sympathizers in January 1996 rekindled awareness of a Circassian identity among particular groups in Turkey. These fears would seem to account for the inclusion of certain key phrases in important Turkish laws. Thus Article 3 of the Turkish Constitution notes that the Turkish state, its territory and nation is an indivisible entity whose language is Turkish. Article 14 prohibits activities which 'violate the indivisible integrity of the state with its territory and nation'. With reference to political parties, Article 68 declares that their statutes and programmes should 'not be in conflict with the indivisible integrity of the state with its territory and nation ...'.[35] A political party based solely on Kurdish ethnicity could thus be banned. Article 125 of the Turkish Penal Code states that: 'Any person...who carries out any action intended to destroy the unity of the Turkish state or to separate any part of the territory from the control of the Turkish state shall be punished by death.'[36] And Article 8 of the Anti-terror Law of April 1991 forbade propaganda, whether written or verbal, and all meetings, demonstrations or 'other acts' which adversely affected the indivisible integrity of the territory and the nation of the Turkish Republic. A revised version of this article agreed upon in October 1995 removed the expression, 'whatever the methods, goals and ideas thereof' from the text. Some Turkish commentators argued that the revision of the text was largely cosmetic, but detainees were released and sentences reduced for future violations of the article.[37]

Concern for the integrity of the Turkish state and 'nation' also explains why Turkey is not a party to several major international conventions which deal with the issue of minority rights. In those conventions that Turkey has acceded to a number of reservations have been made or official statements put on the record. Thus Turkey has signed but not ratified the International Convention on the Elimination of All Forms of Racial Discrimination. Turkey is one of a relatively small number of states that is not a party to the important International Covenant on Civil and Political Rights. Hence neither the Committee on the Elimination of Racial Discrimination nor the UN Human Rights Committee is able to make effective comments on Turkey's Kurdish policy.[38] Turkey has signed and ratified the UN Convention on the Rights of the Child but with reservations on Articles 17, 29 and 30. These articles stated that children belonging to an ethnic, religious or linguistic minority or of indigenous origins have the rights of language, education and cultural identity.

In connection with CSCE/OSCE conventions, Turkey has placed a reservation insisting that the term 'national minorities' should refer only to those recognized in international treaties,[39] i.e., the Treaty of Lausanne and its exclusive reference to religious minorities. Turkey, together with Spain, has also stressed that the OSCE High Commissioner on National Minorities may not intervene in situations involving 'terrorism'.[40] What is meant by 'terrorism' is obviously open to interpretation. Many Turkish officials believe that in Turkey there is no Kurdish problem but rather a problem of terrorism. Turkish governments have expressed their strong opposition to any possible implementation of the Vienna and Moscow Mechanism of the Human Dimension with reference to Turkey and the Kurdish issue. Officials in Ankara have stressed that the invoking of these Mechanisms would be regarded as a hostile act and would be seen as interference in the internal affairs of the Turkish state. In spite of their mounting criticisms of Turkish policy towards the Kurds, OSCE members have not been willing to invoke these Mechanisms hitherto. As noted earlier, this most probably would be done only as a last resort.

In May 1994 Germany called for the convening of a CSCE Conference on the Kurdish problem in Turkey and had pressed for the despatch of CSCE monitors. German Foreign Minister Klaus Kinkel in a meeting with his Turkish counterpart Mümtaz Soysal in September 1994 had again pushed for the sending of CSCE monitors to south-eastern Anatolia.[41] Instead, in order to ease tensions and pre-empt the possible implementation of the Moscow Mechanism, an OSCE delegation led by Willy Wimmer, deputy President of the OSCE Parliamentarians' Assembly, visited Turkey in early

May 1995 at the invitation of the Speaker of the Turkish Grand National Assembly, Hüsamettin Cindoruk. This was in effect a brief fact-finding mission. In its report released in June 1995 the OSCE delegation expressed its respect for Turkey's territorial integrity but urged officials to take political measures to solve the Kurdish problem.[42]

As a member of the Council of Europe Turkey is a party to the ECHR. More significantly, since 1990 Turkish officials have recognized the authority of the European Court of Human Rights. Judgments of this court are binding. Prime Minister Çiller in a luncheon speech to the ambassadors of western European states in December 1994 said that the imprisoned deputies of the pro-Kurdish Democracy Party (DEP) could appeal to the European Commission of Human Rights,[43] from where the case could then go to the European Court. In January 1996 lawyers for the four ex-DEP deputies still being held in custody announced that they would indeed appeal to the European Commission of Human Rights.[44] A number of cases involving alleged human rights violations in south-eastern Turkey have been taken up by the European Commission of Human Rights after requests from the Turkish Human Rights Association (IHD) and the Kurdistan Human Rights Project in London. Cases were being investigated by the European Commission of Human Rights before the exhaustion of existing legal channels in Turkey. The Turkish government was seeking 'friendly settlements' in order to prevent the European Court from taking up the cases. In January 1996, however, the European Court took up the case of the earlier closure by the Turkish authorities of the pro-Kurdish People's Labour Party (HEP). In this particular case the European Commission of Human Rights had not agreed with proposals for a friendly settlement put forward by Turkish officials. The ex-HEP deputies insisted that their party should be re-established.[45] The European Court could force the Turkish government to pay damages to the ex-HEP deputies or even demand the re-opening of the party.

The Turkish government, in line with a number of other governments, finally decided not to sign the Council of Europe's Framework Convention for the Protection of National Minorities in February 1995. Evidently, Turkish officials had originally considered signing but with a number of reservations.

Periodically, as indicated previously, there has been talk among official circles in Turkey about the possibility of recognizing the Kurdish reality. Thus the leaders of the SHP (Social Democratic Populist Party) and ANAP (Motherland Party) have on occasion advocated the opening of Kurdish schools and the broadcasting of radio and television programmes in Kurdish. Even Prime Minister Çiller referred, albeit fleetingly, to the relevance of the Basque model and its provisions for wide-ranging autonomy. The crucial question here, however, is how may these proposals be carried out given the deep-rooted fears that their implementation could endanger the integrity of the Turkish state.

Concerning the Kurds in Turkey, it is not possible to ascertain what exactly most Kurds who regard themselves as Kurds actually want. Are they after recognition of a minority status along with the rights that this would then entail? Some Kurds, feeling themselves to be a separate ethnic group, may not necessarily agree with the views of certain leaders of other Kurdish entities. In March 1994 in Brussels representatives of Kurdish political groups, associations and trade unions, together with other Turkish delegates and participants from several states, attended the Brussels International Conference on North West Kurdistan (South East Turkey). This meeting was the first of its kind. The Final Resolution of the conference called for changes to the Turkish constitution and domestic laws in order to 'guarantee fully and effectively the cultural, social and political rights of the Kurdish people'. A call was made for the lifting of all bans and restrictions on Kurdish organizations in Turkey including the PKK, and an appeal was made for the 'legal recognition of the right to use the Kurdish language'. The repeal of the Anti-terror Law was demanded. The Final Resolution noted the responsibilities of the international community. Specific reference was made concerning the need of the CSCE (now the OSCE) to extend the functions of the High Commissioner on National Minorities to enable him to exercise his mandate in Turkey. A plea was also made to activate the Vienna and Moscow Mechanisms of the CSCE Human Dimension. The delegates requested that all members of the Council of Europe should make use of Article 24 of the European Convention for the Protection of Human Rights and Fundamental Freedoms and submit an interstate application against Turkey concerning violations of the Convention. An appeal was also made to states to support the work of the newly-appointed UN Commissioner for Human Rights.[46] Given the circumstances then, most of these demands were unrealistic. The specific demands of certain Kurdish groups and associations will be examined in more detail later when we discuss recommendations for a possible peaceful solution to the Kurdish question.

The Çiller government has come under increasing international pressure to improve its human rights record. In October 1994 the President of the Parliamentary Assembly of the Council of Europe, Miguel Martinez, released a report on the current human rights situation in Turkey. This called for amendments to be made to several articles of the Turkish Constitution (including Article 14), the Turkish Penal Code, the Anti-terror Law, and the Law on Political Parties with reference to territorial integrity and the rights of political parties. The Martinez Report warned that Turkey's membership of the Council of Europe could be re-assessed.[47] For a period in 1995 Turkish deputies did not attend meetings of the Council of Europe's Parliamentary Assembly. This was until the Ministerial Committee of the Council of Europe overruled a previous decision of the Assembly to suspend Turkey's membership of the Council of Europe. In December 1994 Turkish officials resisted demands at the CSCE/OSCE Budapest Summit to accept observers to investigate allegations of torture and human-rights violations in Turkey. There have been proposals by the UK Parliamentary Human Rights Group, Amnesty International and the International Helsinki Federation for Human Rights to activate the Moscow Mechanism against Turkey. Following the sentences imposed upon the arrested DEP deputies, the European Parliament suspended all contacts in January 1995 with the Turkish Parliament and called for the release of the deputies and the reopening of their party. This effectively suspended the operation of the Turkey–EU Joint Parliamentary Commission and jeopardized the prospects for the final ratification of the Turkey–EU Customs Union accord. In December 1995 the European Parliament finally ratified the accord after fierce Turkish lobbying and after the revision of Article 8 of the Anti-terror Law.

There does seem to be an increasing awareness among some officials in Ankara that they should be seen to be making initiatives with regard to the human rights situation in Turkey. Thus at the Budapest Summit Prime Minister Çiller declared that Turkey was seeking to find a 'national consensus' to improve its human-rights record in line with its undertakings as a CSCE member, noting also: 'We all have shortcomings at the present time'. Çiller added: 'Whether it comes from the state or from terrorist organizations, human-rights violations are similarly unacceptable.'[48] In the case of Turkey, it would seem that rights will only be given – directly, tacitly, or indirectly – to a number of groups and minorities provided that the territorial integrity of the state and 'nation' would not be endangered. Thus these groups and minorities would first need to demonstrate their 'loyalty' to the Turkish state. The terrorist actions of the PKK are clearly not helping the cause of other Kurds in Turkey who are pressing for more rights. The behaviour of the PKK does make it exceedingly difficult for officials to separate the Kurdish issue from what is really a separate terrorist problem. The right to identity of a minority group is linked once again to the problems of self-definition and other-definition. At present, the Kurds in Turkey are an ethnic group which is yet to be recognized as an ethnic minority. With the exception of the recognized religious minorities in Turkey, the official policy of the government is based on an emphasis on the prevention of discrimination against any of its citizens rather than on positive action.

What Is a 'People'?

To many, a 'people' has a higher status than a 'minority'. According to international conventions it seems that peoples have a right to self-determination but not minorities. In practice, the distinction between a minority and a people is blurred. Self-determination is also an imprecise expression. There are several types of self-determination. Self-determination does not necessarily involve the right to establish one's own state. So-called 'internal self-determination', for example, covers much of what are generally known as minority rights without invoking the right of independent statehood.

As noted previously, the Turkish authorities have recently been prepared to admit that a Kurdish 'people' exists. In so doing, perhaps they were unaware of the possible ramifications of this recognition for international law. The problem of defining what is meant by a people in connection with the issue of self-determination was most vividly illustrated in a famous remark at a UN debate on decolonization concerning the ambiguity of 'self-deter-mination': 'On the surface it seemed reasonable: let the people decide. It was in fact ridiculous because the people cannot decide until someone decides who are the people.'[49] A UN report published in 1981 (the Critescu Report) listed the criteria required to qualify for being a 'people' for the purposes of self-determination. These were: a distinctive language, culture or religion; a shared sense of history; a commitment to maintain communal identity; and an association with a defined territory.[50] Once again objective and subjective criteria were deemed important. A people must be self-aware, i.e., self-defined. It would seem then that a people could be a nation, an ethnic group, a national minority or an ethnic minority.

However, like nations, national minorities and ethnic minorities, some form of other-definition is also necessary for a people to secure its rights. In order to enjoy the benefits of self-determination a people needs to be recognized by the central authorities within the state in which it resides (i.e., for so-called internal self-determination), or the recognition of the inter-national community in general is required for a people to secede successfully and establish its own state (i.e., for so-called 'territorial self-determination'). In practice, therefore, self-determination has an important element of 'other-determination'.

Lord Avebury, a keen and well-known advocate of Kurdish rights and the rights of other minority groups, has attempted to identify and define peoples. He has suggested the appointment of a new UN official, a 'High Commissioner for Self-Determination', who could be authorized to report to a new Committee on Self-Determination. This committee could also take over responsibility for the few remaining territories in the list of the Committee on Decolonization. A Committee on Self-Determination should be composed of independent experts and not state representatives, along the lines of the UN Sub-Commission on the Prevention of Discrimination and Protection of Minorities, in order to offset the tendency to make rulings up-holding territorial integrity. If in its considered opinion a self-determination claim was justified, it was proposed that the Committee on Self-Determination could formally notify the state concerned and request the authorities there to discuss with the committee procedures to hold a referendum to let the people decide on their political future.[51] For the foreseeable future, however, this series of mechanisms does not appear to be realizable. The proposal looks too revolutionary for today's still predominantly state-centric world. In addition, as will be seen, the holding of a referendum may be beset by a number of technical problems.

It is therefore no simple task to define what is meant by a 'people'. In October 1970 a UN General Assembly resolution which referred to self-determination stated that a state must be 'possessed of a government representing the whole people belonging to the territory without distinction as to race, creed or colour'.[52] This reference to the 'whole people' belonging to a territory rather than to distinct ethnic groups and minorities is seen by one commentator as evidence of a ruling made to enhance the principle of the territorial integrity of a state.[53] In this context a 'people' is a vague and all-embracing term unlike the definitions and explanations offered by Avebury and Critescu.

An assertion made by Crawford would appear to be relevant here – to ask what is a 'people' is in effect question-begging. The definition of a people would be context-dependent, or open to interpretation at least dependent on the context. What constitutes a people may differ for the purposes of different rights.[54] This line of reasoning, however, does not get us very far. One needs to focus on the definition of a people and its rights within the context of self-determination. An additional complication here, though, is that there are different types of self-determination.

What Is Meant by Self-Determination?

'Self-determination' is another expression whose meaning is far from clear. Several types of self-determination have been identified. A linkage with minority rights is clearly apparent. If self-determination is realized this may mean that a people has obtained its own state or joined up with another state; a people may be granted political or cultural autonomy; a federal system or a form of consociation or power-sharing arrangement may have been agreed upon with a people; or a more democratic, representative form of government may have been established to satisfy the demands of a people. In effect, therefore, the realization of self-determination provides a number of possible recommendations for the peaceful solution – in part at least – to a trans-state ethnic conflict. These end-products as it were of self-determination will be analysed in more detail later and their applicability in the case of Turkey and its Kurds will be assessed. However, here it is important to bear in mind that the close connection between self-determination and secession is particularly problematic.

According to Halperin and his colleagues: 'The principle of self-determination is best viewed as entitling a people to choose its political allegiance, to influence the political order under which it lies, and to preserve its cultural, ethnic, historical or territorial identity.'[55]

Assuming that the identification of a 'people' does not pose a major difficulty, in practice there are a number of means by which these policies may be realized. For example, Shehadi has distinguished between 'internal' and 'external' self-determination. The former regulates relations between rulers and ruled within a community inhabiting a defined territory. It is concerned usually with securing more democratic and representative forms of government. External self-determination regulates relations between a self-defined community and the outside world. This self-defined community need not necessarily have its own state – it could be a minority, for example – and it may seek to develop relations with other states or international organizations and minority groups, for instance.[56] In the case of a people here, its members may also seek to further contacts with others from the same people who live in another (usually neighbouring) state (or states).

Shehadi also has differentiated between territorial and ethnic forms of self-determination. The former focuses on the obtaining of independence for a defined territory or the uniting of this territory with another independent state. The latter concentrates on an identifiable ethnic group which may be given its own state or may be recognized as a distinct political entity within a state.[57]

Other types of self-determination have been catalogued by Halperin and his associates.[58] 'Sub-state self-determination' involves the attempt of a group within an existing state to break away and form a new state or obtain more political/cultural autonomy within an existing state. This would be easier to realize for groups concentrated in a particular area. 'Trans-state self-determination' refers to the self-determination claims of a people scattered in more than one existing state. They may seek to establish an independent state carved out of two or more existing states. Obviously, this would be difficult given that more than one state would be involved. The self-determination of dispersed peoples concerns groups scattered so widely throughout one or more states that it is not possible to provide territorial autonomy arrangements. There is a need here to focus on democracy and the protection of non-territorial minority rights. 'Anti-colonial' and 'indigenous self-determination' refer to peoples striving to secure independence from colonial rule or claiming more power for indigenous groups. 'Representative self-determination' involves the will of the population in general of an existing state to make their government more representative.

Concerning self-determination there is also a debate about whether self-determination is in effect a 'principle', a 'right' or is actually 'ius cogens'. Ius cogens refers to 'peremptory norms of general international law' from which states are not allowed to contract out. These norms must be accepted and recognized by the international community of states as a whole.[59] However, given the difficulty establishing what exactly is meant by self-determination and the uncertainty over to whom it should apply, and, indeed, how it should be applied, it would appear that in practice self-determination does not warrant the label *ius cogens*. Whether self-determination is a principle, or a right, or both, and what significance this may have had and will have on international politics must be examined.

The Development of the Principle and Right of Self-Determination

In his work *Representative Government* J.S. Mill argued in 1861 that: 'Where the sentiment of nationality exists in any force, there is a prima facie case for uniting all the members of a nationality under the same government, and a government to set themselves apart.'[60] This is generally regarded as one of the earliest references to what was, in effect, self-determination, i.e., the right of each community (in this case a 'nationality') to have its own form of government. Self-determination would become politically important when it became closely associated with the speeches of President Woodrow Wilson towards the end of the First World War.

President Wilson declared in February 1918: 'National aspirations must be respected; peoples may now be dominated and governed by their own consent. Self-determination is not a mere phrase, it is an imperative principle of action which statesmen will henceforth ignore at their peril.'[61] At the same time he also stated: 'All well-defined national aspirations can be accorded the utmost satisfaction that can be accorded them without introducing new and perpetuating old elements of discord and antagonism that would be likely to break the peace of Europe and consequently of the world.' But, as Roucek pointed out not long after, herein lay the problem because of uncertainty about what was actually meant by 'well-defined national aspirations' and just what elements might create or perpetuate 'discord and antagonism'.[62]

In reality, it seemed that Wilson and his contemporaries never intended that the self-determination of 'peoples' should have universal application. Self-determination was meant to be limited to areas formerly under the sovereignty of the defeated powers in central and eastern Europe.[63] It was also not clear what was meant by 'peoples' although a linkage between self-determination and peoples had by then been established. Self-determination was not supposed to apply to the colonies of the victorious great powers. The colonies of the defeated Central powers were placed initially under the supervision of the triumphant states of the Triple Entente under League of Nations mandates. Fearing that the prevailing state-centric system could eventually come under threat, the great powers resisted and ensured that the concept of self-determination was not incorporated into the League of Nations Covenant. Wilson had believed that self-determination was needed for the establishment of a democracy based on popular consent. This was in effect a concern for representative self-determination. In practice, none the less, the territorial redrawing of the map of Europe was largely determined by political calculation and the perceived needs of the great powers rather than on the basis of the peoples with the strongest claim to self-determination.[64] However, because of the wide distribution of ethnic groups the revised territorial arrangement led to the formation of new minority groups in new states who would later in turn press for self-determination as the governments of the newly-created states often did not respect democratic rights and freedoms.

Commentators are in general agreement that while in the UN Charter the principles of state sovereignty and territorial integrity and the self-determination of peoples were advocated, in practice the last-mentioned principle would prove to be of less importance. Article 1(2) did state that: 'One of the main purposes of the UN ...' is '... to develop friendly relations among nations based on respect for the principle of equal rights and self-determination of peoples'. Article 55 also noted that the UN aimed to create conditions 'for peaceful and friendly relations among nations based on respect for the principle of equal rights and self-determination of peoples'. The 'principle' of self-determination was thus openly acknowledged, but events would prove that the importance of state sovereignty and the primacy of domestic jurisdiction in the internal affairs of states remained unchallenged. According to a UN report released in 1945, there was the strong assumption that self-determination only referred to the 'self-government' of peoples and did not include the right of secession.[65] Certainly the UN Charter did refer to the self-government of peoples, although this was meant to be applicable to certain territories rather than to distinct ethnic groups or nations. According to Article 73, states administering 'non-self governing territories' (i.e., colonies) should promote self-government there. And Article 76 stipulated that the basic objective of the UN trusteeship system (in effect the successor mechanism to the League of Nations mandate system) was to promote the 'progressive development' in trust territories 'towards self-government or independence'.

Therefore, according to the UN Charter, self-determination, which meant basically the self-government of peoples, only applied originally to colonies and trust territories. The principles of state sovereignty and territorial integrity otherwise prevailed. It was up to the central authorities of states then to choose to recognize or not the existence of other 'peoples' and accord them the right of self-government or self-determination. However, Article 21 of the Universal Declaration of Human Rights did note that: 'The will of the people shall be the basis of the authority of government.'[66] In this reference to the importance of representative government, which, as we have noted, may be accommodated by the principle of self-determination, there is no territorial delimitation. Also, significantly, although the Universal Declaration, like the UN Charter, does refer to individual or universal rights, in Article 21 the Universal Declaration does speak of a particular group – 'the people'.

The General Assembly Declaration on the Granting of Independence to Colonial Countries and Peoples issued on 14 December 1960 declared that: 'All peoples have the right to self-determination; by virtue of that right they freely determine their political status and freely pursue their economic, social and cultural development.' On the other hand, the Declaration also stated: 'Any attempt at the partial or total disruption of the national unity and territorial integrity of a country is incompatible with the purposes and principles of the Charter of the UN.'[67]

At first sight the Declaration appears to be almost contradictory. There is a reference to the right of all peoples to self-determination which is now no longer restricted to certain territories. What is meant here appears to be representative self-determination, where various political and cultural rights (which could include minority rights) should be respected. Independent statehood – i.e., territorial self-determination – does not seem to be implied, especially when the reference in the second clause to the importance of territorial integrity and national unity is taken into account. There is no right of secession here. These references to self-determination, rights and national unity within the same declaration are admittedly confusing. Shehadi has interpreted this to mean that the right of self-determination here is not a right to an independent state, but rather a right to demand one and negotiate for it with states and groups directly affected. A claim to self-determination then should be pursued through peaceful, negotiated means.[68] Another important point to note is that in the declaration self-determination has been elevated from a principle to a right of peoples. The concept had assumed more importance by this time.

To add to the confusion, the very next day another General Assembly Resolution – 1541 (15 December 1960) – was passed in connection with the issue of self-determination. This referred to what has become known as the 'theory of salt-water colonialism'. It reverted to stressing the importance of territory rather than peoples or ethnic groups with regard to self-government. It noted that the reference in Article 73 of the UN Charter to the granting of self-government to 'non-self-governing' territories referred only to that territory which was 'geographically separate' and 'distinct ethnically and/or culturally from the country administering it'.[69] This ruled out the classifying of a certain minority or an ethnic group on a state's territory as a 'non-self governing' entity which could then be entitled to self-government or self-determination. The central authorities of a state could then persecute what were in effect distinct peoples within their territory in the knowledge that the international community would most probably do little to assist the oppressed groups. According to this General Assembly Resolution therefore, the principle and right of self-determination should not threaten the sovereignty and territorial integrity of independent states.

The situation was somewhat clarified by Article 1 of the 1966 UN International Covenants on Civil and Political Rights and Economic, Social and Cultural Rights. This article – common to both Covenants – read: 'All peoples have the right of self-determination. By virtue of that right they freely determine their political status and freely pursue their economic, social and cultural development.'[70] Evidently, self-determination here referred to representative and internal forms of self-determination rather than the territorial variant of self-determination which allowed for the possibility of secession. This was apparent from the 'General Comment' issued by the Human Rights Committee which said: 'With regard to paragraph 1 Article 1, States Parties should describe the constitutional and political processes which in practice allow the exercise of [self-determination].'[71] This form of self-determination here seemed to apply to all territories, as Article 1, paragraph three of the Covenants also noted that it was the duty of states parties to promote self-determination 'including those having responsibility for the administration of non-self-governing and trust territories.'[72]

The General Assembly Declaration on Principles of International Law Concerning Friendly Relations and Co-operation among States in accordance with the Charter of the UN (UN General Assembly Resolution 2625 [XXV], 24 Oct. 1970) was the last major UN declaration specifically referring to the question of self-determination. It spelt out more clearly the different forms of self-determination. This was important since throughout the 1960s the impression had been created that self-determination meant decolonization and little else. The declaration read: 'The establishment of a sovereign and independent state, the free association or integration with an independent state or the emergence into any other political status freely determined by a people constitute modes of implementing the right of self-determination by that people.' Significantly, as mentioned above, the Declaration also noted that a state must be 'possessed of a government representing the whole people belonging to the territory without distinction as to race, creed or colour.'[73]

The problem of what was meant here by 'the whole people' has been referred to previously. What is also of interest is whether this clause implies that if a state does not possess such a government, the whole people or peoples then have a right to self-determination, including possibly even a right to secession, i.e., not just referring to colonial or trust territory but including any territory. Following other commentators, Thornberry has adopted a cautious stance and argued that this clause was meant to apply only to racist regimes such as Apartheid South Africa and not, for instance, to peoples treated in a grossly disriminatory manner by an unrepresentative government.[74]

In practice, since 1945 there has been a close linkage between self-determination and decolonization and the future of the trust territories. Several General Assembly declarations have also advocated the right to self-determination in specific cases of non-colonial peoples such as the Palestinians, the Tibetans and the inhabitants of South Africa.[75] Whether self-determination in any of its possible forms applies to peoples in other states is not exactly clear. There is a problem in the perceptions of many with regard to the association between self-determination and secession and the perceived threat therefore to state sovereignty and territorial integrity, even though self-determination need not necessarily lead to eventual secession. There is no right to secession, as will be seen, even in those cases where it seems that a people's right to self-determination has been denied. Certain groups and peoples have, however, been able to secede.

The Problems of Self-Determination

There are many problems associated with self-determination. As observed, the meaning of the term is not clear and UN texts, for example, referring to the concept are open to differing interpretation. The central authorities in one state could permit one form of self-determination but not another. Peoples are evidently entitled to self-determination, but what is a people anyway? How should the right of self-determination be exercised in practice? For example, if a plebiscite is to be held, how should one be organized? What would constitute a majority? The fears of state authorities that self-determination may lead ultimately to secession have also hindered the prospects of certain peoples from realizing other forms of self-determination.

Although international conventions refer to the right of self-determination, no right of secession is mentioned. This is in spite of the fact that self-determination and secession do overlap in connection with so-called territorial self-determination. But no international convention advocates the right to territorial self-determination per se. International law is against the threat or use of force to change territorial boundaries. What has happened in practice, however, is that certain groups such as the Bengalis and Eritreans have had to wage a successful war in order to secede and secure international recognition of their secession – although the status of Eritrea and the nature of its ties with Addis Ababa were subject to dispute before Ethiopia had fully incorporated the province in the early 1960s. Self-determination, in effect, was achieved through force. This is not always so. The Czechs and the Slovaks, for example, were able to agree to a 'velvet divorce'. The case of 'Yugoslavia' is somewhat complicated. The CSCE ruled – ineffectively as it turned out – that the Yugoslav central authorities should not use force to protect their borders, as the international community recognized the seceding states of Croatia, Slovenia, Macedonia and Bosnia-Hercegovina. The Soviet Union, though, swiftly and relatively peacefully disintegrated after its republics had started to secede and were being recognized by outside states.

In connection with the undoubted linkage between self-determination and secession, it has been argued that the moral and psychological appeal of self-determination has compelled many ethnic groups seeking support for their secessionist ambitions to invoke the principle of self-determination.[76] Certainly the central authorities in states are cognizant of the danger that minorities and other groups may adopt such a policy. But, as Halperin and his colleagues have also pointed out, a paranoid government may create major problems for itself over the issue of self-determination and unwittingly encourage moves towards secession by certain groups: 'The real mistake occurs when a government is so fearful of self-determination – even when it is not aimed at secession – that it denies minority groups the protection of their traditional rights. Such negativist actions can easily trigger minority discontent and upheaval and create the surge toward self-determination that the government so fears.'[77]

It is generally accepted that a group of people may not legally use force to attempt to secede. But, on the other hand, it is contended that force may also not be employed to prevent self-determination. This has been argued for instance by Akehurst in his interpretation of paragraph 4 of the General Assembly Declaration on the Granting of Independence to Colonial Countries and Peoples of December 1960, which read: 'all armed action or repressive measures of all kinds directed against dependent peoples shall cease in order to enable them to exercise ... their right to complete independence.'[78] But, as Akehurst also noted here, a 'people' needs to demonstrate to international law that it is a people possessing a legal right of self-determination, and if a state refuses to allow it to exercise this right, then such a people may justifiably wage wars of national liberation. Of course, one result of a successful war of this type may well be secession. This would seem to imply, indirectly at least, a right to secede under certain conditions. The 'people' concerned first need to be 'other-defined' – or, in this case 'other-determined' – by an outside authority. Self-definition alone is not enough to establish the legal right of self-determination.

An additional complication is the existence of the state loyalty clauses in international conventions which have been discussed above in relation to minority rights. How may these be accommodated with the right of self-determination which is, after all, linked with the possibility of secession and independence for particular groups? One answer here could lie in Akehurst's analysis of the General Assembly Resolution of 1960 in tandem with a generous interpretation of the 1970 General Assembly Declaration on

Principles of International Law Concerning Friendly Relations and Co-operation among States in Accordance with the Charter of the UN. Thus state loyalty clauses could perhaps be disregarded and dispensed with in those cases involving repressive regimes which are grossly discriminating against parts of the population.

There is also the problem of 'never-ending self-determination'. However, what is actually involved here is one form of self-determination, namely territorial self-determination and its close association with secession. The danger is one of chaos through fragmentation and Balkanization. A newly created state formed by the successful secession of a particular ethnic group could have within its territory another, smaller, ethnic group which may, in turn, feel trapped and could attempt to break away. This is quite likely because it is argued that the authorities of a newly-seceded state are likely to be less tolerant of minorities within their population.[79]

How should the varying forms of self-determination be peacefully implemented? It is too easy to say let the people decide. How does one identify the people? A plebiscite assumes that a collective identity already exists. Even if this hurdle is overcome there are also other obstacles. Lapidoth is correct to ask whether members of the 'people' who live abroad should take part in the decision on its future status. Who decides what options, and what questions should be submitted to the people? What is the territorial frame in which self-determination is to be implemented and who decides on the definition of this frame? Since 'majorities' and 'minorities' in a certain territorial frame may change it is important to decide on a 'critical date', namely the specific date at which a person had to live in the area in order to qualify for participation in the vote. Should plebiscites be one-off, or perhaps be held again?[80] There is also the problem of 'authentic voice'. Is a simple majority or say a majority of three quarters of all potential or actual votes needed in order to reach a decision on secession, for example?[81]

It has been suggested by Halperin and his colleagues that a group or people should first attempt to realize self-determination within existing state borders. Only in the event of failure here should the group advocate secession, while at the same time promising to guarantee democracy and protect individual and minority rights in order to secure international support.[82] This step-by-step process will be exceedingly difficult to put into practice in reality. In addition to the legal uncertainties, the central authorities within a state are not likely to accept the role of passive bystanders. In what would be a much more realistic scenario, in the face of these difficulties a particular group or people seeking to secede could attempt to exacerbate the situation through the use of violence. The purpose of such actions would be to attract inter-national attention and possibly support. This could be achieved as the state authorities would most probably respond in kind to acts of violence and thereby set in motion an escalating spiral of conflict. The particular group involved could then perhaps base their claims to self-definition on the pretext that they were fighting a justified war of national liberation against an oppressive state.

We saw previously that Lord Avebury has proposed an arrangement to assist in the management of the problems associated with self-determination by establishing a mechanism to identify what is a people. Halperin and others have suggested that the Security Council should appoint a special committee to monitor self-determination movements and alert it whenever a situation is likely to escalate and become a threat to peace. This may be a useful preventive measure, but it does not address the problem of an already ongoing violent situation. Halperin and his colleagues have also recommended that the Security Council should make the UN Trusteeship Council an advisory body on self-determination issues, or that the Trusteeship Council should be converted into a modern, international clearing-house for self-determination cases.[83]

Shehadi has correctly indicated that self-determination is not necessarily a zero-sum game between the central authorities of a state and a people. 'Shared sovereignty' is possible in which the sovereignty of a state is, in effect, shared with the sovereignty of constituent groups or geographic units in a society. Federations or consociational democracies may be devised here and these could be guaranteed by other states or international organizations.[84] Such arrangements will be discussed in more detail later. Suffice it to say here that these solutions would be dependent, *inter alia*, on historical factors, the current composition and policies of the state authorities, and the groups or peoples involved, and the regional context. Several forms of self-determination could result in the accommodation of the rights of minorities or peoples without any group needing to attempt to secede. The recognition of such rights by the central authorities of the state in question would, however, be necessary first.

Self-Determination and the Case of Turkey and the Kurds

The possibilities, and the advantages or disadvantages of secession or types of power-sharing arrangements within Turkey between the authorities in Ankara and the 'Kurds' will be discussed in more detail later. Some politicized Kurdish groups have claimed that the Kurds are a 'distinct people'. Thus, in the Final Resolution in the International Conference on North West Kurdistan (South East Turkey) held in Brussels in March 1994, paragraph 2 referred to the Kurds as 'a distinctive people with their own history, language and culture, [who are] the fourth largest people in the Middle East'. Paragraph 9 called for amendments to the Constitution of Turkey to recognize the Kurds as a 'distinct people'.[85]

What form of self-determination could apply to the Kurds in Turkey? There is little prospect of the authorities voluntarily agreeing to territorial self-determination or secession in which the Kurds in Turkey could unite with the Kurds in neighbouring states to create a larger 'Kurdistan' – a form of trans-state self-determination, as it were. The central authorities in the other states in question would also most probably endeavour to prevent this realization. The West too would object to such developments, since chaos in the region would be likely to ensue – with a flood of refugees, for instance – thereby endangering its access to oil. For other forms of self-determination to be entertained within Turkey itself, involving a change in the relationship between the rulers and the ruled, officials in Ankara would first of all have to recognize, at least tacitly, the existence of a Kurdish minority or people. This could involve granting additional rights to the Kurds without openly declaring that they were a minority. As a consequence, Turkish officials could then perhaps tolerate official contacts between the Kurds and their kin-groups outside Turkey, i.e., permit a form of external self-determination. Traditionally, unofficial contacts across borders between the several Kurdish tribal groups have been allowed by the Turkish authorities. Perhaps the current small-scale trading along the Turkish–Iraqi border – a new form of transborder co-operation which was a product of the Gulf War – could help to create an atmosphere where such official contacts might eventually commence.

Since the Kurdish issue is a trans-state, ethnic phenomenon, what would be the impact on Turkey if the Kurds in a neighbouring state were granted variants of self-determination other than the form of territorial self-determination? Would this then compel the Turkish authorities to follow likewise? In the 1970s the government in Baghdad had sponsored autonomous arrangements for the Iraqi Kurds. There were provisions for the recognition of a Kurdish nationality and guaranteed Kurdish participation in the central government, together with assurances that the vice-president of Iraq would be a Kurd. At the time the authorities in Ankara did not feel obliged to adopt a similar policy. Autonomy for the Iraqi Kurds was very limited. The more economically-important Kurdish territories, such as the oil-rich region of Kirkuk, were excluded and much of local government within the autonomous areas actually remained under the direct control of the central authorities. It remains to be seen what impact an autonomous Kurdish government of northern Iraq could have on the Kurds in Turkey, although the Turkish authorities are attempting to have a major say in events in northern Iraq, as was seen in the large Turkish armed incursion into that territory in the spring of 1995.

How would a plebiscite be organized in Turkey for the purposes of attempting to provide self-determination for the Kurds? Who would be entitled to vote, bearing in mind the difficulty of identifying who is and who is not a Kurd? What questions should be asked and who would arrange these?

How would one ensure that 'the Kurds' would be able to exercise their choice freely without fear of intimidation possibly from Kurdish nationalist movements or the Turkish security forces? What would be the territorial frame? What sort of majority would be required? The problem of the widely dispersed nature of the Kurdish population within Turkey would need to be taken into account. If a form of self-determination were agreed upon would this result in the large-scale movement – voluntary or otherwise – across the territory of particular groups – such as Kurds to south-eastern Turkey and 'non-Kurds' out of the region? There is a danger of never-ending self-determination in a larger 'Kurdistan' if all other states in the region ever agreed on a common policy of self-determination for the Kurds. This would be because the Azeris, the Turkmens and other groups would become trapped minorities.[86]

Notes

1. J. Mayall, 'Sovereignty and Self-Determination in the New Europe', in H. Miall (ed.), *Minority Rights: the Scope for a Transnational Regime* (London: Pinter, for the Royal Institute of International Affairs, 1994).
2. A. Roberts, 'Humanitarian War: Military Intervention and Human Rights', *International Affairs*, 69, 3 (July 1993) pp.429–49; and K. Kirişci, '"Providing Comfort" and Turkey: Decision Making for Refugee Assistance', *Low Intensity Conflict and Law Enforcement*, 2, 2 (Autumn 1993).
3. UN Doc. E/CN.4/Sub.2/1985/31.para.181 is cited in I. Gyurcsik, 'New Legal Ramifications on the Question of National Minorities', in I.M. Cuthbertson and J. Leibowitz (eds.), *Minorities: the New Europe's Old Issue* (Prague: Institute for EastWest Studies, 1993) p.22.
4. K. Koch, 'The International Community and Forms of Intervention in the Field of Minority Rights Protection', ibid., p.267.
5. *Document of the Copenhagen Meeting of the Conference on the Human Dimension of the CSCE*, 5–29 June 1990, Copenhagen, para.32.
6. H. Miall, 'Introduction', in H. Miall (ed.), op. cit., p.2.
7. For the text of the Polish Minorities Treaty signed by Poland on 28 June 1919 see C.A. Macartney, *National States and National Minorities* (London: Oxford University Press under the auspices of the Royal Institute of International Affairs, 1934) Appendix 1. Here see Article 12, p.506.
8. I. Claude, *National Minorities: an International Problem* (Cambridge MA: Harvard University Press, 1955) p.17.
9. For the full text of the *International Covenant on Civil and Political Rights and its Optional Protocol*, UN GA Res. 2200 A (XXI), 16 Dec. 1966 (entered into force 23 March 1976) see *Collection of International Instruments Concerning Refugees* (hereafter cited as *Collection of International Instruments*), (Geneva: Office of the UN High Commissioner for Refugees, 1988) pp.104–27.
10. A. Fenet, 'The Question of Minorities in the Order of Law', in G. Chaliand (ed.), *Minority Rights in the Age of Nation-States* (London: Pluto, 1989) p.40.
11. P. Thornberry, *International Law and the Rights of Minorities* (Oxford: Clarendon, 1991) p.173.

12. *UN General Assembly Declaration on the Rights of Persons Belonging to National or Ethnic, Religious and Linguistic Minorities*, UN GA Res. 47/135, 18 Dec. 1992.
13. P. Thornberry, 'International and European Standards on Minority Rights', in H. Miall (ed.), op. cit., pp.14–16.
14. T.R. Gurr and B. Harff, *Ethnic Conflict in World Politics* (Boulder CO, San Francisco and Oxford: Westview, 1994) p.141.
15. For the full text of the *International Convention on the Elimination of All Forms of Racial Discrimination*, UN GA Res. 2106 A (XX) 21 Dec. 1965 (entered into force 4 Jan. 1969), see *Collection of International Instruments*, pp.150–62.
16. For further details on the UN Commission on Human Rights and its Sub-Commission see P. Thornberry op. cit., (note 11) pp.124–32; and N.S. Rodley, 'United Nations Non-Treaty Procedures for Dealing with Human Rights Violations', in H. Hannum (ed.), *Guide to International Human Rights Practice* (Philadelphia: University of Pennsylvania Press, 1992) pp.60–85.
17. The Declaration on Principles Guiding Relations between Participating States is a sub-section within the section Questions Relating to Security in Europe in the *Conference on Security and Co-operation in Europe Final Act* (Helsinki, 1975).
18. *Document of the Copenhagen Meeting*.
19. *Report of the CSCE Meeting of Experts on National Minorities*, Geneva, 19 July 1991, Section 2.
20. *Document of the Moscow Meeting on the Conference on the Human Dimension of the CSCE*, Moscow, 10 Sep.–4 Oct. 1991, para.1–16.
21. K. Koch in I.M. Cuthbertson and J. Leibowitz (eds.), op. cit., p.258.
22. *European Convention for the Protection of Human Rights and Fundamental Freedoms*, 4 Nov. 1950 (entered into force 3 Sep. 1953), in *Collection of International Instruments*, pp.274–90.
23. *Framework Convention for the Protection of National Minorities and Explanatory Report*, Council of Europe, Feb. 1995 (Strasbourg: Council of Europe Press, 1995).
24. J. Gyurcsik in I.M. Cuthbertson and J. Leibowitz (eds.), op. cit., p.43.
25. Tribal Feeling', *Economist*, 25 Dec. 1993.
26. A. Eide, *New Approaches to Minority Protection* (London: Minority Rights Group, 1995).
27. I. Gyurcsik in I.M. Cuthbertson and J. Leibowitz (eds.), op. cit., p.26.
28. R.G. Wirsing, 'Dimensions of Minority Protection', in R.G. Wirsing (ed.), *Protection of Ethnic Minorities: Comparative Perspectives* (New York and Oxford: Pergamon, 1981) p.9; and I. Brownlie, 'The Rights of Peoples in Modern International Law', in J. Crawford (ed.), *The Rights of Peoples* (Oxford: Clarendon, 1988) pp.1–16.
29. K. Koch in I.M. Cuthbertson and J. Leibowitz (eds.), op. cit., p.253.
30. P.L. Van den Berghe, 'Protection of Ethnic Minorities: a Critical Appraisal', in R.G. Wirsing (ed.) op. cit., pp.343–55.
31. J. Crawford, 'The Rights of Peoples: "Peoples" or "Governments"?', in J. Crawford (ed.), op. cit., p.60; and J. Crawford, 'The Rights of Peoples: Some Conclusions', ibid., p.172, n.29.
32. I. Claude, op. cit., p.47.
33. For the text of the Treaty of Lausanne and the Accompanying Straits Convention, 24 July 1923, see, J.C. Hurewitz, *Diplomacy in the Near and Middle East: a Documentary Record: 1914–1956*, Vol.2 (Princeton NJ, New York, Toronto and London: Van Nostrand, 1956) pp.119–27.
34. P. Robins, 'The Overlord State: Turkish Policy and the Kurdish Issue', *International Affairs*, 69, 4 (Oct. 1993) p.600.

35. *Constitution of the Republic of Turkey* (official translation into English) (Ankara: 1990). Although the constitution was revised in July 1995 these provisions remained intact.

36. For Article 125 of the Turkish Penal Code (originally passed 1 March 1926), see *Yürürlükteki Kanunlar Külliyatı*, Başbakanlık Mevzuatı Geliştirme ve Yayın Genel Müdürlüğü (Ankara: Başbakanlık Basımevi) (1988, EK-9: [Aug.] 1991), 1, p.464.

37. For the full text of the Anti-terror Law of April 1991 see ibid., (EK-15; [Feb.] 1993), 6, pp.7215–17. For the revised text of 27 Oct. 1995 see *T.C. Resmi Gazete*, 30 Oct. 1995, No.22448. For one critical commentary of the revised text see the comment by Ali Bayramoğlu in *Yeni Yüzyıl*, 31 Oct. 1995.

38. H. Hannum, *Autonomy, Sovereignty and Self-Determination: The Accommodation of Conflicting Rights* (Philadelphia: University of Pennsylvania Press, 1990) p.189.

39. For instance, this applies to Turkey's understanding of the 1991 Geneva Meeting on National Minorities. See R. Dalton, 'The Role of the CSCE', in H. Miall (ed.), op. cit., p.108, n.3. Greece in practice appears to follow a similar policy.

40 P. Thornberry in ibid., p.20. This is actually in line with the CSCE's Helsinki Summit Document of July 1992.

41. *Reuters*, 8 May 1994 (via Internet Wire Service); and *Turkish Daily News (TDN)* 1 Oct. 1994.

42. *TDN* 5 May and 23 June 1995.

43. Ibid., 16 Dec. 1994.

44. Ibid., 9 Jan. 1996.

45. *Yeni Yüzyıl*, 29 Dec. 1995.

46. *International Conference on North West Kurdistan (South East Turkey), 12–13 March 1994, Brussels, Final Resolution*, organized by Medico International (Frankfurt/Berlin) and the Kurdistan Human Rights Project (London).

47. *TDN*, 5 Oct. 1994.

48. Ibid., 6 Dec. 1994.

49. J. Mayall, *Nationalism and International Society* (Cambridge: Cambridge University Press, 1990) p.4, citing I. Jennings, *The Approach to Self-Government* (Cambridge: Cambridge University Press, 1956) p.56.

50. P. Thornberry in H. Miall (ed.), op. cit., p.20, referring to the *UN Report of the Special Rapporteur on the Historical and Current Development of the Right to Self-Determination. Critescu Report*, UN.Doc E/CN.4/sub.2/404/Rev.1 1981.

51. E. Avebury, 'Not a Mere Phrase', paper presented at Evangelischen Akademie, Kamburg-Dammtor, 21 Jan. 1994.

52. *UN General Assembly Declaration on Principles of International Law Concerning Friendly Relations and Co-operation among States in Accordance with the Charter of the UN*, UN GA Res. 2625 (XXV), 14 Oct. 1970.

53. P. Thornberry (note 11) pp.19–20.

54. J. Crawford 'The Rights of Peoples: Some Conclusions', in J. Crawford (ed.) (note 31) pp.168–70.

55. M.H. Halperin, D.J. Scheffer, with P. Small, *Self-Determination in the New World Order* (Washington DC: Carnegie Endowment for International Peace, 1992) p.47.

56. K.S. Shehadi, *Ethnic Self-Determination and the Breakup of States* (London: IISS, Adelphi Paper 283, 1993) p.4.

57. Ibid.

58. M.H. Halperin *et al.* (eds.), op. cit., pp.49–52.

59. M. Akehurst, *A Modern Introduction to International Law* (London: Allen & Unwin, 1987) p.41.

60. J. Mayall (note 49) p.27.
61. C.A. Macartney, op. cit., pp.189–90.
62. J.S. Roucek, *The Working of the Minorities System under the League of Nations* (Prague: Orbis, 1929) p.21.
63. W. Connor, 'Self-Determination: the New Phase', in W. Connor, *Ethnonationalism: the Quest for Understanding* (Princeton NJ: Princeton University Press, 1994) p.5.
64. H. Hannum (note 38) pp.28–30.
65. M.M. Kampelman, 'Secession and the Right of Self-Determination: an Urgent Need to Harmonize Principle with Pragmatism', *Washington Quarterly*, 16, 3 (Summer 1993) p.7.
66. *Universal Declaration of Human Rights*, UN GA Res. 217A (111), 10 Dec. 1948, in *Collection of International Instruments*, pp.99–103.
67. *Declaration on the Granting of Independence to Colonial Countries and Peoples*, UN GA Res. 1514 (XV), 14 Dec. 1960, para.2 and 6.
68. K.S. Shehadi, op. cit., pp.83–4.
69. UN GA Resolution 1541, 15 Dec. 1960, Principles IV and V.
70. *International Covenant on Civil and Political Rights*, and *International Covenant on Economic, Social and Cultural Rights*, UN GA Res. 2200A (XXI), 16 Dec. 1966 (entered into force 23 March and 3 Jan. 1976, respectively), in *Collection of International Instruments*, pp.104–23 and 128–38.
71. P. Thornberry (note 11) p.215.
72. See note 70.
73. See note 52.
74. P. Thornberry (note 11) pp.19–20.
75. For example, at the request of the Afghan delegation the phrase 'alien domination' was inserted into the text of the UN GA Res. 2708 (XX), 14 Dec. 1970, which also referred to the right of self-determination. According to Kirişci, the phrase was generally meant to cover the Palestinian people. See K. Kirişci, *The PLO and World Politics: a Case Study of the Mobilization of Support for the Palestinian Cause* (London: Pinter, 1986) p.136.
76. N. Entessar, *Kurdish Ethnonationalism* (Boulder CO and London: Lynne Rienner, 1992) p.162.
77. M.H. Halperin *et al.* (eds.), op. cit., p.60.
78. M. Akehurst, op. cit., pp.19–20.
79. For a trenchant criticism of self-determination along these lines see A. Etzioni, 'The Evils of Self-Determination', *Foreign Policy*, 89 (Winter 1992/93) pp.21–35. However, Etzioni refers only to what is in effect territorial self-determination. Other forms of self-determination could actually help to fashion a more pluralist society which Etzioni himself strongly favours.
80. R. Lapidoth, 'Sovereignty in Transition' *Journal of International Affairs*, 45, 2 (Winter 1992) pp.341–2.
81. A. Buchanan, *Secession: the Morality of Political Divorce from Fort Sumter to Lithuania and Quebec* (Boulder CO: Westview, 1991) pp.139–43.
82. M.H. Halperin *et al.* (eds.), op. cit., p.9.
83. Ibid., pp.112–13.
84. K.S. Shehadi, op. cit., pp.36–7 and 51.
85. See note 46.
86. N. Entessar, op. cit., p.163.

3

The Origins of the Kurdish Question

UNTIL THE end of the First World War the majority of the Kurds lived within the Ottoman Empire while the remainder resided in Persia. The *vilayets* (administrative provinces) of Bitlis, Dersim, Diyarbakır, Hakkari, Mosul, Mamuretulaziz (Elazığ) and Van in the Empire and the region west of the Uremia lake stretching south down to Iran's Khuzistan region were areas mostly populated by Kurds. In these areas Kurds lived as subjects of the Ottoman and the Persian empires in communities which were feudal and tribal in nature.

The map of the Middle East was completely redrawn in the aftermath of the First World War. By the mid-1920s most Kurds lived in the Turkish Republic, and in Iraq and Syria – two new Arab states under British and French mandate – and in Iran after a change of regime there. A small community of Kurds found themselves under Soviet rule in the southern Caucasus. How did the Kurds become dispersed among five states? What were the political forces that culminated in the drawing of the frontiers of Iraq, Iran, Syria, the Soviet Union and Turkey? Why did the Kurds fail to establish a state of their own?

The Partitioning of the Ottoman Empire

The 'Eastern Question' involved the competition between the great powers for influence over the Ottoman Empire. Its origins may be traced back to the late eighteenth century when the Empire suffered military defeats by Russia and experienced growing internal problems in the Balkans.[1] The major players were Britain and Russia. Russia steadily expanded its territories to the south at the expense of the Empire while at the same time acquiring growing political influence in the Balkans and within the Ottoman Empire. Britain's policy was centred around protecting the integrity of the Empire in an effort to balance Russia in the Near East.[2]

By the end of the nineteenth century the great powers had also begun to take an interest in the Middle Eastern territories of the Empire. Britain had obtained a privileged status in Egypt and together with France had built the

Suez Canal. The opening of the Canal meant that the lands between the Mediterranean Sea and the Indian Ocean assumed considerable strategic importance. For Britain, these were vital for the security of British India. Germany's growing involvement in Ottoman affairs, with the German decision to finance the construction of a railway from Berlin to Baghdad via Istanbul, also drew Britain's attention to the area. The discovery of oil in southern parts of Mesopotamia and Iran further increased the importance of the Middle East.

The competing interests of Britain, Germany and Russia were exploited by successive Ottoman governments which played off these states against each other. This helped to prolong the existence of the Empire. Britain remained committed to the integrity of the Empire even though it continued to lose territories to the newly-emerging Balkan countries and Italy. However, the Ottoman decision to enter the First World War on the side of the Triple Alliance drastically changed this situation. Britain and its allies, France and Russia, saw the dismemberment of the Ottoman Empire as inevitable. The need to avoid conflict among the allies led to a series of agreements between 1915 and 1917 which aimed to partition the Ottoman Empire. With the exception of an area roughly coinciding with central Anatolia and the corresponding Black Sea coast, the rest of the Empire was to be shared between Britain, France, Greece, Italy and Russia. The Kurdish populated areas would come under the control or influence of Britain, France and Russia.

The signing of the Mudros Armistice in October 1918 between the allies and the Ottoman Empire opened the way for the allies to proceed and occupy their particular areas. However, Russia was compelled to sign a separate agreement with the Empire because of the internal disturbances resulting from the Bolshevik revolution. According to the terms of the Brest-Litovsk Treaty, Russia allowed the holding of a plebiscite in those territories the Russians had seized from the Ottoman Empire in the 1877–78 War. The territories voted to return to the Ottoman Empire. The newly-established Soviet Russian government condemned the secret agreements struck in the First World War and renounced claims over the Ottoman Empire. The allies, on the other hand, pressed ahead with their partition plans and during the Paris Peace Conference of 1919 supported the idea of allocating to Armenia and to a future Kurdish state the areas which had been reserved for Russia.

The Sèvres Treaty signed between the allies and the Ottoman government in August 1920 formalized the division of the Empire and was considered at the time as the final settlement of the Eastern Question.[3] The Treaty had provided for local autonomy for 'Kurdish areas lying east of the Euphrates, south of the southern boundary of Armenia as it may be hereafter determined, and north of the frontier of Turkey with Syria and Mesopotamia' and referred to the possibility of independence for the Kurds under certain conditions.[4] However, the Treaty was never ratified by the signatories. Some of the

Ottoman elite and the population in Anatolia would participate in a resistance movement which opposed its terms.

The Struggle for Power and the Redrawing of Frontiers

The secret agreements partitioning the Ottoman Empire had allocated an important part of the territories inhabited by Kurds to France. However, the advances of British forces beyond the Mudros Armistice lines north of Mesopotamia left Britain in occupation of large stretches of Kurdish-populated territories that should have come under French control. Britain had a definite policy towards the Arabs but not towards the Kurds. Initially, the British position on the Kurds seemed to be the product of the personal initiatives of Major William Charles Noel, a military intelligence officer, whose romantic commitment to Kurdish independence had earned him the title of 'Lawrence of Kurdistan'.[5] Soon, however, Britain would pursue a policy which was influenced by its relations with 'Turkey', the geopolitics of the region and the competition between the local British administration in Iraq and the government in London.[6]

Early in the First World War the British government had dismissed the offers of Mohammed Şerif Paşa, the ex-Ottoman Ambassador to Stockholm, to rally 'the Kurdish nation to the allied cause'.[7] Towards the end of the war another prominent member of the Kurdish elite Kiamil Bedirhan evidently promised to create havoc for the Ottoman government if Britain would help him in his quest to become leader of the Kurds.[8] Many other tribal leaders attempted to negotiate deals with the victorious British.[9] But British officials were reluctant to support the political aspirations of the Kurds. Britain refused to allow a number of Kurdish tribal leaders to attend the Paris Peace Conference.[10]

Britain was no longer willing to commit large resources to implement the previous allied decision to keep the Ottoman Empire weak and divided. Neither Britain nor the allies were willing 'to prosecute a long and costly struggle in the interior of Anatolia' which did not enjoy public support.[11] There was also an expectation that the Greek occupation of western Anatolia would still enable the Sèvres Treaty to be implemented in eastern Anatolia.

Percy Cox, a senior British administrator, argued that the British occupation in Mesopotamia should be expanded northwards to include areas populated by Kurds. According to Cox 'the new entity would be a logical addition to Britain's vast empire' and would include the rich oil deposits of Kirkuk and Mosul. This would not only help to reduce the dependence of the Royal Navy on foreign oil but would also make 'Britain's new possession self-supporting'.[12] But Edwin Montagu, the Secretary of State for India, and Winston Churchill, then head of the Colonial Office, were two influential officials who favoured independence for the Kurds. Apparently concerned at the size of the administrative costs which British rule over Kurdish areas would entail, Montagu argued that 'Kurdistan must be left to its own devices'.[13] Churchill believed that an independent Kurdish state could create a buffer zone between the British mandate in Iraq and the successful resistance movement in Anatolia until the day when 'Kurdistan and Iraq would draw closer together, and ... form one State'.[14]

The views of Cox would prevail and the idea of supporting Kurdish independence lost its attraction for the British government. Instead it was decided to incorporate eventually the region north of Mesopotamia with Iraq.[15] Developments on the ground also played an important role. As a result of the policies of Noel, a Southern Kurdistan Confederacy under the leadership of Shaikh Mahmoud was announced in 1919. Mahmoud was a powerful local tribal leader with ambitions to form his own Kurdish kingdom. However, his repeated calls for independence and his frequent efforts to remind British officials of President Wilson's concern about the need to recognize a people's right to self-determination were not well received.

At this time the resistance movement in Anatolia was becoming more organized and had formed itself into the government of the (Turkish) Grand National Assembly in April 1920. The resistance movement secured modest military successes against the French in Cilicia, against the Armenians in eastern Anatolia and against two rebelling Kurdish tribes, the Koçgiri and Milli Aşiret. These victories were achieved while the Greeks were expanding their occupation of western Anatolia. Although one should note that many Kurds were participating in the efforts to liberate the country from foreign occupation.

There were also close contacts between this emerging government of 'Turkey' and prominent Kurdish figures in Iran such as Ismail Agha (Simko). Links were also established in northern Iraq with key Kurdish leaders such as Shaikh Mahmoud. These links were especially significant because the National Pact adopted by the resistance movement in early 1920 considered all the Kurdish populated areas of the Ottoman Empire, and hence the Mosul area, as part of the territories which were to be liberated. This alarmed the British in northern Iraq. Noel's arguments made at the end of the First World War, that the Kurds in eastern Anatolia were willing to co-operate with Britain, were sounding increasingly less convincing.[16]

British officials were becoming more reluctant to support the idea of Kurdish independence in 'Turkey' for other reasons. An independent state in the north could have encouraged Kurds under British rule to unite with this state.[17] This would have jeopardized British strategic interests in northern Iraq and adversely affected its relations with the Arab world. During the First World War Britain had promised the Arabs independence. These promises conflicted with Britain's commitments under the secret agreements to partition the Ottoman Empire. In 1920 France had thwarted the efforts of the Arab nationalist leader Feisal to declare an independent Syrian kingdom. Attempting to compensate for their broken promises to the Arabs, the British offered the Kingdom of Transjordan to Feisal's brother Abdullah and lined up Feisal for the leadership of Iraq. After a contested referendum Feisal was crowned King of Iraq in August 1921 and a treaty was signed in October 1922 committing Britain to support Iraq's territorial integrity.[18] Clearly, the Arabs would have opposed British policies that could have put into question Arab sovereignty over northern Iraq.

Britain's policy towards the Kurds was also influenced by the Bolshevik revolution and the establishment of Soviet Russia. Britain had been actively involved in efforts to reverse the revolution and saw a threat to her interests in the Middle East from Soviet Russia. Britain was heavily involved in the Caucasus at the end of the First World War. Soviet expansion in that area forced the British out in 1920. Growing Soviet influence was seen as a threat to British interests in Iran and Iraq. The close relations that had developed between Soviet Russia and the new government of the (Turkish) Grand National Assembly based in Ankara made Britain fearful of an alliance between the two that could directly threaten the British presence in northern Iraq.

However, Britain did not immediately abandon the idea of supporting the Kurds against the Ankara government. Early in 1921 a conference was convened in London which failed to persuade the Ankara government to accept a peace deal based on a minor revision of the Sèvres Treaty which would have included an amendment of the articles on Kurdish autonomy.[19] Britain then lent further support to Kurdish nationalist groups.[20]

By the end of 1921 the Ankara government had concluded treaties with Soviet Russia and France. The treaty with France had finalized the withdrawal of French forces from Cilicia. This relieved military units which could be deployed by the Ankara government against the Greeks whose advance had already been checked west of Ankara. By summer 1922 Britain's strategy of using the Greeks to keep 'Turkey' divided was about to collapse. Reacting to these developments, the British government shifted its policy and sought to improve relations with Ankara. By the time the Ankara government had defeated the Greeks and the Lausanne Conference had commenced the British were prepared to play the Kurdish card only to neutralize Turkey's claims over Mosul.

As noted earlier, by the terms of the National Pact the resistance movement in Anatolia had staked a claim over Mosul. After its control over eastern Anatolia was consolidated, the Ankara government sent a small military unit during autumn 1922 to the area north of Mosul. The unit was to collaborate with local Kurdish tribes to establish control in this strategically important area.[21] For the Kurds inhabiting territories under the control of the Ankara government, this opened up the possibility of reuniting with their co-ethnics in the Mosul region and returning to the pre-First World War state of affairs.[22] Officials in Ankara clearly believed that if they were unable to control this area the National Pact would be undermined. They also feared that in those circumstances the British might encourage the Kurds to rebel against the Ankara government.[23]

The dispute between Britain and Turkey was not resolved when the Lausanne Treaty was signed in July 1923. The two failed to reach an agreement in a conference in Istanbul in May 1924. The dispute was taken to the League of Nations, which appointed an international commission. By summer 1924 Britain had gained the upper hand in the Mosul district and during the autumn an attempt by Ankara to regain control failed. At that time Turkey faced a rebellion led by the Christian Nastorian tribes. This was followed by a major Kurdish uprising led by Shaikh Said in spring 1925.

Whether or not they were instigated by Britain, these rebellions made it much more difficult for Turkey to press its case with the international commission and the League of Nations. Turkey was not a member of the League at this time. The report prepared in July 1925 by the commission recommended that the district of Mosul should remain part of the League of Nations Mandate and that the Kurds there should be given administrative autonomy. However, Turkey's refusal to accept the competence of the League delayed the final solution of the problem until the signing of a tripartite agreement between Britain, Iraq and Turkey in June 1926. This finalized the separation of the Kurds in Turkey from those in Iraq. This would have profound effects on the future of the Kurdish question.

Compared with the British interest, French involvement with the Kurds was very limited. Nevertheless, French policies had an indirect but significant impact on what would result in the separation of the Kurds into a number of countries. According to the secret agreements to partition the Ottoman Empire, France had been assigned areas populated by Kurds in Anatolia and in the district of Mosul. A number of prominent Kurdish figures were thereby encouraged to approach the French. One such was Şerif Paşa, who, after the dismissive treatment he received from the British, had travelled to Paris during the summer of 1918 to press the case for autonomy for the Kurds.[24]

Even after it became clear that France would not be controlling Kurdish populated areas and the Mosul district, a number of tribal notables sought French help, including the leaders of the Milli Aşiret tribe. This had rebelled against the nascent resistance movement in Anatolia and had demanded from the French a Syrian-style mandate.[25] From the outset the French did not seem very receptive to the idea of Kurdish autonomy as it conflicted with their interests in the region. This was clearly apparent in the position taken by Georges Picot after his meeting with Mark Sykes in Cairo when the latter had advocated Kurdish autonomy under British protection. The French had a much greater interest in the fate of the Armenians, Assyrians and Nastorians, who were all Christians, than with the Kurds.[26]

French policy toward the Kurds seemed to be greatly affected by deteriorating relations between France and Britain. Although they had been allies during the war, disagreements soon surfaced over the distribution of war spoils. France had let itself be persuaded to accept British control over Mosul.[27] In return Britain agreed that Syria should be assigned to France as a mandated territory. Britain also recognized French control of Cilicia. This territory included smaller areas populated by Kurds together also with Armenians and other Christian communities.[28]

This arrangement prevented a rift between the two former allies. France had feared that Britain was attempting to establish control over the territories of the defeated Ottoman Empire and the Middle East at its expense. The secret agreement of September 1919 between the Ottoman government and Britain allowing Britain a greater say over the Straits and Istanbul fuelled these fears. The British decision in May 1919 to encourage Greece to invade and occupy western Anatolia had also undermined French confidence in Britain.[29]

Relations between France and Britain further suffered when Britain supported Feisal in his efforts to declare independence in Syria and become the King of Syria.[30] France reasserted control in Syria with great difficulty. This coincided with a period when France encountered growing problems in maintaining influence in Cilicia in the face of the military advances of the Ankara government. At the same time, France, like Britain, was becoming increasingly concerned about the costs of military occupation and the French public did not seem enthusiastic about supporting overseas military involvements in the aftermath of the war.[31] These considerations and the desire to counter British influence, led to French moves to seek accommodation with the Ankara government.

The French had approached the resistance movement in Anatolia as early summer 1919. Both sides expressed their opposition to the establishment of a Kurdish state. More importantly, the French were particularly pleased to learn that the leadership of the resistance movement in Anatolia did not plan to take over Arab populated areas of the Ottoman Empire in their liberation struggle.[32] In October 1921 an agreement between Ankara and France led to a withdrawal of French troops from Cilicia and the adoption of a new frontier between the French mandate in Syria and territories under the control of Ankara. This was further south than the frontier envisaged in the Treaty of Sèvres.[33] The French, wishing to strengthen the military capabilities of the Ankara government, left substantial amounts of military equipment behind as they withdrew. Evidently, France wanted a strong Turkey to weaken or at least to balance British power in the region. Any British support for the Kurds was perceived by France as an effort to weaken Turkey. Thus France would later oppose the awarding of Mosul to the British mandate over Iraq.[34]

French support for Turkey has been described as anti-Kurdish.[35] However, it seems that the French government was more concerned to protect its interests in Syria and prevent British ascendancy in the Middle East. As a consequence many Kurds were further separated, with a group finding themselves in the French mandate of Syria.

According to the secret agreements to partition the Ottoman Empire, Russia would have received territories in eastern Anatolia with a large Kurdish population. However, the withdrawal of Russia from the First World War and the military expansion of the Ottoman Empire into the Caucasus after the signing of the Brest-Litovsk agreement brought the Kurds of the Caucasus as well as north-western Iran under the control of the Empire. The Ottomans were forced by Britain to evacuate this area after the signing of the Mudros Armistice in October 1918. Independent republics of Azerbaijan, Georgia and Armenia were established. The Treaty of Sèvres had allocated most of the territories that Russia would have received in eastern Anatolia to Armenia. Armenian efforts to expand into these areas were pre-empted by the resistance movement in Anatolia and the expansion of Soviet Russia into the Caucasus. Soviet support for the Ankara government again led to the division of the Kurds.

As early as May 1920 Ankara attempted to establish contact with the new Soviet state. Mustafa Kemal argued in a letter that the government was willing to support Soviet Russian expansion into the Caucasus. He added that the government was prepared to form a buffer state between Soviet Russia and the allies in return for Soviet military and financial support. The Ankara government was in dire need of military assistance and desperate for a secure border in the east in order to confront the Greeks in the west. Officials in Moscow, on the other hand, realized that supporting the Ankara government would help them in their struggle against the allies. The Soviets preferred that Ankara rather than Britain should control the strategically important Straits, especially at a time when the British were involved in military operations to weaken Soviet Russia and establish small buffer states in the Caucasus. Moscow also hoped to Bolshevize Turkey.[36] However, it was pragmatic considerations that eventually led to the signing of an agreement between Moscow and Ankara in March 1921.

Through this agreement Moscow was able to consolidate its control of the Caucasus and gain the goodwill of Ankara with regard to talks on the final status of the Straits. The two parties recognized the need to co-operate in their struggle against 'imperialists'. The Ankara government received invaluable military and financial assistance. The agreement also enabled Ankara to transfer large numbers of military units which could be redeployed against the French in Cilicia and then eventually against the Greeks. It also brought much needed prestige and credibility to the government. The frontier between Soviet Russia and the territories controlled by the Ankara government was fixed to include the districts of Ardahan and Kars within the jurisdiction of Ankara. Batum remained in Georgia although there were guarantees of autonomy for the local population. This arrangement left some Kurdish communities on the Soviet side of the frontier. By this agreement the establishment of a Greater Armenia in parts of eastern Anatolia had become exceedingly unlikely.

When the Mudros Armistice was signed the Ottoman army was in occupation of parts of Azeri- and Kurdish-populated areas of north-western Iran, including the city of Tabriz. As the Ottoman army completed its withdrawal in December 1918 most of these areas came under the control of Ismail Agha (Simko), the leader of the Shakak tribe. Within a year all the Kurdish tribes in the area recognized the authority of Simko. Mostly out of fear of British plans to use against them the Assyrians, Armenians and Kurds, the Ottoman Empire and the Ankara government extended assistance to Simko. Simko's rule lasted until July 1922 when, following his defeat by the Iranian army, Iran re-established control over the whole area.[37] Subsequently, in an agreement negotiated in October 1922 between Ankara and Tehran both sides decided to co-operate to increase security in the border area.

However, British influence over Iran made the officials of the newly-established Turkish Republic at first reluctant to develop close relations with Iran. Once Reza Shah had consolidated his power in Iran (by 1925) relations between Turkey and Iran gradually improved. In 1926 the two signed an agreement of friendship and non-aggression and recognized the frontiers that the Persian and the Ottoman Empire had agreed upon as early as 1639. A minor frontier revision was arranged in a treaty signed in 1932 soon after the Turkish government had suppressed a major Kurdish rebellion in an area along the Iranian border.[38] This treaty reinforced the centuries-old division of the Kurds in the area.

The Emergence of a National Resistance Movement and the Establishment of the Turkish Republic

The formation in 1919 of an effective resistance movement composed of both Kurds and Turks, as well as other Muslim groups of different ethnic backgrounds such as the Albanians, Circassians and Laz, would ultimately forestall the establishment of Kurdish autonomy or independence as envisaged by the Treaty of Sèvres. The resistance movement in 1920 formed an alternative government in Ankara to the Ottoman one based in Istanbul. By 1923 the Ankara government succeeded in expelling the occupying powers from the country and obtained international recognition of Turkey's independence.

Soon after the signing of the Mudros Armistice the allied fleet sailed into

Istanbul and established control over the Straits. The Sultan and the Ottoman government were at the mercy of the allies, who, in accordance with the armistice, proceeded to occupy parts of Anatolia. The Ottoman government acted submissively in the hope that this would lead to the signing of a more favourable peace treaty.

By spring 1919 Greece had landed its army in western Anatolia. Along the eastern Black Sea coast the Greeks living in the district of Trabzon were hoping for support from the Greek government to set up a Greek dominated Pontus state. In eastern Anatolia, aiming to establish a Greater Armenia, Armenians were occupying areas vacated by the Ottoman armies.

In these circumstances local defence organizations, often known as societies for the defence or preservation of national rights, were formed throughout Anatolia and eastern Thrace in areas that fell within the lines determined by the Mudros Armistice. The local defence societies from Erzurum in eastern Anatolia and from Trabzon were the first to attempt to pre-empt the establishment of an Armenian and a Pontus state.[39] These developments coincided with the arrival of Mustafa Kemal in eastern Anatolia. At the time he was a high-ranking Ottoman army officer who had originally been sent by the government to calm the agitation in Anatolia after the British had complained and threatened to send allied forces into the area.[40]

The news of the landing of Greek troops in İzmir in May 1919 under the protection of British, French and American warships accelerated efforts to co-ordinate the many resistance societies across the country. In July 1919 in Erzurum a congress was convened and attended by representatives of provinces from Kurdish-populated areas in eastern Anatolia (Bitlis, Erzurum, Sivas and Van) and from the district of Trabzon. Mustafa Kemal played a central role in the organization of the congress which elected him as its leader. The congress chose a representative executive committee (*Heyet-i Temsiliye*) and adopted measures which stressed loyalty to the Ottoman Sultan-Caliph. The indivisibility of the country (*vatan*) within its boundaries was declared. Resistance to foreign occupation was pledged.[41]

The Erzurum Congress was immediately followed by a series of local meetings held by defence societies throughout the country. These laid the groundwork for the Sivas Congress which was held in September 1919.[42] Representatives from 17 provinces participated together with members from the committee elected at the Erzurum Congress.[43] It was decided to unify all the local defence societies and form one Society for the Defence of Rights of Anatolia and Rumelia (SDRA-R). The Sivas Congress also agreed to oppose the establishment of Armenian and Greek states on Ottoman lands; to protect the indivisibility of the country; to preserve the Islamic Caliphate and the Ottoman Sultanate; and to establish provisional administrations in any part of the country which the Ottoman government might surrender to occupying forces.[44]

The Sivas Congress allocated more powers to the representative committee that had been originally set up by the Erzurum Congress. The representative committee was thus able to function more as a government.[45] It was able to persuade the government in Istanbul to hold new elections for the Ottoman parliament in October 1919. Most of the seats were won by members or sympathizers of the resistance movement in Anatolia. This was reflected in the parliament's unanimous adoption of the National Pact on 28 January 1920.

The National Pact was a short document which laid down the principles and aims of the resistance movement. The major objective was to ensure 'the continued existence of a stable Ottoman Sultanate and society'. The movement aimed to achieve this within the boundaries fixed by the Mudros Armistice of October 1918. The National Pact also noted that the future of the Ottoman lands with an Arab majority under foreign occupation should be determined by a free vote, while the status of western Thrace was left to a plebiscite that would be held once peace was established. It was stated that the people of the three sanjaks of Kars, Ardahan and Batum (who had already voted in July 1918, according to the terms of the Treaty of Brest-Litovsk, in favour of rejoining the country) would be given another opportunity to hold a plebiscite.[46] However, after the signing of the March 1921 treaty between Soviet Russia and Ankara, the intended plebiscite was never held.

The adoption of the National Pact precipitated the allied decision to occupy Istanbul, arrest many deputies of the Ottoman parliament and deport them. Allied pressure made it impossible for the parliament to continue to function and on 11 April 1920 it was closed down. This increased the rift between the Ottoman government and the committee representing the resistance movement. The government declared Mustafa Kemal a rebel after he had succeeded in persuading the resistance movement to hold elections across the country and form a new parliament in Ankara. This parliament, composed of newly elected representatives as well as deputies from the defunct Ottoman parliament, met in Ankara on 23 April 1920 and adopted the title 'Grand National Assembly'. The deputies during their oath-taking ceremony swore loyalty to the Caliphate and Sultanate. Mustafa Kemal was elected president of the assembly.

The rift between the Ottoman government and the resistance movement further deepened after the establishment of the assembly. On 20 January 1921 the assembly in Ankara adopted the Law on Fundamental Organization (*Teşkilat-ı Esasiye Kanunu*) which amended the 1876 Ottoman constitution. This provided a legal structure for the *de facto* government whose main aim remained 'the liberation of the Caliphate and the Sultanate'. However, by emphasizing that the parliament and its government would derive authority and legitimacy from the people, it formalized a major departure from the form of government under the Ottoman Empire.[47]

During the course of 1921 the Ankara government brought the country under its control after suppressing a number of rebellions. It was able to sign the agreements with Soviet Russia and France already described. By the end of summer 1922 the Greeks in western Anatolia had been forced to evacuate the country and by November 1922 the government was in a position to start peace negotiations with the allies in Lausanne.

The peace treaty signed at the end of the Lausanne Conference recognized Turkey's independence and settled most of the outstanding problems between it and the allies. In preparation for this eventuality and in defiance of the Preamble to the National Pact, the 'Turkish' Grand National Assembly, the new title for the assembly, had broken finally with the Ottoman Empire and its government when it abolished the Sultanate in November 1922. This opened the way in October 1923 for the assembly to declare Turkey a republic with Mustafa Kemal elected as its first President.

The only outstanding territorial issue concerned the final status of the district of Mosul. The Lausanne Conference had failed to resolve the problem and had left the settlement to negotiations between Britain and Turkey. Turkey's military and diplomatic efforts failed to ensure the inclusion of Mosul within Turkey. The settlement that was reached in 1925, leaving the area to Iraq, caused considerable disappointment especially among Kurdish deputies to the Turkish Grand National Assembly. Many Kurds who had participated in the resistance movement felt cheated out of a deal that had promised to keep them united. Other Kurds, especially those with nationalist convictions, regarded the Lausanne Treaty and the establishment of Turkey as an allied conspiracy to keep the Kurds disunited by denying them the autonomy or independence they had been promised by the Treaty of Sèvres.

The Failure of the Kurds to Form a Unified National Movement

Olson has traced the origins of Kurdish nationalism back to the 1870s when Shaikh Ubaydallah attempted to break away from the Ottoman Empire and set up an independent Kurdish state to be called 'Kurdistan'.[48] According to Van Bruinessen, there was no evidence that Ubaydallah had succeeded in establishing a sense of national consciousness among the Kurds.[49] Apparently Shaikh Ubaydallah had led a localized revolt in reaction to attempts by the Ottoman authorities to impose more centralized control. In the late nineteenth century within the Ottoman Empire, the typical Arab, Albanian or Turk was not aware of his separate ethnic identity. Likewise, the Kurds were not ethnically self-conscious. The population of the Ottoman Empire rather identified themselves on religious grounds.

In the period up to the establishment of the Turkish Republic in 1923 the Kurdish nationalists who did emerge failed to form a unified national movement. This was largely because of the lack of ethnic self-awareness among the Kurds. Disunity among the Kurds was another reason which accounted for the success of the Ankara government in resisting the terms of the Treaty of Sèvres and preventing the establishment of an autonomous or independent Kurdish state. During the First World War the Kurds had remained loyal to the Empire. In the immediate aftermath of it one group of Kurds came to identify themselves with the resistance movement in Anatolia and supported it. Another small group of nationalists aspired for an independent state or at least aimed for autonomy within an Ottoman or Turkish state. A third group included powerful Kurdish tribal leaders who were mostly interested in creating their own 'kingdoms' over the parts of Kurdish-populated territories they controlled. The second and the third Kurdish group were unable to co-operate and organize themselves into an effective movement.

At the 1919 Erzurum Congress 22 of the 56 delegates who attended were Kurds.[50] The delegates focused on the need to resist allied efforts to create Armenian and Greek states in Anatolia. Islam and 'Ottoman patriotism' constituted an important common bond between the Kurds and other delegates. Kurds were represented in the executive committee that was formed to represent and co-ordinate the activities of the resistance movement. Subsequently, Mustafa Kemal, the elected leader of this body, sent a series of letters and telegrams to numerous tribal chief and shaikhs to secure their support.[51]

Kurdish participation in the resistance movement was further strengthened after news arrived from the Peace Conference in Paris in November 1919 that the Kurdish nationalist representative Şerif Paşa had reached a deal with the Armenians. Şerif Paşa had agreed to accept the formation of an Armenian state in areas that included Kurds in return for Kurdish independence in a small part of eastern Anatolia.[52] The revulsion among Kurds at this news led to a number of telegrams being sent to Paris. In these it was argued that the Kurds did not want to separate from the Turks.[53] Ten Kurdish tribal leaders from Erzincan sent a telegram to the French High Commissioner in Istanbul protesting at Şerif Paşa's actions. They declared that Turks and Kurds were 'brothers in terms of race (soy) and religion'.[54] Similar telegrams critical of Şerif Paşa and expressing solidarity between Kurds and Turks were also sent to the Ottoman parliament in January 1920, two days before the adoption of the National Pact.[55] In March 1920 a declaration stressing Islamic solidarity and opposition to efforts to separate Kurds and Turks was signed by 22 Kurdish tribal leaders.[56]

This strong feeling of solidarity between Turks and Kurds was not surprising. The SDRA-R was an organization based on 'Ottoman patriotism'.[57] The importance of the Islamic bond was reiterated by Mustafa Kemal soon after the opening of the Grand National Assembly when he noted that those who composed the assembly were not simply Turks, Circassians, Kurds or Laz but were rather elements of a united Islamic community.[58] The Kurds were represented with about 74 deputies in the Grand National Assembly.[59]

However, there were also Kurdish tribes which rebelled against the Ankara government represented by the Grand National Assembly. Between 1919 and the end of 1921 there were 23 revolts directed against the efforts of the resistance movement and then the Ankara government to centralize its authority across the country outside occupied areas. Only four of these uprisings occurred in Kurdish-populated areas and three involved Kurdish tribes and clans.[60] These were the rebellions of Cemil Ceto's clan in May 1920, by the Milli Aşiret during summer 1920 and by the Koçgiri tribe between March and June 1921.

These three Kurdish rebellions were inspired or influenced by the activities of Şerif Paşa and the nationalists in the Society for the Progress of Kurdistan (Kurdistan Teali Cemiyeti) based in Istanbul.[61] The most serious was the Koçgiri rebellion. Its leader, Alişan Bey, was actually a member of the Society for the Progress of Kurdistan. He had demanded the implementation of Article 64 of the Treaty of Sèvres with its provisions on Kurdish autonomy. The Koçgiri rebellion failed to attract support from Kurdish deputies and from other Kurdish tribes and was eventually suppressed.[62] However, these manifestations of Kurdish discontent, with the possibility that Britain and France might provide support, were viewed at the time with such concern by Mustafa Kemal that he went as far as briefly toying with the idea of granting limited autonomy to territories where there was a Kurdish majority.[63] As regards the Koçgiri rebellion, Kurdish tribes of Sunni Moslems were reluctant to support what they considered to be an Alevi uprising.[64] Mustafa Kemal would exploit these rebellions, particularly the Koçgiri rebellion, in order to strengthen the cohesion of the resistance movement. He referred to the rebels as traitors who were trying to undermine efforts to liberate the country and the Caliph/Sultan.

A number of the Kurdish members of the Ottoman elite in Istanbul had founded organizations in 1908 which would in time promote Kurdish national aspirations. The Society for the Progress of Kurdistan was one such. These bodies published newspapers and magazines in Kurdish in Istanbul, Cairo and Geneva. Initially, many members of them were actually pressing for the development of the eastern provinces of the Ottoman Empire under the banner of 'Ottomanism'. The term 'Ottomanism' will be examined in detail later. When the more reformist Ottoman government led by the Committee of Union and Progress (CUP) began to press for centralization and developed an interest in Turkification, these Kurdish organizations turned away from Ottomanism and began to focus on ideas associated more with Kurdish nationalism.[65] However, some prominent Kurds such as Ziya Gökalp and Süleyman Nazif would eventually become ardent supporters of Turkish nationalism of a civic kind.

The Society for the Progress of Kurdistan and other Kurdish organizations were closed down for a period by the Ottoman government. In 1918, soon after the Mudros Armistice was signed, the Society for the Progress of Kurdistan was reactivated. Şerif Paşa, Emir Bedirhan and Seyid Abdul Kadir were among the key individuals who had been actively involved in these organizations before their closure. In contrast to its former practice, the Society for the Progress of Kurdistan after 1918 opened branches outside Istanbul and included younger people with radical views among its members.[66]

Şerif Paşa had been an Ottoman ambassador to Stockholm in the 1890s and had been a close supporter of the Sultan.[67] When the Young Turks came to power he fell out with the CUP government and was denied the post of ambassador to Paris.[68] This may well have made Şerif Paşa more receptive to Kurdish nationalist ideas and may have led him to play a central role in the formation of the early Kurdish nationalist societies in Istanbul. By the end of the First World War he had become much influenced by the ideas of President Wilson and was directly involved in efforts to convince the Paris Peace Conference to include provisions for Kurdish autonomy or independence in the Treaty of Sèvres. In the face of allied anxieties about the territorial overlap between the planned Armenian state and 'Kurdistan', he had not hesitated to sign an agreement with Boghas Nubar, the Armenian representative, in November 1919 in order to leave the settlement of boundaries to the Peace Conference. As noted earlier, Şerif Paşa's readiness to allow many Kurds to come under Armenian rule and also under the control of the British in Iraq precipitated criticisms from many Kurdish circles. Members of the Society for the Progress of Kurdistan denounced Şerif Paşa's actions. In April 1920 he was forced to resign from the society 'and renounce all his dreams of one day becoming the ruler of Kurdistan'.[69]

One of the critics of Şerif Paşa was Seyid Abdul Kadir who was a member of the Ottoman parliament and also a high-ranking official in the government. Abdul Kadir represented the autonomist faction among the Kurdish nationalists. He remained too attached to the Ottoman Empire and the Sultan to contemplate full independence except when he once approached the French in Istanbul to submit a document demanding access to the sea for an independent 'Kurdistan'.[70] The document was prepared in support of Şerif Paşa whose map had left 'Kurdistan' landlocked. Abdul Kadir quickly abandoned the idea of independence and became critical of Şerif Paşa's deal with the Armenians. He argued that all the Kurds wanted was the possibility to develop freely and stated that the Turks were the co-religionists of the Kurds. In his opinion, Şerif Paşa's idea of separating Kurds from Turks was unacceptable. However, Abdul Kadir's close association with Şerif Paşa got him into a difficult situation in the Ottoman parliament as he faced calls for resignation from other Kurdish deputies. Abdul Kadir subsequently declared that he would stop supporting Kurdish separatism and instead expressed sympathy with the patriotism of his co-religionists in Anatolia.[71]

Emir Ali Bedirhan was a descendant of the famous Bedirhan Bey, the Emir of Botan in 1821, who to some is considered as the father of Kurdish nationalism.[72] It was Emir Bedirhan and Abdul Kadir who had founded the first Society for the Progress of Kurdistan. However, the two quickly differed over its objectives. Unlike Abdul Kadir, Emir Bedirhan was much more supportive of the idea of the independence of 'Kurdistan'. He did not share Abdul Kadir's loyalty to the Sultan. Emir Bodirhan and his family were eager to re-establish control over the territories that his ancestors had ruled in the first half of the 1800s.[73]

Shaikh Mahmoud, the leader of the Barinja of Suleimania, and Ismail Aǧha (Simko), leader of the Shakak tribe in western Iran, were two other prominent Kurds who aspired for independence. The vacuum created by rivalry between the Ankara government and Britain in the Mosul district enabled Shaikh Mahmoud to increase his power in the area and he attempted to establish control over parts of southern 'Kurdistan'. Soon after they had occupied parts of the Mosul district, the British decided in May 1919 to create 'autonomous Kurdish States under Kurdish chiefs' which were to be advised by 'British officers'. This led to Shaikh Mahmoud's appointment as a district governor.[74] However, Shaikh Mahmoud's demands for effective autonomy or independence and his references to Wilson's concern for the right to self-determination strained his relations with the British.

Shaikh Mahmud's decision soon afterwards to proclaim independence led to his expulsion from the area by the British in August 1919. However, British supremacy in the area was short-lived. With the support of some local Kurdish tribes the Ankara government began military operations in the northern parts of the contested district of Mosul. This led the British to evacuate Suleimania in September 1922.[75] In an attempt to rally the Kurds against Ankara the British brought back Shaikh Mahmoud. However, he refused to submit himself fully to the authority of the British and instead attempted to rule the area with the self-proclaimed title of 'King of Kurdistan'. Shaikh Mahmoud even announced a government of 'Kurdistan'.[76] His rule lasted until March 1923 when he was forced out of Suleimania by British bombing. In the meantime the British succeeded in defeating the forces of the Ankara government. Although Shaikh Mahmoud returned to Suleimania again in July 1923 he enjoyed little of his previous authority and soon after the formal establishment of Iraq was forced to flee to Iran in July 1924.

Shaikh Mahmoud's interest in independence seemed limited to his area of control in southern 'Kurdistan'. He appeared disinterested in the plans of Şerif Paşa when the latter approached him in 1919 about Kurdish independence.[77] Shaikh Mahmoud did not seem to entertain ideas of nationhood that transcended Kurdish tribal identities. At one time for a short period he co-operated with the British in the belief that he could have his own tribal 'kingdom'. When this did not seem feasible he then responded favourably to the approaches made by the Ankara government to enlist his military support in an effort to try to force the British out of Mosul.[78] He even went as far as expressing a desire to be a representative of Suleimania at the assembly in Ankara.[79] The fluctuations in Shaikh Mahmoud's policies were best captured by a British official serving in the area who noted that Shaikh Mahmoud maintained 'a foot in both British and Turkish camps with an increasing bias towards the latter'.[80] Ultimately none of Shaikh Mahmoud's schemes would materialize, as the district of Mosul together with the Kurds of the area became part of British-mandated Iraq.

At the end of the First World War, soon after the Ottoman Empire withdrew from north-western Iran, Ismail Agha (Simko) established control over an area extending from the Ottoman border to Tabriz. Simko never made clear what form his rule would take. According to him, independence seemed only to signify 'the establishment of his personal despotic rule over the other Kurdish tribes of Iranian Azerbaijan'.[81] The lack of a sense of attachment to a unified 'Kurdistan' made him reluctant to assist the efforts of the Society for the Progress of Kurdistan to establish such a state. Simko appeared to prefer to be the ruler of an area under his control rather than to support a Greater Kurdistan that might be run by someone else.[82]

In July 1922 Simko was defeated by the Iranians and forced to seek refuge in Turkey. He subsequently went to Suleimania where he was received as a king by Shaikh Mahmoud in January 1923. It seems that a sense of nationhood had not developed among the Kurds during Simko's short rule even though at one time he was able to field almost 10,000 fighters. Nevertheless, his rule 'may be considered as the first attempt by the Kurds in Iran to create an independent or autonomous region', even if Simko had 'neither the desire nor the ability to create a state in the modern sense of the word, with an administrative organization'.[83]

Independence for 'Kurdistan' had been entertained by some Kurdish members of the Ottoman elite in Istanbul as early as 1908. In general, the societies established by this group did not seek to mobilize a mass movement among the Kurds in the period leading up to 1923 and the establishment of the Turkish Republic. In practice, this Kurdish elite had not progressed beyond Phase A of Hroch's nation-building process. Some members of it, instead of garnering popular support, sought rather to collaborate with the allies in order to establish an independent Kurdish state of sorts. The example of Şerif Paşa was a clear case in point. The deal Şerif Paşa had unsuccessfully attempted to strike with the Armenians was initiated without attempting to secure support among the Kurdish population at large. Politics for this elite was too much of 'a gentlemen's game' to involve the masses.[84]

However, as noted above, the activities of Şerif Paşa and other Kurdish nationalists active in the Society for the Progress of Kurdistan had apparently in part encouraged the three popular Kurdish rebellions in 1920 and 1921. A form of mass mobilization was in evidence, although this was only at the tribal level. It was not possible to mobilize support among the Kurds as a whole on account of the lack of modern leadership and because tribal and religious loyalties and personal interests prevailed over any sense of genuine nationhood. It was not possible to speak of the formation of a politicized Kurdish ethnic group in this period. Ethnic identity formation had scarcely been set in motion. The Ottoman Kurdish elite, as one of their sons observed, had 'one foot in nationalism and the other in Ottoman and Islamic identities and in the ambition to be ministers'.[85]

President Wilson's ideas and the provisions for Kurdish autonomy and even possibly independence in the Treaty of Sèvres did seem to encourage some Kurdish tribal leaders to rebel and attempt to establish their own personal kingdoms or statelets. Evidently the lobbying of Şerif Paşa and a handful of other active Kurdish nationalists had convinced allied officials that a separate Kurdish group of peoples did exist which could be entitled to self-determination. Although a Kurdish 'nation' as such was not explicitly acknowledged, the officials who drew up the terms of the Treaty of Sèvres were prepared to recognize a Kurdish entity which in reality at that time had not taken shape. In this particular instance, for a brief period between 1920 and 1923 in effect, 'other definition' preceded 'self definition'. Ironically, therefore, it was in 1920 that the then disunited Kurds, of whom the great majority were scarcely aware of their common ethnic as opposed to tribal identity, came closest to securing outside recognition of a right to nationhood. But without the necessary ethnic let alone national self-awareness of a body of the population the realization of a Kurdish state and nationhood could not materialize.

Events showed that the complex web of intrigues and rivalries between Kurdish tribal leaders prevented the Kurds as a whole from mustering enough support to select a modern leadership and organize a nationalist struggle.[86] The original division of Kurdish tribes in separate Ottoman and Persian camps had meant that unity among the Kurds would be difficult to achieve. The further redistribution of the Kurds into a number of other states made the prospects for Kurdish unity much more unlikely. By 1923 the trans-state nature of the Kurdish question had become more complex. Within the region as a whole and within the newly established Turkish Republic itself sectarian divisions between the Sunni and the Alevi Kurds was another complication. Yet, on the other hand and within Turkey specifically, the majority of Kurds more importantly still had a strong sense of allegiance to Islam as a common uniting religion. Most Kurds identified themselves closely with their fellow Moslem Turks.

The Ankara government led by Mustafa Kemal was successful in co-opting

Kurdish tribal leaders into the resistance movement and in mobilizing Kurdish loyalty to the Caliph-Sultan and the country. Mustafa Kemal not only offered to protect these tribal leaders but he also 'had power that he might delegate to them, whereas the [Kurdish] nationalist organizations did not'.[87] Mustafa Kemal also enjoyed the benefit of the support of a number of advisers with experience in state affairs and organizational work. It was a combination of these factors which prevented Kurdish nationalism from developing and which forestalled the possibility of the establishment an independent Kurdish state.

It would be misleading to attribute the division of the Kurds into a number of countries to the triumph of Turkish nationalism and Western conspiracy. The division of the Kurds was rather a complex political process brought about by the conflicting interests of wartime allies, the emergence of the Soviet Union, the geostrategic characteristics of the area, Greek/Armenian nationalism and the nature of the resistance to the partitioning of the Ottoman Empire. In other words, the Kurds found themselves separated from each other by default rather than by design.

Notes

1. M.S. Anderson, *The Eastern Question 1774–1923* (London: Macmillan, 1966).
2. M.E. Yapp, *The Making of the Modern Near East, 1792–1923* (London: Longman, 1987) p.87.
3. H. Howard, *The Partition of Turkey: a Diplomatic Analysis 1913–1923* (Norman OK: University of Oklahoma, 1931) p.217.
4. J.C. Hurewitz, *Diplomacy in the Near and Middle East: a Documentary Record: 1914–1956*, Vol.2 (Princeton NJ, Toronto, New York and London: van Nostrand, 1956) p.82.
5. U. Mumcu, *Kürt-İslam Ayaklanması 1919–1925* (Istanbul: Tekin Yayınevi, 1992) p.18; and R. Olson, *The Emergence of Kurdish Nationalism 1880–1925* (Austin: University of Texas Press, 1991) p.52.
6. For a detailed analysis of these developments see U. Sipahioğlu, *The Mosul Question and Anglo-Turkish Relations, 1922–1926* (PhD thesis, University of Cambridge, 1995) pp.22–61.
7. D. Korn, *The Men who Put the Kurds into Iraq: Percy Cox and Arnold Wilson* (Silver Spring MD: KNC Publications, 1993) p.7.
8. C. Kutschera, *Le Mouvement National Kurde* (Paris: Flammarion, 1979) p.34.
9. H. Arfa, *The Kurds: A Historical and Political Study* (London: Oxford University Press, 1968) p.27.
10. C. Kutschera, op. cit., p.25.
11. A. Powell, *The Struggle for Power in Moslem Asia* (New York: Century, 1923) pp.99–100.
12. D. Korn, op. cit., pp.4–5.
13. Quoted in ibid., p.24.
14. U. Sipahioğlu, op. cit., pp.36–7.
15. Ibid., pp.40–57. See also R. Olson, op. cit., pp.52–85.
16. R. Olson, op. cit., p.53.

17. H. Arfa, op. cit., p.113; and U. Sipahioğlu, op. cit., p.38.
18. M.S. Anderson, op. cit., p.384.
19. A.J. Toynbee, *The Western Question in Greece and Turkey* (Boston MA: Houghton Mifflin, 1922) p.95.
20. R. Olson, op. cit., p.65.
21. U. Sipahioğlu, op. cit., pp.62–72.
22. During the debate concerning Mosul and Kirkuk in the National Assembly in Ankara there were a number of Kurdish deputies who stressed the importance of ensuring that these areas were not left to the British. See particularly the speech by Yusuf Ziya Bey, Deputy for Bitlis, *Türkiye Büyük Millet Meclisi (TBMM) Gizli Celse Zabıtları* 3, (Ankara: Türkiye İş Bankası Kültür Yayınları, 1985) pp.1317–18 and ibid., 4, p.163.
23. H. Howard, op. cit., p.298.
24. C. Kutschera, op. cit., p.24.
25. Ibid., p.35; and H. Yıldız, *Fransız Belgelerinde Sevre-Lozan-Musul Üçgeninde Kürdistan* (Istanbul: Koral, 1992) p.117.
26. H. Yıldız, op. cit., pp.54–5.
27. A. Powell, op. cit., p.296.
28. Ibid., p.224.
29. A.J. Toynbee, op. cit., p. 74.
30. A. Powell, op. cit., p.220.
31. Ibid., p.99.
32. H. Yıldız, op. cit., p.94.
33. H. Howard, op. cit., p.261.
34. H. Yıldız, op. cit., p. 87.
35. Ibid., p.66.
36. S. Sonyel, *Türk Kurtuluş Savaşı ve Dış Politika I* (Ankara: Türk Tarih Kurumu Basımevi, 1973) p.84.
37. Ibid., pp.44–54.
38. H. Arfa, op. cit., pp.40–1.
39. A. Demirel, *Government and Opposition in the First Grand National Assembly* (PhD thesis, Department of Political Science and International Relations, Boğaziçi University, Istanbul, 1993) pp.31–2.
40. Ibid., p.31.
41. For the Erzurum Declaration see M. Goloğlu, *Erzurum Kongresi* (Ankara: Nüve Matbaası, 1968) pp.201–3.
42. For the coverage of a list of the local societies and the regional meetings see T.Z. Tunaya, *Türkiye'de Siyasi Partiler* (Istanbul: Doğan Kardeş, 1952) pp.472–527.
43. For the list of delegates see V.C. Aşkun, *Sivas Kongresi*, (Istanbul: Inkilap ve Aka, 1963) p.147.
44. H. Howard, op. cit., p.255.
45. A. Demirel, op. cit., p.34.
46. The original text in French as well as its translation into English may be found in A.J. Toynbee, op. cit., pp.207–10. In the literature there seems to be some confusion over the geographical location of these three sanjaks. In Toynbee the French text lists the names of the three while the English translation does not. This might explain why in some of the subsequent references to the Pact some authors have thought that these three sanjaks were located in Kurdish populated eastern or south-eastern Anatolia rather than in the north-eastern corner of Anatolia where traditionally no Kurdish communities of any significant size lived. See, for example, J.C. Hurewitz,

op. cit., pp.74–5.

47. A. Demirel, op. cit., p.112.

48. R. Olson, op. cit., pp.1–7.

49. M. Van Bruinessen, *Kürdistan Üzerine Yazılar* (Istanbul: Iletişim Yayınları, 1993) p.137.

50. H. Yıldız, op. cit., p.34. For a list of the delegates see M. Gologlu, op. cit., pp.78–80.

51. M. Gologlu, op. cit., pp.113–14 and K. Öke, *Musul ve Kürdistan Sorunu 1918–1926* (Ankara: Türk Kültürü Araştırma Enstitüsü, 1992) p.48.

52. H. Yıldız, op. cit., p.23. For the details of the deal see C. Kutschera, op. cit., p.29.

53. M. Van Bruinessen, *Agha, Shaikh and State* (London: Zed, 1992) p.279.

54. U. Mumcu, *Kürt Dosyası* (Istanbul: Tekin Yayınevi, 1993) p.14.

55. For an excerpt from these telegrams see K. Öke, op. cit., p.76.

56. H. Yıldız, op. cit., p.104.

57. M. Tunçay, *Türkiye Cumhuriyeti'nde Tek Parti Yönetimi'nin Kurulması* (Ankara: Yurt Yayınları, 1981) p.28.

58. K. Öke, op. cit., p.77.

59. There were 437 deputies in the first Grand National Assembly. With 74 deputies the highest proportion of the deputies came from the south-eastern region, the region mostly populated by Kurds. For the distribution of deputies by regions see A. Demirel, op. cit., p.82.

60. For a detailed analysis of these rebellions see *Türk İstiklal Tarihi VI ncı Cilt: İstiklal Harbinde Ayaklanmalar (1919–1921)* (Ankara: Gnkur. Basımevi, 1974).

61. For a detailed analysis of the formation, activities and membership of this Society see I. Göldaş, *Kürdistan Teali Cemiyeti* (Istanbul: Doz Yayınları, 1991).

62. For a detailed analysis of the Koçgiri rebellion from the Kurdish perspective written in modern Turkish see, N. Dersimi, *Kürdistan Tarihinde Dersim* (Istanbul: Zel Yayıncılık, 1994) pp.84–114.

63. *TBMM Gizli Celse Zabıtları* 3, op. cit. p.551. Mustafa Kemal also talked about autonomy for Kurds during a press conference in Izmit in January 1923. The records of this autonomy plan were banned from publication in Turkey until they appeared in 'Gizlenen Tutanak, Atatürk, Kürtlere Özerklik' *2000'e Doğru*, 30 Aug.–6 Sep. 1987, pp.1–6. R. Olson, op. cit., Appendix II provides a summary of a 'Draft Law for a Proposed Autonomy of Kurdistan as Debated in the Grand National Assembly on 10 February 1922'. Although this Draft Law was much more comprehensive compared with other plans it was not possible to find any reference to it in the Records of the Turkish Grand National Assembly. These records do not report a meeting of 10 Feb. 1922. However, two Turkish historians familiar with Turkish and Ottoman archives, Mete Tunçay and Zafer Toprak, during discussions with the authors argued that this Draft Law was most probably misinformation fed to the British Embassy by the resistance movement.

64. M. Van Bruinessen (note 53) p.278.

65. For a detailed analysis of the place and role of Kurds in Ottoman politics during the period of the CUP movement see, N. Kutlay, *İttihat Terraki ve Kürtler* (Ankara: Beybun, 1992).

66. M. Van Bruinessen (note 53) p.277.

67. H. Arfa, op. cit., p.31.

68. C. Kutschera, op. cit., p.23.

69. Ibid., p.26.

70. H. Yıldız, op. cit., p.60.

71. K. Öke, op. cit., p.76; and C. Kutschera, op. cit., p.31.
72. C. Kutschera, op. cit., p.13.
73. H. Yıldız, op. cit., pp.108–9.
74. H. Arfa, op. cit., pp.111–12.
75. U. Sipahioğlu, op. cit., p.67.
76. Ibid., p.73; and C. Kutschera, op. cit., pp.63–5.
77. H. Arfa, op. cit., p.112.
78. *Türk İstiklal Harbi IV ncı Cilt, Güney Cephesi* (Ankara: Gnkur. Basımevi, 1966) p.277.
79. U. Sipahioğlu, op. cit., p.76.
80. Ibid., p.85.
81. H. Arfa, op. cit., p.57.
82. C. Kutschera, op. cit., p.49.
83. H. Arfa, op. cit., pp.63–4. C. Kutschera, op. cit., pp.47–51 also regards Simko as a Kurdish nationalist and notes that he unwillingly 'accepted the assistance of Turks'. Simko's grandson, who is now a retired local administrator and a local historian in Van, has contested Kutschera's view of his grandfather during an interview with the authors in June 1995. He argued that Ismail Agha was a local tribal leader loyal to the Ottoman and Turkish state who had not entertained any Kurdish nationalist aspirations.
84. M. Van Bruinessen (note 53) p.276.
85. C. Kutschera, op. cit., p.26.
86. H. Yıldız, op. cit., pp.107 and 117.
87. M. Van Bruinessen (note 53) p.279.

4

The Evolution of the Kurdish Question in Turkey

THE KURDISH question in Turkey today is highly complex. Economic, social and political (domestic as well as international) factors must be taken into account. The Kurdish question is also tied up with the transformation of Turkey from a traditional society, where identities were religiously determined at a communal level, to a modern society, where the aim was to define an individual's identity at the state level. The driving force behind this transformation was Turkish nationalism. In its early stages it seemed that the Turkish nationalist elite had in mind the creation of a national identity which would be territorially defined. This could have developed into a form of civic nationalism in which there was scope for multiculturalism and expressions of Kurdish cultural and ethnic identity. However, the nation-building and state-building processes culminated in the establishment of a strongly centralized regime.

Some of the traditional Kurdish elite struggled to resist this state-building process. The Kurdish populated areas of eastern Turkey were the scene of a series of rebellions until the beginning of the Second World War. By the 1950s, much of the traditional Kurdish elite had either been eliminated or incorporated into the new regime in Turkey which was becoming relatively more democratic. The modernization of society assimilated many Kurds. But another product of this modernization was the emergence of a small yet steadily growing new, Kurdish elite which sought recognition of a separate Kurdish identity. By the 1980s this elite was able to generate a sense of Kurdish identity among other Kurds. The divisions of the traditional Kurdish society of the pre-Second World War period were to an extent transcended. This growing awareness of Kurdish identity and the difficulty of the Turkish political system in accommodating it lie at the heart of the Kurdish question.

The Origins of Turkish Nationalism

In Ottoman society nationality was determined on the basis of a person's membership in a religious community. This was not much different from western Europe in the sixteenth century when religion constituted the basis of an individual's identity. At a time when Europeans referred to the Ottoman Empire as 'Turkey' and to its subjects as 'Turks', 'the Turks thought of themselves primarily as Moslems; their loyalty belonged ... to Islam and to the Ottoman house and state'.[1] Moslems basically belonged to the 'community of Islam', and were the subjects of the Sultan, their Caliph. For most Moslems ethnic and national identity were not as salient as religious affiliations. As Ziya Gökalp, a leading ideologue of Turkish nationalism, noted 'before [1908], there were Turks, but there was no idea "we are the Turkish nation" in the collective consciousness of that people: in other words, there was no Turkish nation at that time.'[2]

The Turks were basically an 'ethnic category'. Outside observers were able to identify the Turks as a distinct group with their own, separate language, culture and history. Many Turks themselves though had little or no self-awareness of an ethnic identity. Only in the late nineteenth century did a number of leading Ottoman figures take an interest in Turkish language and culture.[3]

A growing European interest in Turkology led to the publication of a number of works which examined the ancient Turkish language, culture and history which originated in Central Asia. These included *Travels in Asia* (1871) by Arminius Vambery, and *Introduction a l'histoire de l'Asie* (1896) by Leon Cahun. The deciphering of the Orhun inscriptions by the Danish philologist Vilhelm Thomsen in Central Asia in 1893 provided additional evidence of a Turkish language and civilization dating from the sixth century.

In addition to this 'other-labelling' of 'Turks' by outside scholars and historians, Ottoman writers and diplomats also began to produce literature in the late nineteenth century which focused on Turkish language and identity. The scholar and statesman Ahmet Vefik Paşa wrote *Şecere-i Evşal-i Türkiye* (undated) (*Genealogy of Turkey*). The military officer, diplomat and writer Mustafa Celaleddin (who was a former Polish refugee) wrote *Les Turcs Anciens et Modernes* (1869). Süleyman Paşa, a military officer, scholar and director of the Harbiye Cadet School, wrote extensively on the Turkish language and advocated that the language of Turks was Turkish and not Ottoman. His works included *Tarih-ı Alem* (*History of the World*) (1874) and *Ilm-i Sarf-Türki* (1876) (*Science of Turkish Grammar*). The appearance of this growing literature about Turks and the Turkish language at a time when nationalist uprisings were taking place in the Balkans and the Middle East led some of the Ottoman elite to question their own identity in ethnic terms.

There were also intellectuals, mostly émigrés from Russia, who arrived in Istanbul around the the time of the First World War and began to advocate political Turkism. Gaspıralı Ismail Bey not only talked about the unity of Turkish speakers but also thought in terms of a Turkish nation.[4] He became famous for advocating the cultural and political unification of all Turks and Tatars. Yusuf Akçura was another émigré from Russia who pressed for the political unification of Turkish people in the Ottoman Empire and Russia. He believed that pan-Turkism rather than pan-Islamism or Ottomanism could save the Empire.[5] It was Ziya Gökalp, a Kurd from Diyarbakır, who was to 'systemize Turkish thinking on pan-Turkism'.[6] Gökalp became an influential intellectual in the circles of the governing CUP. However, he did not consider pan-Turkism as a viable policy. Instead he promoted the idea of a Turkish nation that stressed common culture and education rather than ethnicity.[7] As we have discussed previously, common culture is one of the features shared by a particular ethnic group.

The origins of the idea of Turkish nationalism as a political force in government may be traced back to the development of a reformist movement in the Ottoman Empire. This movement, originally launched by two Kurds, a Tatar and a Circassian, in 1889 had aimed to develop a sense of Ottoman patriotism which would transcend religious and ethnic differences.[8] It was hoped that a multi-denominational nationalism could be nurtured to 'save the Ottoman Empire' from disintegrating under the pressure of nationalist uprisings in the Balkans. However, the movement which became known as the CUP soon began to show signs of an ideological disagreement between those advocating Ottomanism and those supporting Turkism. Proponents of different forms of Turkish nationalism came to the fore. For example, Tekin Alp who was by birth a Jew, advocated different forms of Turkish nationalism at one time stressing common culture – in line with Gökalp – and on other occasions stressing rather ethnicity and race.[9]

In the war against the occupying forces the resistance movement in Ankara stressed the need to save the country (*vatan*) as well as the Ottoman Sultan and Caliphate. It was Ottoman patriotism that provided the basis of popular mobilization. But the leadership which had led the struggle against foreign occupation would come to regard Turkish nationalism as a vehicle for establishing a modern and secular Turkey in place of the defunct Ottoman Empire. The population of Turkey would need a new identity which would replace that based on religion. Eventually an identity based on Turkish ethnicity was emphasized. In these circumstances little opportunity would be given for the free expression of a separate Kurdish identity.

From Ottoman Patriotism to Turkish Nationalism – 1919–23

The protection of the Sultan and Caliph and a commitment to the independence of Ottoman territories and the Ottoman nation within the Mudros Armistice lines were the basic elements of Ottoman patriotism. As Tunçay has noted, the term 'nation' used in this context did not signify nation in the modern sense of the word but rather referred to the 'nation of Islam'.[10] In the case of the Turkish War of Independence, the symbols and values employed to mobilize people were still very much religiously determined. This was clearly evident in the content of the telegrams written to most of the participants by Mustafa Kemal before the Erzurum and the Sivas Congress. In his efforts to mobilize support Mustafa Kemal stressed the common religious bonds between Turks and Kurds as well as with other groups such as the Laz and the Circassians.[11] The Erzurum and the Sivas Congress were opened with prayers and speakers emphasized the need to rescue the Caliph from captivity and drive non-Moslems out of the holy territories of Islam. The Declaration of Principles of the SDRA-R adopted during the Sivas Congress in September 1919 included references to numerous religious values and considered all Moslems as natural members of the association.[12]

The emphasis on religion and Ottoman patriotism was also evident in the National Pact adopted in January 1920. This was all the more significant because this document has been considered by some historians as a 'Declaration of Independence of the Turkish Nation'.[13] However, it referred to 'Turkey' only once – in Article 3 in the context of the status of western Thrace – and the term 'nation' was used to denote a community of Moslem believers. Hence Lewis was correct to note that 'the Pact still speaks of "Ottoman Muslims" and not of Turks, and the word Turk appears nowhere in the document.'[14] The purpose of the pact was to identify the territories to be liberated and to provide a basis for mobilizing the maximum possible support to defeat the occupiers and achieve independence. The document did not refer to the form and nature of the state and society that would follow independence. By implication it seemed that little would change given the emphasis put on preserving the Sultanate and the Caliphate.

The opening ceremony of the Grand National Assembly in Ankara in April 1920 incorporated several Islamic rituals and particular care was given to ensure that the assembly would open after the Friday prayer.[15] At its first session the assembly committed itself to the National Pact and it became the main decision-making and legitimizing body for the resistance movement. However, the assembly did not officially take on the name 'Turkish' until the following year when the Law on Fundamental Organization, an amendment of the 1876 Ottoman Constitution, was adopted.

Mustafa Kemal was elected president of the assembly and during his speech summarizing recent events he underlined that the purpose of the assembly would be to lead the struggle to reinstate the independence of the seven-centuries-old Ottoman state and nation. He defined the nation he had in mind as being composed of all Islamic elements living within the National Pact boundaries.[16] A few days after this speech Mustafa Kemal intervened in a heated debate between deputies concerning the responsibilities of the health ministry which was to be established. Several deputies had become disturbed by the exclusive references made by one member to the term 'Turks'. These deputies called instead for the use of the terms 'Moslem' or 'Ottoman'.

Mustafa Kemal noted that the assembly was not composed of representatives of Turks, Circassians, Kurds and the Laz but consisted of members of an Islamic community held together by a powerful bond.[17]

The first article of the Law on Fundamental Organization adopted in January 1921 declared that 'sovereignty, without any preconditions, belongs to the nation'.[18] Accordingly, the nation would become the source of the assembly's authority and legitimacy. This was a major departure from the Ottoman understanding of government which had been based on the divine authority of the Sultan/Caliph. Article 3 of the Law on Fundamental Organization identified the assembly as the governing body of the 'state of Turkey'. This was the first occasion that the name 'Turkey' was officially employed by the resistance movement in more than just a passing sense.

These references to 'the nation' and to 'Turkey' led the way to the mentioning of a 'nation of Turkey' (*Türkiye Milleti*). This expression was used with increasing frequency in the Turkish Grand National Assembly and particularly by Mustafa Kemal. It was never clearly defined. It seems to have been employed in a manner that suggested a national identity which incorporated all the Islamic groups of different ethnic backgrounds in Turkey. Oran has argued that the expression was employed by Mustafa Kemal to stress the common bond and solidarity between Turks and Kurds.[19] At this time there was a conspicuous absence of any mention of the terms 'Ottoman' or 'Ottoman nation' in Mustafa Kemal's speeches.

The Turkish Grand National Assembly adopted decisions in November 1922 which in effect abolished the Sultanate and replaced the Ottoman Empire by the Turkish Republic. The continued importance of religion at the time demanded that the Office of the Caliphate should be retained. These two decisions were also of interest because they introduced new terms such as the 'Turkish Nation' (*Türk Milleti*) and the 'Turkish Government' (*Türk Hükümeti*).[20] The fact that these terms appeared in decisions that were adopted immediately after a long speech by Mustafa Kemal that focused on the '1500-years-old history of Turks' in place of the past references to '700 years of Ottoman history' was especially significant.[21]

The introduction of these terms and the stress on 'Turkishness', instead of on Ottoman identity, may have suggested that an emphasis was being placed on Turkish ethnicity. However, the text of the decision abolishing the Sultanate included more generic terms such as the 'People of Turkey' (*Türkiye halkı*). Furthermore, a number of deputies continued to make references to the 'nation of Turkey' and also employed the term 'Turkish nation'.[22] It is exceedingly difficult to ascertain what exact meanings were attributed to these words. For many deputies the term 'Turk' would still have been associated with the notion of being a Moslem, and could thus have included all the Moslems of different ethnic backgrounds in Turkey, including the Kurds.

However, for Mustafa Kemal and his closest associates the terms 'Turk' and 'Turkish' were acquiring new meaning. Although they continued to remain ambiguous, by late 1922 there was a definite attempt to dissociate 'Turkishness' from its previous link to the traditional notion of 'nation' associated with Islam and the Ottoman Empire. In a speech Mustafa Kemal gave to a group of teachers in October 1922 he noted that until 'three-and-a-half years ago we were living as a religious community. … Since then we are living as a [Turkish] nation.'[23]

Mustafa Kemal and his supporters seemed to have been thinking of 'Turkishness' increasingly in a functional manner. For them 'Turkishness' would become the basis of a new national identity that would be needed to transform a traditional society inherited from the Ottoman Empire into a modern one. The first clear articulation of how this would be brought about came immediately after the April 1923 assembly decision to hold new elections. In preparation for these Mustafa Kemal issued a Declaration of Nine Principles which was to constitute the election programme for the SDRA-R.[24] In this emphasis was put on the principle of the 'unconditional sovereignty of the people' and on the need to introduce reforms in areas ranging from education to the civil service.

A new assembly was convened in August 1923 after the elections. This assembly was to all intents and purposes handpicked by Mustafa Kemal himself. The elimination of opposition enabled a republic to be declared in October 1923. Reforms would be introduced accompanied by efforts to build a national identity.

Turkish Nationalism – 1923–38

As we have indicated previously, it is not easy to carry out simultaneously nation-building and state-building. As the Ottoman Empire was disintegrating Mustafa Kemal and his supporters were confronted with the need to build a new order. In the war of Turkish independence a resistance movement had been mobilized. Mustafa Kemal and his followers would aim to transform this into a national movement which would lend support to the consolidation of the Turkish Republic. It was far from clear at first what form of nationalism would be adopted by the founders of the Republic. With regard to the formation of Turkish nationalism, Hroch's model of three separate, structural phases of development seems oversimplified. The resistance movement in Anatolia was proof of a mass mobilization encouraged initially by the activities of the SDRA-R. But this was not a movement based on Turkish nationalism. Turkish nationalism would appear only after the founding of the Republic in what was in effect a fourth phase of national development. Moreover, as a further complication there were several popular uprisings against the original resistance movement. As discussed earlier, the majority of these, which were instigated by the Ottoman government in Istanbul, did not involve Kurdish groups. In spite of the activities of a few Kurdish nationalists, those few mass mobilizations against the resistance movement which occurred in Kurdish-populated areas were largely the product of tribal divisions and personal rivalries.

The Declaration of the Turkish Republic took the form of the introduction of an amendment to the Law on Fundamental Organization. This defined the Turkish state as a republic whose official language would be Turkish and its religion Islam.[25] The opposition that built up against the declaration of the republic, particularly in circles close to the Caliphate, revealed the continuing hold of Islam over society. As Toprak has noted: 'An institution which had its theoretical base in a supra-national concept of solidarity was, of course, inimical to the interests of the nationalist movement.'[26] But Mustafa Kemal and his leadership were determined to press on with reforms which would require the abolition of the Caliphate, the introduction of a new education system and the definition of a new national identity.

In a law adopted in March 1924 the assembly abolished the Office of the Caliphate and ordered the members of the Ottoman dynasty to leave Turkey. The office of the Caliphate had been under the control of the Ottoman dynasty since 1517 and had become an important source of legitimacy for the Ottoman Empire. More importantly, the Caliphate was a source of identification for the Moslem subjects of the Empire.

On the day that the assembly abolished the Caliphate it also adopted the Law on the Unification of Education (*Tevhid-i Tedrisat*) and a law abolishing the Ottoman Ministry of Religious Affairs and Pious Foundations was passed. All schools were brought under the control of the government. Medreses and religious schools were closed down. Kazamias has noted that 'to those who wanted to modernize the society the medrese symbolized reaction, conservatism, and a static state of affairs.'[27] Mustafa Kemal gave much importance to the secular education of youth. He saw education as a powerful tool for transforming people's hearts and minds in a country where literacy rates stood at around ten per cent.[28]

Not surprisingly, considerable emphasis was placed on unifying the education system and introducing policies that would nurture a sense of nationhood among the population. Previously, a highly diffused education system had existed. There were many foreign missionary schools. Educational instruction was offered in several languages. There were many schools run by religious minorities which often did not teach any Turkish. Winter has noted that the new law on education marked 'a fundamental step in the establishment of a unified, modern, secular, egalitarian and national education system. Its nation building role was especially vital in a country where identity was often Islamic rather than national, and which was fragmented into numerous tribal, racial and linguistic units.'[29]

The changes introduced to the education system and the emphasis put on the Turkish language were clear manifestations of the growing importance of Turkish nationalism. In the new constitution adopted in March 1924, which was mostly based on the Law on Fundamental Organization of 1921, a deliberate attempt was made for the first time to define the term 'Turk'.[30] According to Article 88 of the Constitution 'the people of Turkey regardless of their religion and race were, in terms of their citizenship, to be Turkish'. However, the wording of this article was the product of a heated debate which revealed the continuing importance of religion and language in the definition of a Turk.

The draft of this article had not referred to citizenship but used a much broader definition simply calling 'the people of Turkey Turkish regardless of their religion and race'. A number of deputies objected to this formulation, arguing that nationality and citizenship were not the same. One deputy, Hamdullah Suphi Bey, declared that the Jews in England and France could be considered as being part of the English and French nations because they had adopted as their own the language and culture of both countries. However, according to Hamdullah Suphi Bey, in Turkey the Armenians, Greeks and Jews had chosen to act to the contrary. Hence, until they adopted as their own the language and culture of Turkey they could not be considered part of the Turkish nation.[31]

Another deputy, Celal Nuri Bey, seemed confused and argued that the 'real' citizens of Turkey were Hanefi Moslems who spoke Turkish. But even he could not see what term other than 'Turkish' could be used to refer to Christians and Jews. He was interrupted from the floor with calls of '*Türkiyeli*' ('someone from Turkey'), something very different from being 'Turkish'. Celal Nuri Bey called this term nonsense and insisted that Armenians, Greeks and Jews be called Turkish too.[32] Religion still seemed to be an important factor for at least some of the deputies. The reference to Hanefi Moslems speaking Turkish as 'real' citizens was interesting because an overwhelming majority of Kurds were and still are Shafi Moslems and at the time at least many of them did not speak Turkish. Shafi and Hanefi Moslems belong to different schools within the same Sunni branch of Islam.[33] However, there was no discussion of the case of the Kurds. Instead, concern focused on the non-Moslem minorities.

Within a short period the Turks, who had been in effect only an ethnic category, came to form the dominant ethnic core of a Turkish nation. Initially, Ziya Gökalp had an impact on the formulation of Turkish nationalism as well as on Mustafa Kemal's thinking on the subject.[34] According to Gökalp a nation was 'not a racial, ethnic, geographical, political, or voluntary group or association'. A nation was a group composed of people who had gone through the same education and had 'received the same acquisitions in language, religion, morality, and aesthetics'.[35] Mustafa Kemal defined a nation as consisting of a group of people who inhabited the same piece of land, who were bound by the same laws, and shared a common morality and language. Mustafa Kemal placed considerable emphasis on the 'will to live together' as a characteristic of a nation.[36] The emphasis on morality, language and education was clearly inspired by Gökalp's ideas. However, the conspicuous absence of any reference to religion and the importance attributed to a territory in Mustafa Kemal's definition were striking. He did not consider ethnicity and race to be constituent elements of a nation.

The 1931 programme of the Republican People's Party (CHP) – established by Mustafa Kemal in 1924 after the earlier disbandment of the SDRA-R – defined a nation as a 'social and political whole formed by citizens that are united by a common language, culture and objective'.[37] The influence of Mustafa Kemal was evident. Again, there was no reference to ethnicity. The importance of a will to live together was stressed. The General Secretary of the party, Recep Peker, in his analysis of the programme dwelt upon these two points and noted: 'In today's political and social community of the Turkish nation, we consider of our own those citizens whose minds have been inculcated by ideas of Kurdish, Circassian or even Laz or Pomak ethnicity.' He added that the party included in its understanding of a nation Christian and Jewish citizens as long as they accepted 'a common language and objective'.[38]

Mustafa Kemal and his leadership appeared to have developed a theoretical definition of a nation which could have moulded together the remnants of Ottoman society – which had been in effect a type of multicultural and multiethnic society – into one nation. Such a definition of a nation could have replaced the role that religion had played during Ottoman times in generating a sense of togetherness among Moslems of different ethnic backgrounds. Were these theoretical formulations actually put into practice? In other words, did this declaratory civic nationalism actually take the form of a real civic nationalism in practice?

It seems that especially from the late 1920s to the mid-1940s successive Turkish governments did not practise civic nationalism. Developments in the Republic in this period were not conducive to the development of a genuine civic nationalism. There was a further series of popular uprisings against Ankara's attempts to centralize and modernize the Turkish state. The absence of a democratic tradition in the Ottoman and then the Turkish polity would make it exceedingly difficult for decision-makers in Ankara to pursue a policy based on real civic integration as opposed to ethnic nationalism. Ironically, Islam had functioned as a kind of transcending bond of national unity among the Moslem population of the Ottoman Empire. The attempt to replace Islam by Turkish nationalism as a new transcending bond to establish a political community would be only partially successful.

Governmental practice departed from a civic understanding of Turkish nationalism in two respects. First, in spite of the official commitment not to emphasize religion as a defining characteristic of Turkish nationalism non-Moslems were discriminated against. Christians and Jews were excluded from military schools and academies. As Oran has noted: 'The most important requirement for joining military schools here was not Turkish citizenship but membership of the Turkish race', which often meant the need to be a Moslem. Oran added though that at times this practice even led to Moslem Circassians being excluded from these schools.[39] During the Second World War the government introduced a Wealth Tax (*Varlık Vergisi*) which aimed to tax those people who allegedly made excessive profits. Although the tax was supposed to be levied without any discrimination, in practice it was mostly used against non-Moslems. Non-payment of taxes resulted in many people being sent to labour camps in eastern Anatolia. In 1930 all the non-Moslem personnel of Turkish Railways with the exception of a handful of experts were laid off.[40] In a similar practice 26 Jewish employees of the Anatolian Press Agency were dismissed with one day's notice in May 1942.[41]

However, the bias against non-Moslems was not directed solely towards Armenians, Greeks and Jews. During the exchange of population between Greece and Turkey in the mid-1920s a whole community of Turkish-speaking members of the Greek Orthodox Church near the central Anatolian city of Konya were sent to Greece even though they practised their religion in Turkish and did not speak any Greek. On the other hand, in the 1930s when Turkish ethnic nationalism was on the rise, the requests of the Christian Orthodox Gagauz Turks to emigrate from Romania to Turkey were turned down by Turkish officials on the grounds that the Gagauz Turks were Christians.[42] In contrast, many Moslems from Balkan countries who did not speak Turkish and were not of Turkish ethnicity, such as the Albanians, Bosnians and Pomaks, were admitted to Turkey as immigrants.[43] Civic nationalism was not carried out in practice. For many officials and people in Turkey, Turkishness remained very much associated with Islam.

There was also an emphasis put on Turkish ethnicity and language. Oran has argued that Mustafa Kemal's reference to expressions such as, 'One Turk equals the whole world', may be considered as manifestations of an ethnically-based nationalism.[44] Mustafa Kemal's famous 'address to the nation' on the tenth anniversary of the Republic was filled with references to the high virtues of Turks. In a similar vein, when a Turkish woman was chosen as Miss World in 1931 Mustafa Kemal argued that this was evidence of 'the Turkish race being the most beautiful race in the world'.[45] These references to Turkish ethnicity and race were clear departures from Gökalp's notion of civic nationalism. This has led Parla to conclude that beside a benign civic face Kemalist Turkish nationalism also had a second 'racist-ethnic' visage.[46]

An example of government policy that emphasized Turkish ethnicity and language was the Settlement Law (No. 2510) adopted in 1934.[47] The law divided people in Turkey into three groups: those who spoke Turkish and were of Turkish ethnicity; those who did not speak Turkish but were considered to be of Turkish culture,[48] and finally those who neither spoke Turkish nor belonged to the Turkish culture. The law and the debate before its adoption made no reference to the Kurds. However, the term 'not belonging to the Turkish culture and not speaking Turkish' with regard to Turkish citizens was used mostly to refer to Kurds and Arabs.

The Settlement Law also divided the country into three zones. One was inhabited by those who spoke Turkish and who were of Turkish culture and ethnicity. This zone could receive immigrants from any part of the country and from abroad. A second zone included people whose Turkishness, in terms of culture and language, needed to be enhanced by resettlement policies. A third zone was designated as areas closed for security reasons to any form of civilian settlement.

Beşikçi has argued that this Settlement Law was basically adopted to assimilate Kurds into a Turkish identity.[49] However, the lawmakers were not only concerned about Kurds. One of the deputies, Ruseni Bey, bitterly complained during the parliamentary debate about the failure of the government to assimilate Jews, without actually referring to the Jews by name. The same deputy also noted angrily that there were still large numbers of immigrants from the Balkans and the Caucasus who had been settled in Turkey by successive Ottoman governments and who could still not speak Turkish and hence had maintained their ethnic identities.[50] Similar remarks were also made by the drafters of the law. The Interior Minister Şükrü Kaya stated that the assimilation of these immigrants was one of the goals of this law. Another objective was to settle nomadic tribes, both Kurdish and Turkish. Kaya noted that there were more than one million nomads in eastern as well as in southern and western parts of Anatolia and that he considered it paramount to settle them and 'make the benefits of the Republic accessible to them'.[51]

Clearly, the purpose of the law was to assist the nation-building process taking place in the country. In the words of one deputy, the law aimed at creating 'a country which would speak one single language, think and feel alike'.[52] What was striking was the privileged status extended to individuals of Turkish ethnicity. Article 7 authorized immigrants of Turkish ethnicity to settle where they wished except in areas closed to settlement. The settlement of other immigrants would be regulated by the government. In practice, some Kurds were relocated in western Turkey and some Turks were settled in traditionally Kurdish-populated areas in the east.

Why was so much emphasis placed on Turkish ethnicity and language? It seems that one should examine the difficulties arising from efforts to transform a traditional, religious society into a modern nation and state. Modernization required the construction of a centralized state capable of providing a wide range of services. And 'a revolution in values' was essential to replace the

Ottoman way of thinking with one which would stress rationality, science and individualism in place of superstition, religion and communalism.[53] Instead of a decrepit empire, a dynamic, modern republican state was required.

In order for modernization to be carried out reforms had to be introduced in government, administration and the law. This clashed with the views of a rural elite who had their interests vested in the traditional order. A revolution in values was mostly centred around the process of the secularization of society and the introduction of a unified, modern education system. This, on the other hand, deeply affected the identities of the masses with regard to their religious beliefs and cultural identities. As Mersin-Alıcı has noted, the transformation 'was rather abrupt and quite unnatural. For it did not come about smoothly as a result of gradual evolution in the nature of the society itself but was designed and imposed on the people by a reforming elite'.[54]

Opposition to these developments led to a wave of rebellions in the 1920s and the 1930s. Of the 18 rebellions that broke out between 1924 and 1938 17 were in eastern Anatolia and 16 of them involved Kurds.[55] The first and most significant of the Kurdish rebellions was the one led by Shaikh Said. It started on 13 February 1925 and was not fully suppressed until the arrest of the leadership on 15 April. According to Tunçay, the military operation to suppress the rebellion was more costly in human and financial terms than the war of independence.[56] The impact that this rebellion had on the evolution of Turkish nationalism was profound. The uprising occurred at a time when two world views clashed. One stressed modernism and secularism, the other emphasized religion and traditionalism.

Mustafa Kemal and his leadership regarded the Shaikh Said rebellion as an attempted counter-revolution.[57] The rebellion had been preceded by calls for the restitution of the religious *sharia* courts which had been closed down the previous year. The uprising was perceived as a threat to the very foundation of the nascent state. It left Mustafa Kemal and his supporters feeling insecure about how they could realize the transformation of society in Turkey. This insecurity led to the introduction of new legislation in the second half of the 1920s. By the 1930s officials in Ankara were emphasizing more the importance of Turkish ethnicity and language to create a sense of nationhood.

Immediately after the rebellion there was a government reshuffle followed by the adoption of the Law for the Maintenance of Order (*Takrir-i Sükun Kanunu*) and the formation of two *ad hoc* courts called Independence Tribunals. These courts were used to try the leaders of the rebellion. Many received the death penalty including Shaikh Said himself. The Law for the Maintenance of Order gave the government special powers which were used to suppress all opposition in the country. The government also used this law to pass legislation aimed at encouraging further the secularization and modernization of the country.

The Hat Law (October 1925) ordered the wearing of rimmed hats and

Western clothing. This was followed by a law which ordered the closure of religious orders, lodges and cells (*tarikats, tekkes* and *zaviyes*) and banned religious titles (December 1925). The Hat Law was of particular significance because the hat which replaced the fez symbolized Westernization and progress. The law ordering the closure of religious orders together with adoption of a Western Civil Code (*Medeni Kanun*) in October 1926 led to the introduction of an amendment in April 1928 to Article 2 of the 1924 Constitution. The reference to Islam as the official religion of the Turkish state was removed.

Another important reform concerned the Turkish language. In November 1928 the Arabic script was replaced by the Latin alphabet. This was ostensibly on the grounds that the latter was better suited to the Turkish language and that the simplicity of this script would help to improve the low literacy rates in the country. But, as Lewis has noted, 'the basic purpose of the change was not so much practical as pedagogical, as social and cultural – and Mustafa Kemal, in forcing his people to accept it, was slamming a door on the past as well as opening a door to the future.'[58] The language reform was not well received in all circles. The advocates of the Latin script were accused of giving the West an opportunity to declare 'that the Turks have adopted ... foreign writing and turned Christian'.[59]

These reforms were opposed by those who supported the old order. There was a sudden rise in the number of rebellions in Turkey. Of the 18 uprisings that took place between 1924 and 1938, eight occurred between May 1929 and December 1930. One involved an incident in the western Anatolian town of Menemen, where a group of men tried to incite the population to rebel against the government and reinstate the *sharia* law. The other revolts occurred in Kurdish populated areas in eastern Anatolia.

The emphasis put on modernization, centralization and secularization contributed to the spread of Kurdish ethnic awareness which became an important source of opposition to the governing elite. Major rebellions erupted around Mt. Ararat in summer 1930. These were led by Captain İhsan Nuri, a deserter from the Turkish army, and were supported by the Kurdish nationalist movement, the Khoybun. The rebels declared a 'Kurdish Republic', but this was crushed by the Turkish military in September 1930.[60]

Efforts to weaken the role of religion in Turkey encouraged Kurdish secessionism in this period. In the Ottoman Empire the social-political order based on Islam had held the Turks and Kurds together. Abdülmelik Fırat, Shaikh Said's grandson, would note that with the abolition of the Caliphate there was no reason left to stay in the Turkish Republic.[61] Kurdish rebellions and opposition to Mustafa Kemal's reforms from conservative circles fuelled the growing insecurity of the regime.

Toprak has noted that 'the state, by its secular policies and its program of Westernization, had threatened the dominant value system of a traditional

Islamic society without providing, at the same time, a new ideological framework which could have mass appeal.'[62] The solution that Mustafa Kemal and his leadership adopted was to emphasize Turkish nationalism as an alternative source of mobilization. One deputy, Ruşeni Bey, whom we have mentioned earlier, declared that the new religion of Turks would be nationalism. This was received with great enthusiasm by Mustafa Kemal.[63] However, the nationalism that emerged was one which emphasized Turkish ethnicity and language. In the early 1930s this manifested itself in the introduction of the Turkish History and Sun-Language Theses, both of which had the full blessing of the government.

The Turkish History Thesis was first elaborated in 1930 in a book entitled *Türk Tarihinin Ana Hatları* (*The Principal Characteristics of Turkish History*) prepared by a study group under the auspices of the *Türk Ocakları* (Turkish Hearths).[64] The thesis argued that Turks originated from Central Asia and migrated to different parts of the world spreading civilization. Continuity was established between the Turks living in Anatolia and their ancestors in Central Asia by arguing that all previous ancient civilizations in Anatolia, including the Hittites and the Sumerians, were Turkish-inspired. The Turkish History Institute (*Türk Tarih Kurumu*) developed this thesis through the creation of historical 'myths'. Turkish school textbooks were rewritten to incorporate this thesis and People's Houses (*Halkevleri*) were set up across the country to educate the people about their history and 'Turkishness'.

The Sun-Language Theory was based on the argument that only one language, Turkish, was spoken in Central Asia. According to the theory, Turkish constituted the basis of all languages. Current Anatolian Turkish was supposedly a continuation of this original form of Turkish. Language had become another tool for mobilizing national consciousness. The Turkish Language Institute (*Türk Dil Kurumu*) was established. Its purpose was to purify the language. A law was even passed which required the *ezan* (call for prayer) to be read in Turkish. According to Mersin-Alıcı these were attempts to create 'a nation by design through the employment of the tools of the ethnic model with the aim of arriving at a Western type of national identity'.[65]

In a survey of students conducted in 1958 Hyman and others concluded that these policies had been largely successful in substituting a Turkish national identity in place of religion.[66] Similar observations were also made by Frey concerning the rural areas of Turkey.[67] The likelihood of conflict increased as the Turkish History Thesis and the Sun-Language Theory led to the development of an argument that the Kurds were really Turks.

Gökalp had concluded at the end of an ethnographic field survey of tribes in the vicinity of Diyarbakır that there were a large number of Turkmen tribes that had become Kurdified over many years.[68] However, at no point had he suggested that Kurds themselves were Turks. Yet in the 1930s intensive efforts were made to prove that Kurds were Turks. This 'scientific' reality was to be instilled into the hearts and minds of 'confused' Kurds. Accordingly, Kurds were 'mostly comprised of Turks who had changed their language', and the term Kurd 'was the name of a community that spoke a broken Persian and that lived in Turkey, Iraq and Iran'.[69] In another study in the 1930s Candar provided a long list of tribal names and villages from eastern Anatolia. On the basis of an etymological study he concluded that people who thought of themselves as Kurds were in reality Turks.[70]

In December 1936 the Governor of Tunceli (Dersim), Army General Abdullah Alpdoğan, argued that Kurds were in essence 'mountain Turks'. He criticized the practice of 'calling them Kurds. Of treating them as though they are of a different race'.[71] In a book originally completed in 1945, M.S. Fırat, himself an ethnic Kurd, observed that the descendants of the ancient Turkish and Turkmen tribes who spoke Kourmanji and Zaza and who were referred to as Kurds were actually 'mountain Turks'.[72]

With opposition to modernization, particularly from religious circles, and the conviction held by Mustafa Kemal and his followers that Turkey continued to face serious domestic and foreign challenges to its integrity and security, more officials in Ankara were determined to encourage nation-building with a heavy emphasis on Turkish ethnicity, history and language. Ethnic nationalism rather than civic integration was clearly the order of the day. The government was relatively successful in neutralizing religious opposition. Likewise, most of the population who were not of Turkish ethnic background went along with these nation-building policies with little resistance. However, there was violent opposition from parts of the mainly Kurdish-populated areas of eastern Turkey.

Kurdish Nationalism – 1923–38

Oran has argued that the development of Kurdish nationalism was largely a reaction to the rise of a Turkish nationalism with its growing emphasis on Turkish ethnicity and language.[73] Kurdish nationalism would evolve gradually. The lack of unity among the Kurds in the period before 1923 has been discussed in detail earlier. In March 1923 Yusuf Ziya, a Bey Kurdish deputy in the Grand National Assembly, during a debate concerning the future of Mosul, could still deliver a moving speech which stressed Turkish and Kurdish fraternity and the inseparability of the two peoples.[74]

As indicated earlier, the greatest challenge to the newly formed Republic was the major rebellion in spring 1925 led by the Kurdish religious leader Shaikh Said. The origins of this revolt may be traced to the establishment in May 1923 of a Kurdish nationalist party called Azadi. This was founded by Kurdish nationalists and officers from the Ottoman Army and was led by Hacı Musa, once a prominent member of the resistance movement and then the head of the Mutki Tribe from Muş. Azadi's members included one-time Kurdish members of the Turkish Grand National Assembly who had failed to be re-elected in the 1923 elections.[75] Azadi mobilized support among the Zaza-speaking tribes and also received the backing of Shaikh Said. Followers of Azadi opposed the new Turkish government's policies especially those concerning the abolition of the Caliphate and the introduction of a modern education system based on Turkish. They looked for independence and aimed to secure this through a rebellion which they hoped would be assisted by the British.

Mumcu believed that the Shaikh Said rebellion was a religious uprising. He quoted Shaikh Said's statement made under interrogation when he stated that the aim of the rebellion was to ensure the restitution of the *Sharia* Law.[76] Abdülmelik Fırat later contended that his grandfather was a prominent religious leader and scholar who could not have entertained nationalist ideas.[77] Van Bruinessen and Olson concluded that the rebellion had religious as well as nationalist motives.[78] On the other hand, Aybars and Tunçay argued that Shaikh Said was primarily a nationalist. According to Aybars, once caught Shaikh Said supposedly attempted to deceive the authorities by alleging that the rebellion was a religious one.[79]

The Shaikh Said rebellion was connected with resentment against the centralizing policies of the Turkish government. According to Arfa, the dire economic situation in the east, the frustration of the tribal leaders who had failed to be elected to the Turkish Grand National Assembly in 1923, and 'the fear of the feudal landowners and chiefs of tribes of having their privileges curtailed' by the government were responsible for the rebellion.[80]

Some of the leaders who were involved in the Shaikh Said rebellion were very conscious of their distinct Kurdish identity and clearly had articulated a separatist political agenda, albeit with a heavy dosage of religious discourse. Shaikh Said, under interrogation, appeared to have shied away from expressing separatist aspirations. But his brother Abdurrahim and others openly declared that their aim was the establishment of an independent, Moslem, Kurdish government.[81] It seems that religion was an important distinguishing characteristic of Kurdishness at a time when the reforms of the Turkish government were seen to be undermining Islam. When referring to Turkish government troops, it was not surprising that Shaikh Said had declared 'in terms of religious law killing one Turk was worth more than killing seventy infidels'.[82]

This emphasis on religion may also partially explain why the rebellion did not receive much support from Alevi Kurds. Van Bruinessen has noted that the rebellion was mostly supported by Zaza-speaking Sunni Kurds and that Alevi Kurds from areas with a reputation for Kurdish nationalist ideas by and large did not support Shaikh Said.[83] A number of tribal leaders sent telegrams to the Turkish Grand National Assembly expressing their readiness to support the government in suppressing the rebellion. Hence it is difficult to speak of a widespread national consciousness among the Kurds in Turkey at the time of the rebellion. Arguably this revolt was an example of a charismatic religious figure playing a critical role in uniting several Kurdish tribes to resist the centralization which the authorities in Ankara were seeking to impose.

There were other Kurdish rebellions in the period between 1925 and 1938. These were uprisings against the attempted forceful assimilation of the Kurdish population by the dominant Turkish ethnic core. Some Kurdish nationalist leaders were involved. But these outbreaks of violence were sporadic and unco-ordinated. Cleavages among the Kurds along tribal, religious and regional lines still persisted and worked against the formation of a Kurdish ethnic and national identity in Turkey.

The government became increasingly intolerant of any opposition to its policies. Mustafa Kemal and the leadership of the CHP, the single party in power, handpicked all parliamentary deputies. As a result, the constituencies mostly populated by Kurds had the lowest percentage of locally-born deputies.[84] A Kurd who refused to support government policies on modernization and nation-building could not participate in the work of the assembly and government.

In 1930 the government accepted the recommendations of the Head of the Turkish General Staff, Field Marshal Fevzi Çakmak. According to Çakmak, civil servants of Kurdish descent in eastern Anatolia should be dismissed from their jobs and Kurds who had been involved in rebellions should be moved to western Turkey.[85] In December 1935 the assembly adopted a law granting the government emergency powers to administer the area around Tunceli. People could be detained indefinitely and individuals refusing to abide by the laws and regulations of the country could be deported from the area.

These measures which aimed to assimilate Kurds and punish those who resisted led to deep resentment and frustration among the Kurdish nationalist elite. This was well captured by Dr Nuri Dersimi who complained to the governor of Tunceli, General Abdullah Alpdoğan, that 'on the one hand when we say we are "Turks" we are told "no, you are not Turks, you are Kurds". Yet, when we, the people of Dersim, say we are Kurds, they hit us hard and say that "no you are not Kurds, there are no Kurds".'[86] This frustrated Kurdish elite was involved in the formation of the Kurdish nationalist Khoybun group in 1927 which participated in the rebellion around Mt. Ararat in 1930.

By 1939 the government had consolidated its rule over Kurdish populated areas in Turkey. As Van Bruinessen noted: 'All the rebellions had remained regional and in many cases it was Kurds themselves who had played an active role in suppressing these rebellions.'[87] When Turkey had its first competitive election in 1950 which brought in a new government led by the Democrat Party (DP), there was little evidence of Kurdish nationalism in the country. Many Kurds by this time appeared to have been assimilated and the tribal leaders co-opted into the Turkish political system.

The Development of Kurdish Nationalism in Post-World War Two Turkey

In the post-World War Two period a Kurdish ethnic identity would eventually emerge. To some extent this was the product of the further modernization of society in Turkey. Consciousness of an ethnic identity would become less the exclusive preserve of a handful of Kurdish nationalists. Some of the educated and urbanized Kurdish youth would become radicalized and would burst on to the political scene. This politicized Kurdish youth would ultimately press for the formation of an independent Kurdish state. The gradual development of an ethnic self-awareness among the Kurds would at times clash with and on other occasions complement tribal allegiances. Tribal divisions and rivalries among the Kurds would persist. And the often more conservative and traditional Kurdish notables still based in the countryside would not necessarily share the views of urbanized and politicized youth.

The transition from a single to a multi-party system with competitive elections increased popular participation in politics. The participation rates in the elections during the 1950s in the provinces where more than 15 per cent of the population declared their mother tongue to be Kurdish, was high (Table 4.1). Özbudun has attributed this to the role of feudal and tribal leaders

TABLE 4.1

AVERAGE PARTICIPATION RATES AND DISTRIBUTION OF
VOTES BY POLITICAL PARTIES IN NATIONAL ELECTIONS

Election year	Participation rate (%)	CHP (%)	DP (%)	Others (%)
1950 country average	89.3	39.9	53.3	6.8
average for 15 provinces	87.7	53.4	43.7	2.9
1954 country average	88.6	34.8	56.6	8.6
average for 15 provinces	89.5	36.4	52.8	10.6
1957 country average	76.6	40.6	47.3	12.1
average for 15 provinces	77.9	45.3	45.5	6.3

Source: *Milletvekili: Genel ve Cumhuriyet Senatosu Üyeleri Yenileme Seçimi Sonuçları, 5 Haziran 1977* (Ankara: Başbakanlık, Devlet İstatistik Enstitüsü [DIE], 1977) and *1965 Genel Nüfus Sayımı* (Ankara: DIE, 1969)

Note: the 15 provinces are those where more than 15 per cent of the population declared during the 1965 national census that their mother tongue was Kurdish.

in Kurdish-populated areas who made people vote.[88] According to him, the governing elite in the centre throughout the 1930s and the 1940s had been able to work with many rural notables. Local interests were recognized and in return reforms promoted by the centre were supported by these notables.[89] However, by 1945 this political alliance encountered problems over the issue of land reform.[90]

In the case of Kurdish-populated areas, however, this alliance between the CHP and the local elite continued in the 1950 elections. In the province of Hakkari the CHP received 100 per cent of the votes. By and large, the DP was less successful in Kurdish populated provinces. According to Van Bruinessen, the DP was more successful in these provinces in the 1954 elections because of the relaxation of forced assimilation policies by the government.[91] By the 1957 elections economic difficulties in the country led to a general fall in the votes for the DP, but the CHP was particularly successful in the Kurdish-populated provinces.

Serious economic problems and political instability in Turkey resulted in military intervention in 1960. The military had been disturbed by the liberalization that had taken place under the DP, especially in eastern parts of the country. The armed forces believed that this had led to an increase in Kurdish national consciousness. The military arrested and deported to western Turkey 55 Kurdish notables, of whom 54 were members of the DP.[92]

The military also introduced a law to give villages Turkish rather than Kurdish names.[93] They further considered introducing policies similar to the assimilation and resettlement policies of the one-party era. However, according to Van Bruinessen the liberal nature of the 1961 Constitution prevented this.[94] This gave people more civil rights, the universities greater autonomy, and permitted students to organize their own associations. In this environment, some Kurds began to be increasingly aware of their ethnicity.

Change was gradual. The political participation patterns of the 1950s to a large extent persisted during the 1960s. Özbudun has noted that, unlike other parts of the country, voting participation rates continued to remain high in eastern regions in the 1960s.[95] He attributed this to the persistent influence of tribal leaders and local notables. In her analysis of the 1965 elections, Abadan concluded that voting in eastern parts of Turkey was heavily dominated by a local elite closely associated with the dominant parties of the time.[96]

There were indications in voting behaviour, though, of an increasing awareness of Kurdish ethnicity. The New Turkey Party (YTP), composed mostly of members of the local elite in eastern parts of the country, received more than 30 per cent of the votes in 1961 in the east. With six ministers the YTP was a member of the CHP-led coalition government between July 1962 and November 1963. Under the influence of the YTP one of the first important decisions that the government took in September 1962 was to allow the 55 notables to return to eastern Turkey from western parts of the country to where they had been deported by the military.[97] The coalition collapsed when the YTP decided to pull out after poor returns in the local elections held in November 1963. The performance of the YTP dropped in the following local and national elections but it still received more than 15 per cent of the votes from provinces with a high proportion of Kurdish-speaking voters. According to Özbudun, in the 1969 elections the YTP received more than ten per cent of the votes in almost a quarter of the villages where Kurdish was spoken.[98]

The Turkish Workers' Party (TIP) and the Reliance Party (GP) were two other small political parties that received votes in Kurdish-speaking areas. At its fourth party congress in 1970 the TIP discussed the Kurdish problem and became the first legal party to recognize openly that 'there is a Kurdish people living in eastern Turkey'.[99] The Marxist credentials of the TIP prevented it from making many inroads into rural areas, but during the 1965 and the 1969 election the highest percentage of its votes came from Diyarbakır and Tunceli, two provinces much associated with Kurdish ethnicity. The TIP was forced to close down in 1971. By contrast, political parties which stressed Turkish nationalism, such as the Turkish National Action Party and its predecessor the Republican National Peasant Party, received low percentages of votes in these areas.

Awareness of a Kurdish identity seems also to have manifested itself in increased votes for independent candidates. This trend was already evident in the 1950s as may be seen from the 'Others' column in Table 4.1, which included independent candidates. Unlike 1961, in the 1965 and 1969 elections these independent candidates received a quite substantial vote, especially in Kurdish speaking rural areas. For example, in south-eastern Turkey in the 1969 elections independent candidates received 22.8 per cent of the votes while on average for the country these candidates picked up 5.6 per cent. In south-eastern Turkey the independents constituted the second largest group in terms of percentage of votes after the Justice Party (AP) (which took the place of the DP after 1960), while the CHP trailed fourth after the YTP.[100]

Under their new leader Bülent Ecevit, the CHP performed well in the 1973 elections in Kurdish-speaking areas of eastern Turkey. Ecevit seemed much more sensitive to the problems of eastern Turkey and his social democrat position was popular among the Kurds. In the 1973 election campaign Ecevit promised to solve the problems of eastern Turkey. However, shortly after he came to power the CHP's Kurdish supporters began to make use of moderate nationalist slogans. This compelled Ecevit to renege on his campaign promises. As a result, in the 1977 elections the Kurdish electorate favoured those independent candidates who were mostly former members of the CHP but who were then willing to adopt a more nationalist stance.

Ergüder tentatively noted the growing 'impact of ethnicity and sect on voting behavior' in the 1970s and concluded that 'the Turkish culture and society may not be as homogeneous as the Turkish Kemalist elite portrayed it to be'.[101]

Outside parliament, the political discourse that had once stressed under-development as the source of the problems of eastern Anatolia had begun by the 1970s to focus on Kurdish ethnicity and discrimination. Paradoxically, the modernization of Turkey opened the way for the emergence of a new form of consciousness among some of the Kurds who had become urbanized and better educated. It was among this group of young people that the seeds of a new discourse were sown in the late 1960s. This approach was at first mainly couched in a leftist and class-based analysis which became known as 'Eastism' (*Doğuculuk*). The problems of eastern Anatolia were attributed to exploitation and lack of development.

A series of large public meetings were held in 1967 to draw attention to the problems of eastern Anatolia. These 'meetings of the East' (*Doğu mitingleri*) were supported by the TIP and many left-wing groups. The government accused the organizers of seeking to divide the country and called them traitors. A young Kurdish participant noted that these meetings were not about Kurdish nationalism and separatism but about the need to introduce policies to develop the east.[102]

The meetings raised public consciousness about the problems of eastern Anatolia. Cultural and student organizations were formed which started to promote Kurdish ethnicity.[103] The largest and most effective of these was the Revolutionary Cultural Society of the East (*Devrimci Doğu Kültür Ocakları*), established in 1969. Originally the aim of these organizations seemed to be to persuade the government to recognize the Kurdish language and grant cultural rights to the Kurds. Instead of religious, tribal and traditional themes which Kurdish groups had made use of in the inter-war period, the leaders of these cultural and student organizations would in time turn to more revolutionary, radical and secessionist rhetoric.

It was argued that the pursuit of capitalist and imperialist policies had led to the denial of Kurdish identity and the lack of economic development in eastern Anatolia. Initially there was solidarity between Turkish and Kurdish revolutionaries. The Federation of Turkish Revolutionary Youth, known as *Dev Genç*, an organization notorious for its use of violence, supported the 'struggle against fascism and imperialism, for ideological independence and the liberation of peoples, including that of Turks and Kurds'.[104] Kurdish Marxist revolution-aries seemed to have more in common with their Turkish 'comrades' than with the more traditional Kurds. Some of the most radical and violent leftist groups in Turkey were led by Kurds such as Deniz Gezmiş. Gunter has noted that although individuals like Gezmiş spoke openly of 'a Kurdish people' and virtually incited the Kurds in eastern Turkey to secede, they were clearly Marxist radicals first before being Kurdish nationalists.[105]

The radical Marxist rhetoric employed by these groups and the escalating violence between them and right-wing nationalist forces led to serious instability in Turkey. In March 1971 the military clamped down and arrested many members of these organizations. When the pre-1971 radical organizations began to resurface in the mid-1970s after a general amnesty, it was evident that the ideological congruence that had once existed between Kurdish and Turkish Marxists had been weakened.

Turkish leftists argued that the cultural and economic liberation of the Kurds would come about as a result of a Marxist revolution led by the Turkish proletariat. Many of these leftists considered the Kurdish nationalists' demands as untimely if not reactionary. Kurdish leftists, on the other hand, wanted the Kurds to be recognized as a separate nation capable of leading their own proletarian revolution.[106] One consequence of this rift was that the number of radical Kurdish leftist groups multiplied. İmset listed at least 12 Kurdish separatist groups in Turkey with Marxist-Leninist sympathies which were active in the 1970s.[107] The PKK would became the most radical and influential.

The origins of the PKK may be traced to a meeting in 1977 in Diyarbakır organized by Abdullah Öcalan, who would become the PKK leader. At this meeting he and his immediate supporters adopted a document titled 'The Path of the Kurdish Revolution'.[108] This depicted the Kurdish-populated areas of Turkey as a colony and argued that the Kurdish feudalists and bourgeoisie had chosen to collaborate with the Turkish ruling classes to exploit the Kurdish peasantry and working class. According to the document, a radical revolution was required to establish an independent, Marxist-Leninist Kurdistan where the peasantry and proletariat could enjoy true independence. This document subsequently became the programme of the PKK after its establishment in November 1978. The PKK's early activities were limited to small-scale armed operations and to the recruitment of young sympathizers in a small area around Siverek, the hometown of Öcalan. The 1980 military intervention in Turkey interrupted the activities of the PKK, forcing its leadership to flee abroad. It resumed its armed activities in 1984 and would play an important role in raising the Kurdish question to the top of Turkey's political agenda.

Van Bruinessen has pointed out that by the end of the 1970s the activities of Kurdish nationalist groups were 'changing the self-perception of a considerable section of the Kurds. People who had long called themselves Turks started re-defining themselves as Kurds.'[109] This development, together with the economic chaos, political instability and violence that characterized the late 1970s in Turkey, paved the way for the military intervention in September 1980.

The military were in favour of reintroducing what they regarded as strict Kemalist policies. The political discourse derived from these policies put clear emphasis on the 'Turkishness of Turkey', the unity of the nation and its territorial integrity. There was a major backlash against the conspicuous growth of expressions of Kurdish ethnicity and Kurdish nationalist ideas. Even a former CHP deputy and one-time member of the Ecevit government, Şerafettin Elçi, was sentenced to a year of imprisonment by a military court in March 1981 for having said in an interview that 'There are Kurds in Turkey. I am a Kurd.'[110]

The harsh reaction against manifestations of Kurdishness was also reflected in the new Constitution adopted in 1982.[111] This defined one of the fundamental tasks of the Turkish state as the safeguarding of 'the independence and integrity of the Turkish Nation, the indivisibility of the country, the Republic' (Article 5). This effectively made it illegal to express any idea that could be interpreted by the authorities as amounting to a recognition of a separate, Kurdish, ethnic identity. Another article noted: 'No language prohibited by the State shall be used in the expression and dissemination of thought' (Article 26). Subsequently in October 1983 Law 2932 was introduced to ban the use of Kurdish for the dissemination of information.[112] The Constitution also made the establishment of associations and political parties very complicated. As already noted, political parties which supported activities 'in conflict with the indivisible integrity of the state' were banned (Article 68).

This Constitution was submitted to a national referendum in July 1982. Little public debate was permitted and participation in the referendum was meant to be compulsory. The Constitution was adopted by an overwhelming majority of more than 91 per cent with a similar rate of participation (Table

TABLE 4.2

PARTICIPATION RATES AND THE DISTRIBUTION OF
VOTES IN THE 1982 REFERENDUM

	Country average (%)	Average for 15 provinces (%)
Participation rates	91.3	88.9
'Yes' votes	91.4	88.1
'No' votes	8.6	11.9

Source: T.C. Anayasa Halkoylaması Sonuçları (Ankara: Devlet İstatistik Enstitüsü, 1983) pp.1–3

Note: see note to Table 4.1.

4.2). Many people voted 'yes' believing that the alternative was chaos of the kind that Turkey had experienced during the late 1970s. Furthermore, the stark 'yes' or 'no' options gave people little room for choice. The average approval and participation rates for the 15 provinces with Kurdish speakers of more than 15 per cent was a little lower than in the rest of the country. In some of the eastern provinces, such as Bingöl and Tunceli, acceptance rates were as low as 76.5 and 82.6 per cent, respectively, although ironically one of the highest acceptance rates of 96.4 per cent came from Ağrı, a province with a majority of Kurdish-speaking people according to the 1965 national census. The results in these provinces were of a mixed nature although it seems that Harris was largely correct when he argued that 'the prospect of increased limitations on ethnic expression' may well have induced people in provinces predominantly inhabited by Kurds to turn in lower approval rates.[113]

The Constitution also revitalized the Turkish Language Society and the Turkish History Society. They were expected to reintroduce the political discourse of the 1930s which had argued that Kurds were Turks. Articles and books claiming common ancestry for Turks and Kurds, as well as arguments that a separate Kurdish language did not exist suddenly proliferated. It was claimed that efforts to distinguish a Kurdish identity from a Turkish one were simply fabrications on the part of Western intelligence agencies and separatist groups which were seeking to divide up the country.[114] When, in 1988, several parliamentary deputies of the SHP voted in favour of the 'Minority Languages' report of the Council of Europe they were accused of having fallen prey to the conspiracies of European countries to create a Kurdish minority in Turkey where one did not exist.

Besides encouraging the revival of Turkish nationalism, the military leadership also viewed religion as a political tool to boost national unity and weaken the influence of Marxist and separatist ideas. This new approach came to be known as the 'Turkish–Islamic Synthesis'. The military hoped that by strengthening the 'national culture', society and particularly the young would be shielded from the dangerous and divisive influences of foreign ideologies. Many intellectuals in Turkey considered this practice as an erosion of secularism and a major departure from the practices of Mustafa Kemal and his leadership. These policies did not prevent the Kurdish-populated areas of eastern Turkey from gradually sliding into violence once the PKK began to launch terrorist operations in 1984. The spiral of violence and counter-violence fuelled the growth of Kurdish national consciousness. According to Shaikh Said's grandson and parliamentary deputy Abdülmelik Fırat, the government's repressive policies in the eastern parts of the country played a greater role in enhancing Kurdish national consciousness than the propaganda work of the PKK.[115]

In January 1988 Ali Eren, an SHP deputy, boldly asserted that the existence of the Kurds in Turkey was being continually denied and that parallels could be drawn between the situation of the Turks in Bulgaria and Greece and the Kurds in Turkey. Eren claimed that the Kurds were a national minority who could not speak nor write in their own language nor give their children the names of their choice. His remarks precipitated harsh criticisms from the floor of the parliament. Some accused Eren of violating the constitution. Others charged that he was drunk.[116]

However, by the late 1980s more books and publications were appearing in Turkey which focused on Kurdish ethnicity and challenged the official line. A growing number of journalists, politicians and citizens were becoming increasingly critical of the official denial of a Kurdish identity. In June 1989 President Turgut Özal announced that he himself had Kurdish blood. This marked a significant first step toward an eventual recognition of the Kurdish reality. In April 1991 the ban on the Kurdish language was lifted immediately after more than one and half million Kurdish refugees from Iraq poured into Iran and Turkey.

The 1991 elections brought to power a coalition government which included the SHP who had formed an electoral pact with the HEP. The HEP had been originally set up in 1990 by a group of nationalist Kurdish deputies most of whom had been expelled from the SHP for having attended a conference on Kurdish national identity in Paris in October 1989. The government programme promised major reforms for eastern Anatolia which would also address the 'Kurdish problem'. In December 1991, the deputy Prime Minister Erdal İnönü called for the recognition of the cultural identity of Turkey's Kurdish citizens. In March 1992 Prime Minister Süleyman Demirel openly announced that he recognized the reality of a Kurdish ethnic presence in Turkey.[117] Seventy years previously Mustafa Kemal had openly talked about a Kurdish identity. After a long period of denial the Kurdish reality in Turkey was finally recognized.

Since the founding of the Republic, a political system had gradually evolved which accepted individuals with a good command of the Turkish language as 'Turks'. Their ethnic background was not important. The system had aimed to integrate many of these 'Turks' into the ruling elite. However, any expression of ethnicity – other than Turkish ethnicity – was perceived by officials in Ankara as a threat to the existence of the state itself. Therefore, while many Kurds were promoted to high positions in government, they were able to do so only as members of the Turkish nation. This included the children, grandchildren and relatives of those who led the Shaikh Said rebellion. Kurds served as deputies in the parliament, ministers in the cabinet, mayors of cities, state prosecutors and directors of large state enterprises.[118] However, those Kurds who were conscious of what they perceived to be a Kurdish national identity were penalized by the state. This was the case of the 55 Kurdish tribal chiefs after the 1960 military coup and the fate of Şerafettin Elçi, former deputy and minister, in 1981.

In the late nineteenth century the ordinary people of Anatolia had not perceived themselves as Kurds or Turks. As Abdülmelik Fırat has noted: 'There were no Kurds and Turks then.'[119] The unifying factor was Islam. Only in the last days of the Ottoman Empire did the Ottoman elite of both Kurdish and Turkish descent become more familiar with the concept of ethnic identity. During the war against the occupiers of Anatolia, Mustafa Kemal and his supporters succeeded in mobilizing the support of Turks and Kurds as well as of many other Moslems of different ethnic backgrounds. These wartime leaders became the 'founding fathers' of the new Republic.

At the declaratory level Mustafa Kemal and his supporters had aimed to achieve unity and modernization by mobilizing the population of Turkey behind a civic- and territorially-determined national identity. They had believed this would help to unite different ethnic groups under a common identity. In the pursuit of this objective, Mustafa Kemal and his followers planned to use the Turkish language as a key instrument. However, through the course of events talk of developing a civic, national identity was replaced by a policy which was increasingly perceived by Kurds as emphasizing secularism and Turkish ethnic identity. To some Kurds this was seen to be at the expense of their own religious, traditional and ethnic identity. Kurdish and religious opposition movements only reinforced the resolve of the regime to pursue its modernization plans.

In the late 1960s alternative voices on Kurdish identity began to emerge. The expression of Kurdishness came to be wrapped in a Marxist-Leninist rhetoric. The regime reacted by reasserting its standard political discourse and by denying the existence of a separate Kurdish identity in Turkey. Attempts to express Kurdishness were seen as direct threats to the cohesion and unity of the state, instigated by external forces that sought to revive the Sèvres Treaty. There was a major departure from standard practice though when the Turkish government recognized the existence of a 'Kurdish reality'. The political system in Turkey is going through a slow and painful transformation which may eventually allow for expressions of Kurdish identity. But current socio-economic problems and the growing conflict between Kurdish and Turkish nationalism aggravated by PKK terrorism need to be considered.

Notes

1. B. Lewis, *The Emergence of Modern Turkey* (London: Oxford University Press, 1962) p.2.
2. Z. Gökalp, 'Historical Materialism and Sociological Idealism' in N. Berkes (ed.), *Turkish Nationalism and Western Civilization* (London: Allen & Unwin, 1959) p.62.
3. For one discussion which lays particular emphasis on the awareness of a Turkish ethnic identity before the twentieth century see, S. Deringil, 'The Origins of Kemalist

Nationalism: Namık Kemal to Mustafa Kemal', *European History Quarterly*, 23, (1993) p.137.

4. S. Zenkovsky, *Pan-Turkism and Islam in Russia* (Cambridge MA: Harvard University Press, 1960) pp.31–2.
5. Y. Akçura, 'Üç Tarz-ı Siyaset', *Türkiye Günlüğü*, 31, (Nov.–Dec. 1994). This article was originally published in 1904 in a newspaper called *Türk* in Cairo.
6. J. Landau, 'The Ups and Downs of Irredentism: the Case of Turkey' in N. Chazan (ed.) *Irredentism and International Politics* (Boulder CO and London: Lynne Rienner and Adamantine Press, 1991) p.84.
7. His ideas on this topic were eventually compiled in Z. Gökalp, *Türkçülüğün Esasları* (Istanbul: Arkadaş Basımevi, 1939).
8. E.J. Zürcher, *The Unionist Factor* (Leiden: Brill, 1984).
9. T. Alp, *Türk Ruhu* (Ankara: Remzi Kitabevi, 1944) pp.202–3.
10. M. Tunçay, *Türkiye Cumhuriyeti'nde Tek-Parti Yönetimi'nin Kurulması (1923–1931)*, (Ankara: Yurt Yayınları, 1981) p.30, n.6.
11. B. Oran, *Atatürk Milliyetçiliği: Resmi İdeoloji Dışı Bir İnceleme* (Ankara: Bilgi Yayınevi, 1990) p.123.
12. M. Tunçay, op. cit., pp.341–6.
13. A.J. Toynbee and K. Kirkwood, *Turkey* (London: Benn, 1926) p.85.
14. B. Lewis, op. cit., p.346.
15. S. Kili, *Türk Devrim Tarihi* (Istanbul: Tekin Yayınevi, 1982) p.54–5.
16. *Türkiye Büyük Millet Meclisi (TBMM) Zabıt Ceridesi*, I: 2, 24.4.1336 (1920), C: 1, pp.8–30.
17. *TBMM Zabıt Ceridesi*, I: 8, 24.4.1336 (1920), C: 2, pp.162–5. Ibid., p.165.
18. For a copy of the law see Ş. Gözübüyük and S. Kili, *Türk Anayasa Metinleri* (Ankara: Ajans-Türk Matbaası, 1957).
19. B. Oran, op. cit., p.125.
20. For the texts of these two decisions see Ş. Gözübüyük and S. Kili, op. cit., pp.89–91.
21. *TBMM Zabıt Ceridesi*, I: 130, 1.1.1338 (1922), C: 1, pp.305–11.
22. See for example a speech made by the Deputy of Erzurum, Hüseyin Avni in, *TBMM Zabıt Ceridesi*, I: 130, 1.11.1338 (1922), C: 2, pp.314–15.
23. 'Öğretmenlere (27.X.1922)' in *Atatürk'ün Söylev ve Demeçleri (1906–1938)* (Ankara: Türk Tarih Kurumu Basımevi, 1959) p.45.
24. The SDRA-R operated as an unofficial political party led by Mustafa Kemal. It was composed of his most trusted supporters. The group formed itself into the People's Party (*Halk Fırkası*) in Sept. 1923. Subsequently, the term 'Republican' was included in Nov. 1924. See M. Tunçay, op. cit., pp.354–6.
25. For the texts of these amendments see Ş. Gözübüyük and S. Kili, op. cit., p.95.
26. B. Toprak, *Islam and Political Development in Turkey* (Leiden: Brill, 1981) p.45.
27. A. Kazamias, *Education and the Quest For Modernity in Turkey* (Chicago: University of Chicago Press, 1966) pp.91–2.
28. Ibid., p.116.
29. M. Winter, 'The Modernization of Education in Kemalist Turkey' in J. Landau (ed.), *Atatürk and Modernization of Turkey* (Boulder CO: Westview, 1984) p.186.
30. For the text of the constitution see Ş. Gözübüyük and S. Kili, op. cit., pp.101–24.
31. For details of the debate see Ş. Gözübüyük and Z. Zengin, *1924 Anayasası Hakkındaki Meclis Görüşmeleri* (Ankara: Balkanoğlu Matbaacılık, 1957) pp.436–41.
32. Ibid., pp.439–40.
33. For a detailed analysis of religion among the Kurds see M. Izady, *A Concise Handbook:*

the Kurds (Washington DC: Taylor & Francis, 1992) pp.131–66.

34. U. Heyd, *Foundations of Turkish Nationalism* (London: Luzac, Harvill Press, 1950).
35. Z. Gökalp, 'What is a Nation?' in Berkes N. (ed.), op. cit., p.137.
36. T. Parla, *Türkiye'de Siyasal Kültürün Resmi Kaynakları Cilt 3: Kemalist Tek-Parti İdeolojisi ve CHP'nin Altı Ok'u* (Istanbul: İletişim Yayınları, 1995) p.188.
37. Ibid., p.128.
38. Ibid., p.110.
39. B. Oran, op. cit., p.187.
40. M. Tunçay, op. cit., p.301.
41. J. Glasneck, *Türkiye'de Faşist Alman Propagandası* (Ankara: Onur Yayınları, undated) p.26.
42. B. Oran, op.cit., p.159.
43. K. Kirişci, 'Post Second World War Immigration from Balkan Countries to Turkey', *New Perspectives on Turkey*, 12, (Spring 1995).
44. B. Oran, op. cit., p.187.
45. Quoted in M. Tunçay, op. cit., p.228, n.36.
46. T. Parla, op. cit., pp.171–5, 210, 218.
47. For the full text of the law see *T.C. Resmi Gazete*, 21 June 1934, No. 2733.
48. This group included past immigrants from the Caucasus and the Balkans who were considered Turkish even if ethnically they might have been Albanians, Circassians, Pomaks, Tatars etc. These did not or could not speak Turkish for a variety of reasons. In respect to new immigrants the law authorized the government to determine who would be considered as 'belonging to the Turkish culture'.
49. I. Beşikçi, *Kürtlerin Mecburi İskanı* (Ankara: Yurt Kitap Yayın, 1991).
50. *TBMM Zabıt Ceridesi* I: 65, 7.6.1934, C: 1, pp.69–70.
51. Ibid., p.141.
52. *TBMM Zabıt Ceridesi* I: 68, 14.6.1934, C:1, p.141.
53. Ş. Mardin, 'Ideology and Religion in the Turkish Revolution', *International Journal of Middle East Studies*, 2 (1971).
54. D. Mersin-Alıcı, *The Impact of Turkey's Nationalistic Culture on Turkish Foreign Policy Making as Observed in Turkey's Relations with the Central Asian Turkic Republics* (MA thesis, Department of Political Science and International Relations, Boğaziçi University, 1995).
55. Each of these rebellions is covered in detail in a book published by the Turkish General Staff, *Türkiye Cumhuriyeti'nde Ayaklanmalar (1924–1938)* (Ankara: Gnkur. Basımevi, 1972). B. N. Şimşir (ed.), *Ingiliz Belgeleriyle Türkiye'de 'Kürt Sorunu' (1924–1938* (Ankara: Türk Tarih Kurumu, 1981) has provided British intelligence and diplomatic reports that cover these rebellions.
56. M. Tunçay, op. cit., p.136.
57. S. Kili, op. cit., p.161.
58. B. Lewis, op. cit., p.273.
59. Quoted in G.L. Lewis 'Atatürk's Language Reform as an Aspect of Modernization in the Republic of Turkey' in Landau J. (ed.), op. cit., p.198.
60. C. Kutschera, *Le Mouvement National Kurde* (Paris: Flammarion, 1979) pp.90–101.
61. Interview in *Aktüel* 11 Dec. 1991.
62. B. Toprak, op. cit., p.70.
63. G.D. Tüfekçi, *Atatürk'ün Okuduğu Kitaplar* (Ankara: Türkiye İş Bankası Kültür Yayınları, 1983) pp.170–1.
64. M. Tunçay, op. cit., p.325. For a recent study of this thesis see B. Ersanlı-Behar *İktidar*

ve Tarih :Türkiye'de 'Resmi Tarih' Tezinin Oluşumu (1929–1937) (Istanbul: Afa Yayınları, 1992).
65. D. Mersin-Alıcı, op. cit., p.19.
66. H. Hyman, A. Payaslıoğlu and F. W. Frey, 'The Values of Turkish College Youth', *Public Opinion Quarterly*, (Fall 1958), pp. 275–91.
67. F.W. Frey, 'Socialization to National Identification among Turkish Peasants', *Journal of Politics*, 30, 4, (Nov. 1968).
68. His work has been recompiled and published in Sevket Beysanoğlu, *Kürt Aşiretleri Hakkında Sosyolojik Tetkikler* (Istanbul: Sosyal Yayınları, 1992).
69. P. Andrews (ed.), *Ethnic Groups in the Republic of Turkey* (Wiesbaden: Reichert, 1989) p.36, n.49.
70. A. A. Candar, *Türklüğün Kökleri ve Yayılışı* (Istanbul: Necmi İstikbal Matbaası, 1934) p.41.
71. For a summary of a meeting chaired by Kaya, the interior minister at the time, at which the Governor of Dersim made these remarks see, U. Mumcu, *Kürt Dosyası*, (Istanbul: Tekin Yayınevi, 1993) pp.137–59.
72. M.S. Fırat, *Doğu İlleri Varto Tarihi* (Ankara: Milli Eğitim Basımevi, 1961) p.7.
73. B. Oran, op. cit., pp.204–5.
74. *Türkiye Büyük Millet Meclisi (TBMM) Gizli Celse Zabıtları*, 4, (Ankara: Türkiye Iş Bankası Kültür Yayınları, 1985) p.163.
75. U. Mumcu, op. cit., pp.56 7.
76. Ibid., p.124.
77. Ibid., p.174.
78. M. Van Bruinessen, *Kürdistan üzerine Yazilar* (Istanbul: Iletişim, 1993) p.167; and R. Olson, *The Emergence of Kurdish Nationalism 1880–1925* (Austin: University of Texas Press, 1991) p.154.
79. E. Aybars, *İstiklal Mahkemeleri* (Izmir: Ileri Kitabevi, 1995) pp.310–27; and M. Tunçay, op. cit., p.129.
80. H. Arfa, *The Kurds: a Historical and Political Study* (London: Oxford University Press, 1968) p.37.
81. U. Mumcu, *Kürt-İslam Ayaklanması 1919–1925* (Istanbul: Tekin Yayınevi, 1992) p.161.
82. Quoted in E. Aybars, op. cit., p.317.
83. M. Van Bruinessen, op. cit., p.155.
84. See analysis and tables in F.W. Frey, *The Turkish Political Elite* (Cambridge MA: MIT Press, 1965) pp.184–92.
85. *Türkiye Cumhuriyetinde Ayaklanmalar (1924–1938)*, op. cit., pp.351–2.
86. Quoted in V. Timuroğlu, 'Dersimlinin kimlik bilmecesi' *Cumhuriyet*, 29 May 1991.
87. M. Van Bruinessen, op. cit., p.123–4.
88. E. Özbudun, *Türkiye'de Sosyal Değişme ve Siyasal Katılma* (Ankara: Ankara Üniversitesi Hukuk Fakültesi Yayınları No. 363, 1975) p.95.
89. See E. Özbudun, 'Established Revolution versus Unfinished Revolution: Contrasting Patterns of Democratization in Mexico and Turkey' in S.P. Huntington and C.H. Moore (eds.), *Authoritarian Politics in Modern Society* (New York: Basic Books, 1970) pp. 380–405.
90. E. Özbudun (note 88) pp.37–8.
91. M. Van Bruinessen, op. cit., p.340.
92. I. Beşikçi, *Doğu Anadolu'nun Düzeni: Sosyo/Ekonomik ve Etnik Temeller* (Ankara: E Yayınları, 1969) p.218.

93. N. Entessar, *Kurdish Ethnonationalism* (Boulder CO, Lynne Rienner, 1992) p.88.
94. M. Van Bruinessen, op. cit., p.341.
95. E. Özbudun (note 88) pp.90–1.
96. N. Abadan, *Anayasa Hukuku ve Siyasi Bilimler Açısından 1965 Seçimlerinin Tahlili* (Ankara: Siyasi Bilimler Fakültesi Yayınları, 1967) p.246.
97. *20 Yüzyıl Ansiklopedisi*, 4 (Istanbul: Tercüman Gazetesi, 1990) p.813.
98. E. Özbudun (note 88) p.163.
99. For coverage of the congress see H. Öcar, 'TIP kuruluşundan bügüne, no.8', *Ulus*, 4 Nov. 1970; and, M. Belge, 'Türkiye Işci Partisi', *Cumhuriyet Dönemi Türkiye Ansiklopedısı*, 8 (Istanbul: Iletişim Yayınları, 1983) pp.2120–31.
100. E. Özbudun (note 88) p.93.
101. Ü. Ergüder, 'Changing Patterns of Electoral Behavior in Turkey' *Boğaziçi University Journal*, 8–9, (1980–1981) p.65.
102. Quoted in I. Beşikçi (note 92) pp.251–2.
103. For a detailed coverage of these groups see R. Ballı, *Kürt Dosyası* (Istanbul: Cem Yayınevi, 1992).
104. J. Landau, *Radical Politics in Modern Turkey* (Leiden: Brill, 1974) p.86.
105. M. Gunter, *The Kurds in Turkey: a Political Dilemma* (Boulder CO, Westview, 1990) p.17.
106. Ibid., pp.63–8.
107. I. İmset, *The PKK: a Report On Separatist Violence In Turkey* (Ankara: Turkish Daily News Publications, I, 1992) pp.380–406.
108. *PKK, Kürdistan Devriminin Yolu, Program* (Köln: Serxwebun Yayınları, 1983).
109. M. Van Bruinessen, 'The Ethnic Identity of Kurds' in Andrews P. (ed.), op. cit., p.621.
110. U. Mumcu (note 81) p.238.
111. *The Constitution of the Republic of Turkey* (official English translation) (Ankara: 1990)
112. *T.C. Resmi Gazete*, 22 Oct. 1983, No. 18199.
113. G. Harris, *Turkey: Coping with Crisis* (Boulder CO, Westview, 1985) pp.18–19.
114. I. Giritli, *Kürt Türklerinin Gerçeği* (Istanbul: Yeni Forum Yayıncılık, 1989).
115. Interview in *Aktüel* 11 Dec. 1991.
116. *TBMM Tutanak Dergisi*, Dönem 18, Cilt 1, 19.1.1988, B: 10, O:1, pp.451–61.
117. *Turkish Daily News*, 18 Mar. 1992.
118. For a list of such persons and positions they held see U. Mumcu (note 71), pp.201–2, 222.
119. Interview in *Aktüel* 11 Dec. 1991.

5

The Kurdish Question and Recent Developments in Turkey

T HIS CHAPTER will focus primarily on developments in the 1990s concerning the Kurdish question in Turkey. However, the trans-state nature
of this particular ethnic conflict should be borne in mind. Events in Turkey
with regard to the Kurds cannot be totally divorced from activities elsewhere
in the region. In particular, the ever-changing situation in northern Iraq has
had an important influence. The regional dimension of the Kurdish question
will be analysed separately later. One should note that the socio-economic
problems, the escalating violence in south-eastern Anatolia and the increasing
scale of migration within and out of the area have been adversely affected by
developments in Iraq especially. The trans-state nature of the Kurdish
question has had significant repercussions on politics in Turkey. How Western
governments have perceived and reacted to policies adopted by the authorities
in Ankara with regard to the Kurdish question in the country and in the region
in general, and how Turkish officials in turn have responded to these reactions
will also be examined in more detail later.

The Kurdish Question in Turkey Today: Preliminary Remarks

According to Andrews there are 49 identifiable ethnic groups in Turkey.[1] The
Kurds constitute the largest of these after the Turks. However, the size of the
Kurdish population in Turkey remains disputed. According to Turgut Özal
there were 12 million Kurds in Turkey. Two Kurdish deputies Muzaffer
Demir from Muş and Mahmut Alınak from Şırnak have put the Kurdish
population at 15 and 20 millions respectively.[2] Van Bruinessen has argued
that a 'reasonable and even conservative' estimate for the size of the Kurdish
population in Turkey in 1975 was 7.5 millions, which amounted to 19 per
cent of the total population.[3] This would put the population of Kurds in 1990
at 10.7 millions out of total population of 56.4 million. According to Izady
the figure was 13.7 millions for the same year.[4] There is a considerable discrepancy in these figures because they are based on intuitive guesses.

The Turkish national censuses stopped collecting data on the basis of ethnicity after 1965. Before then, people were asked questions during each national census about their mother tongue. This provided a statistical basis for establishing the number of Kurds even though the figures were not completely reliable. Mutlu has provided a thorough analysis of some of the inconsistencies associated with these figures before reconstructing the size of the Kurdish population for 1965. After readjustments, the Kurdish population then, according to him, stood at 3,130,390, representing 9.97 per cent of the population. This was compared with the census figure of 2,370,233 which accounted for only 7.55 per cent of the total.[5] Accordingly, Mutlu estimated the size of the number of Kurds in Turkey in 1990 at just over 7 millions, more than 12 per cent of Turkey's total population (Table 5.1).

TABLE 5.1

BREAKDOWN OF ESTIMATED KURDISH POPULATION
BY GEOGRAPHICAL REGIONS IN 1990

	Number (000)	As % of total Population
Eastern	2,230.29	41.96
South-eastern	2,365.04	64.98
Aegean	296.99	3.93
Black Sea	37.88	0.50
Central Anatolia	579.38	5.53
Marmara	810.13	6.09
Mediterranean	726.55	8.95
Total for all Turkey	7,046.26	
As % of population for all Turkey		12.60

Source: Figures adopted from S. Mutlu, 'The Population of Turkey by Ethnic Groups and Provinces', New Perspectives on Turkey, 12 (Spring 1995) p.49

This is a figure higher than the one calculated by Özsoy, Koç and Toros who introduced no adjustments into their calculations. They put the projected number of people whose mother tongue was Kurdish in 1992 at 3,620,458. This figure increased to 6,232,234 when the projected number of people whose second language was Kurdish was added to the earlier sum.[6] On the basis of these two estimates the number of Kurds in Turkey would, respectively, amount to 6.2 or 10.7 per cent of the total population in 1992.

The large discrepancy between the figures cited for the size of the Kurdish population is also probably connected with the fact that there are different definitions of who is a Kurd. Mutlu has defined Kurds as those people 'who declared their mother tongue as Kurdish including Zaza, in the 1965 population census'.[7] Zaza is generally considered to be a dialect of the Kurdish language mostly spoken by Kurds in the province of Tunceli; but there are also some Kurds who speak Zaza in the provinces of Erzincan, Bingöl and Diyarbakır. Zaza speakers are mostly Alevis. On occasions the larger grouping of Sunni Kurds have not considered Zaza speakers as Kurds or even Moslems. Van Bruinessen has noted that little research has been done to warrant a definitive statement on the relationship between Kurdish and Zaza.[8]

There are many Kurds in Turkey who are conscious of their Kurdish identity but do not speak any Kurdish. This was even recognized by the leader of the PKK Abdullah Öcalan. In an interview he argued that, even if a separate Kurdish state were set up, Turkish would have to be used there for a considerable period.[9] Many prominent public figures and politicians in Turkey are of Kurdish ethnic background but do not necessarily speak fluent Kurdish. A good case in point would be Hikmet Çetin who has served in government as Foreign Minister as well as Deputy Prime Minister. Furthermore, there are also many Kurds who are of mixed ethnic background. The late Turgut Özal had publicly stated that he was partly Kurdish. Given that Turks and Kurds have lived in the same area for many centuries intermarriage was probably quite common.

Kurdish nationalists tend to exaggerate the number of Kurds in Turkey. Turkish nationalists either tend to deny the existence of Kurds or to understate their numbers. One may argue that a Kurd is someone who considers him/herself to have a Kurdish ethnic identity, irrespective of whether Kurdish is the mother-tongue or not. However, in the case of Turkey, this inevitably raises the question of who is a Turk. Does the label 'Turk' refer to an ethnic background or to citizenship? How individuals perceive themselves is important. As noted earlier, individuals may perceive that they have a multiple identity. Which identity a person may choose to stress could be dependent on a particular context. And the largely psychological 'boundaries' between ethnic groups are not fixed. Different generations within a certain family could thus perceive themselves as either Kurdish or Turkish, or they may feel that they belong to both identities. A Kurd could consider him/herself to be a member of a specific tribe, hold a Kurdish ethnic identity and also feel him/herself to be a Turkish citizen. On the other hand, a Kurd who is a citizen of Turkey may reject a Turkish identity in any form. Therefore someone like Hikmet Çetin would consider himself an ethnic Kurd of Turkish nationality (citizenship). He would regard himself as a Turkish Kurd. There are a number of Kurds, though, who not only refuse a Turkish identity in any form, but also publicly take offence against Hikmet Çetin for holding a multiple identity.

By the 1990s a significant proportion of the population in Turkey considered themselves to be Kurds and they have been increasingly demanding the recognition of the right to express their identity. Although the government in Ankara recognizes the Kurdish reality in Turkey, and has gradually allowed the Kurdish question to be more discussed and debated in the open, the demands from a growing number of Kurds for broadcasting and education in Kurdish have not yet been seriously addressed. The confrontation between the Turkish government and the PKK, which aspires to set up a Kurdish state through armed struggle, is a major complicating factor.

Many Turkish officials argue that Turkey is facing a terrorism problem stemming from the activities of the PKK. Some believe that once terrorism is contained the Kurdish question will by and large be resolved. However, to others the issue is a socio-economic one. Some officials and politicians believe that the terrorism problem is connected with the fact that the Kurds have been unable to express their ethnic identity. These officials are of the opinion that the problem of terrorism would diminish considerably once the Kurds were allowed education and radio and television broadcasting in Kurdish.

In the mid-1990s the prevailing view held that if cultural concessions were to be granted to the Kurds this could be the first step towards the disintegration of the Turkish state. The conspicuous lack of leadership in the country and a preference for populism among both Turkish and Kurdish politicians have aggravated the situation. In the meantime, the violence in eastern and south-eastern Turkey has continued unabated. Violence leads to migration and a further deterioration of the socio-economic and political situation. This feeds back into the Kurdish question, making it even more difficult to resolve.

Socio-Economic Factors and the Kurdish Question in Turkey

The areas traditionally inhabited by the Kurds have been the least developed parts of Turkey. The eastern and south-eastern regions where most Kurds currently live today have the lowest scores for two socio-economic indicators (Table 5.2). Illiteracy rates of 35.5 and 44 .0 per cent for these regions in 1985 were much higher than elsewhere in Turkey. Similarly, the number of medical doctors per thousand people in 1990 was lower in the less-developed eastern and south-eastern regions than elsewhere.

Gross per capita income figures for 1979 and 1986 in relation to the two most prosperous western regions, the Marmara and the Aegean region (indexed as 100), are shown in Table 5.3. The combined per capita income scores for the eastern and the south-eastern region were the lowest for both years. Car ownership is generally highly income-elastic and in Turkey it is considered to be an important sign of economic prosperity. Only just over six out of every 100 privately-owned cars in 1991 were registered in the eastern and the south-eastern regions. These two measures would appear to indicate the relative lack of prosperity in the mostly Kurdish populated areas of Turkey.

However, it would be wrong to suggest that this was the product of a deliberate policy on the part of the Turkish government. The Black Sea region,

TABLE 5.2

PERCENTAGE OF ILLITERATE POPULATION IN 1985 AND
NUMBER OF MEDICAL DOCTORS IN 1990 BY REGIONS

	% of illiterate population in 1985	Number of medical doctors per 1,000 in 1990
Eastern	35.5	4.0
South-eastern	44.0	4.0
Aegean	18.6	9.0
Black Sea	24.7	5.0
Central	18.3	12.0
Marmara	14.2	12.0
Mediterranean	22.1	5.0

Source: Figures were compiled from *İl ve Bölge İstatistikleri* (Ankara: Devlet İstatistik Enstitüsü [DIE], 1993) p.45 and *İller İtibariyle Çeşitli Göstergeler* (Ankara: Devlet Planlama Teşkilatı, 1993) p.37

TABLE 5.3

CARS NEWLY REGISTERED IN TURKEY IN 1991 AND RELATIVE
PER CAPITA GNP IN 1979 AND 1986 (AT 1979 CONSTANT PRICES)

	Cars newly registered in 1991 (%)	Per capita GNP in 1979 and 1986 in relation to two most prosperous regions	
		1979	1986
Eastern +South-eastern	6.4	34.4	29.2
Aegean	11.0	100.0	100.0
Black Sea	6.3	56.2	47.4
Central	21.6	53.8	2.1
Marmara	46.5	100.0	100.0
Mediterranean	8.7	69.1	61.6

Source: *İller İtibariyle Çeşitli Göstergeler*, op. cit., p.67 and *Türkiye Gayri Safi Yurt İçi Hasılasının İller İtibariyle Dağılımı* (Istanbul: Istanbul Sanayi Odası, 1988) p.367

which is not highly populated by Kurds (Table 5.1), also has low socio-economic scores compared with the western regions of Turkey. If anything, the government's public spending in the eastern and the south-eastern regions has been proportionally higher compared to other regions. Between 1986 and 1990 the government spent 78.2 million TL in the eastern and south-eastern regions while the total revenues received from the two regions came to 26.2 million TL. During the same period, while the ratio of budget expenditures to public revenue was 1.4 on a nationwide basis, the regional ratio for eastern and south-eastern Anatolia was 3.0 (Table 5.4).[10] In other words, the government spent three times more money than the revenues it collected from these two regions. Clearly, between 1986 and 1990 there has been a transfer of national budgetary funds from the developed western parts of Turkey to the less developed areas of the country.

The government's efforts to develop the area were also supported by other indicators. As Table 5.4 shows, an overwhelmingly large proportion of public investment expenditures were channelled to the eastern and the south-eastern region between 1983 and 1992. A significant portion of this has gone to finance the gigantic South-East Anatolia Development Project (GAP). This ambitious project, when completed, will have 21 dams, 19 hydro-electric power plants and a complex network of irrigation canals covering eight provinces, seven of which are mostly populated by Kurds.[11] However, a number of economic factors have prevented the mobilization of these public resources to improve the socio-economic situation in the eastern and the south-eastern region.

TABLE 5.4

THE PROPORTION OF EXPENDITURES OVER REVENUES
IN THE NATIONAL BUDGET BETWEEN 1986 AND 1990
AND PER CAPITA PUBLIC INVESTMENT EXPENDITURES
FOR 1983–92

	Ratio of consolidated budget expenditures to budget revenues 1986–90	Per capita public investment expenditure for 1983–92; index (Turkey) = 100
Eastern + South-eastern	3.0	303.0
Aegean	0.7	145.0
Black Sea	1.2	36.0
Central	0.7	131.0
Marmara	0.3	71.0
Mediterranean	0.7	60.0
Turkey	1.4	

Source: İller İtibariyle Çeşitli Göstergeler, op. cit., p.1 and p.16

First and foremost the investment in these two regions has not been matched by private investment. As Table 5.5 indicates, the area is characterized by low levels of savings and credits.

TABLE 5.5

TOTAL BANK DEPOSITS AND CREDITS FOR 1991
AND INVESTMENT CERTIFICATES FOR 1992 BY REGIONS

	% of total bank deposits in 1991	% of total bank credits in 1991	% of investment certificates in 1992
Eastern	2.1	1.5	1.6
South-eastern	1.6	1.1	2.3
Aegean	12.2	11.2	9.6
Black Sea	6.6	7.3	7.0
Central	28.0	27.8	13.8
Marmara	42.9	40.0	55.5
Mediterranean	6.7	10.8	8.3

Source: *İller İtibariyle Çeşitli Göstergeler* op. cit., pp.17, 22 and 16

The first two columns show there is little saving in the form of bank deposits and credits taken out from banks compared with the rest of the country. In a newspaper report on the banking sector in eastern and south-eastern Turkey it was noted that a growing number of banks were closing their local branches and that the banking sector there was fast becoming eroded.[12] To some extent this suggests that there is little capacity for capital accumulation and private investment in the area. This is also reflected in the extremely low levels of investment allowance certificates obtained for these regions. This seems to indicate that private investors prefer to invest in the more developed and prosperous parts of Turkey, where they find larger and more dynamic markets as well as a relatively more skilled labour force. The low levels of purchasing power and education in the eastern and the south-eastern region as represented by the socio-economic indicators presented in Tables 5.2 and 5.3 seem to be discouraging private investment.

Another important factor that has affected the economy of the area concerns the sanctions imposed on Iraq as a result of the Gulf War. Before the sanctions, in 1988, Iraq was Turkey's most important trading partner. Turkish exports to Iraq amounted to more than $1.5 billion. Inevitably, this trade benefited particularly the south-eastern area of the country and provided the basis for an important amount of economic activity that disappeared with the sanctions. The government's decision during the summer of 1994 to reopen the border with Iraq for border trading – it had been closed in 1992 due to PKK activities in the region – has brought some economic activity to an area where there were at least 10–12,000 idle trucks.[13] However, this border trade, which has been limited to the transportation of relatively small quantities of foodstuffs to Iraq in return for 2 to 2.5 tons of petroleum per truck, in no way matched earlier levels of activity.

Robins has noted that the socio-economic disparity between these regions and the western parts of Turkey, especially since the early 1980s, 'has left the Kurds of the south-east with little stake in the prosperity of the new Turkey'.[14] The depressed nature of the economy in the area has also led to high levels of unemployment, particularly among the youth. According to a study prepared by the Diyarbakır Chamber of Commerce and Industry, the unemployment level in the provinces covered by GAP averaged 36 per cent.[15] A frustrated youth is more likely to support the PKK. This contributes to a rise of violence in the area which in itself adversely affects economic activity as investors shy away; and violence leads to a migration of people and a flight of capital out of the area.

Violence and the Kurdish Question in Turkey

In August 1984 the PKK launched its first attack on military installations near Eruh and Şemdinli in south-eastern Turkey. The PKK had been involved in limited acts of violence previously. As a result of PKK attacks and clashes between the PKK and the Turkish security forces 20,181 people have been killed between 1984 and the end of 1995 including 5,014 civilians (Table 5.6).

TABLE 5.6

CIVILIAN, PKK AND SECURITY FORCES CASUALTIES
BETWEEN 1984 AND 1995

	Civilians	PKK	Security forces	Totals
1984–91	1,278	1,444	846	3,568
1992–95	3,736	10,102	2,775	16,613
Total	5,014	11,546	3,621	20,181

Source: The figures for 1984–94 were compiled from *Yeni Yüzyıl*, 6 July 1995 and for 1995 from *Turkish Daily News* 8 Jan. 1996

As early as 1977 Abdullah Öcalan and his colleagues had adopted a pro-gramme which stressed the need to use violence. Their targets would be members of Turkish extreme nationalist groups and 'social chauvinist' groups (Turkish and Kurdish radical left-wing groups) as well as state collaborators and feudal landlords.[16] With the military coup in Turkey in 1980 the leadership of the PKK fled to Syria and Lebanon where they opened training camps. In 1984 when the PKK returned to Turkey the range of their targets had expanded to include economic and military as well as civilian targets. It seemed that they aimed to polarize society along Kurdish and Turkish lines.

Economic targets have included electric power and communication lines, irrigation facilities, factories, petroleum installations, and road construction and maintenance equipment. The purpose was to weaken the presence of the state and disrupt its ability to provide basic public services. Tourism facilities and businesses catering to Turkish tourism in and outside Turkey have also been considered economic targets. According to reports prepared by the US State Department, in 1993 the PKK kidnapped 13 tourists and 'bombed hotels, restaurants, and tourist sites and planted grenades on Medi-terranean beaches'. In 1994 during numerous bombing attacks the PKK injured ten tourists, killed three, and kidnapped two Finnish holidaymakers.[17] The PKK was determined to undermine an important source of foreign currency income for the government.

Attacks on military targets have usually taken the form of raids on remote gendarmerie stations as well as ambushes of units on patrol. The PKK had aimed to challenge the state's ability to maintain security in south-eastern Turkey and thus impose itself as an alternative source of authority. The PKK has also attacked civilian targets to secure the submission of villagers in particular. In March 1987 the PKK issued instructions to raid and burn villages. This strategy continued until early 1990 when Öcalan dissociated himself from the extremely unpopular raids.[18] The brutality of the raids had earned the PKK a similar reputation to that of the Shining Path guerrillas in Peru.

After a brief ceasefire unilaterally declared by the PKK had ended, violence intensified between 24 May 1993 and early October 1993 resulting in a death toll of 1,600 people which was unusually high.[19] By autumn 1993 the PKK's penetration of eastern and particularly of south-eastern Turkey was such that it had begun to introduce a clandestine administration of its own in the area. The Turkish press resembled this repressive administration to martial-law rule.[20] This situation led to a government crisis after a Turkish general was killed during skirmishes with the PKK in the town of Lice. Calls for a decla-ration of martial law were averted with a reshuffle of the cabinet and a decision to harden the struggle against terrorism. The military was given *carte blanche* to combat the PKK more effectively. By late spring 1994 the military had considerably weakened the PKK and, according to a group of Turkish journalists who visited the south-east, relative calm and security had returned to the region.[21] Since then PKK attacks have been mostly directed toward the intimidating of villages that provide militias to the government and against Kurds whom the PKK defines as 'state collaborators'. It seemed that compared with the period between 1991 and 1994 the PKK's activities had diminished considerably in 1995.[22] The organization declared another unilateral ceasefire before the national elections were held in December 1995. The government interpreted this as proof that the PKK's influence over the eastern and the south-east had weakened.

Teachers and schools have been another target of the PKK. According to a report prepared by the IHV, 128 teachers were killed between August 1984 and November 1994. The report attributed more than 80 per cent of these deaths directly to the PKK and noted that the families of these teachers were also attacked.[23] The Turkish Minister of the Interior declared that 5,210 schools had been closed down in eastern and south-eastern Turkey in the period between 1992 and 1994 because of general insecurity there. According to government statistics the PKK burned down 192 of these schools,[24] and according to İmset schools were targeted because the PKK believed that Ankara was using its national education system to assimilate the Kurds. The PKK had pledged to disrupt all educational activities until the teaching of the Kurdish language was allowed.[25]

At the start of the 1994 academic year the PKK announced that only teachers who received their permission could work. The announcement came after the killing of six teachers in Tunceli and was followed by the killing of another four in Erzurum.[26] However, since then attacks on schools and teachers appear to have subsided in spite of the threat issued by the PKK.

The government's reaction to the PKK threat was largely military in nature. The security policies introduced in eastern and south-eastern Turkey were based on the declaration of a state of emergency issued in July 1987. The emergency rule applied to ten provinces and must be renewed every four months by the Parliament. In March 1996 it was renewed for the twenty-sixth time. The law on which the emergency rule is based gives civilian governors the right to exercise 'certain quasi-martial law powers, including restrictions on the press and removal from the area of persons whose activities are believed inimical to public order'.[27] The introduction of the state of emergency has also meant that the application of the ECHR has been suspended in those parts of the country. Furthermore, as Robins has pointed out, this state of affairs has 'curbed the application of Turkey's emerging political liberalization process in the region'.[28]

The Anti-terror Law of April 1991 was also intended to deal with threats to domestic security and order caused by the PKK. A terrorist act was defined as actions involving repression, violence and force, or the threat to use force, by one or several persons belonging to an organization with the aim of changing the characteristics of the Turkish Republic including its political, legal, social, secular and economic system (Article 1). This broad and ambiguous definition coupled with the ban on any dissemination of ideas (Article 8), as previously noted, led to many detentions and human rights abuses. According to a list prepared by the IHV at the end of 1994, there were 95 intellectuals, politicians and academics under detention as a result of violations of the Anti-terror Law.[29] One academic İsmail Beşikçi has set a record for receiving sentences totalling up to 200 years in prison for his publications in violation of this law.[30] An amendment to Article 8 of the law passed by Parliament in October 1995 has led to the reduction of some prison sentences. Subsequently, a number of cases in the courts were dropped and some convicts were released. However, commentators argued that the amendment had not brought about freedom of thought in Turkey.[31]

The broad powers that this law gave to the authorities also led to allegations that the government has been implicated in 'mystery killings'. These appear to have started in 1990 with 11 unsolved murders. Since then 31 cases in 1991, 362 in 1992, 467 in 1993, 400 in 1994 and 92 in 1995 have been reported. In addition to the government, the outlawed religious group known as Hizbullah – an Islamic terrorist group active in south-eastern Turkey – and the PKK are also suspected of involvement in the mystery killings.[32] A report prepared by the Turkish Parliament's Unsolved Political Killings Commission has also implicated Hizbullah and village guards in many of the killings. The report alleged that the military had given support to Hizbullah training camps in south-eastern Turkey. It claimed that most of the village guards were involved with arms smuggling and that they would kill rival members of their tribe and claim that they were members of the PKK.[33]

The controversial village-guard system was introduced in April 1985 because of the enormous logistical difficulties of ensuring security in the mountainous and rural areas of eastern and south-eastern Turkey. The aim was to enable villages to defend themselves against attacks from the PKK. Originally it was believed that the village-guard system would provide income to areas that were economically depressed. İmset has likened the village guard-system to the Ottoman Hamidiye regiments which functioned between 1905 and 1908. The role of those regiments was 'to discipline the nomadic people of the region' and maintain 'the loyalty of Kurdish tribes to the central authority'.[34]

As in the case of the Hamidiye regiments, the government has used the village-guard system not only to improve security in the rural areas but also to determine the loyalty of the villagers. Villages or tribes who have refused to join the system are suspected of being PKK sympathizers. However, over the years the village-guard system has become a source of serious complaint. Sadık Avundukoğlu, a member of the Parliamentary commission investigating 'mystery killings', has even argued that the abuses committed by the village guards helped to swell the ranks of the PKK fighters.[35] In spite of frequent calls for its abolition, the number of village guards increased from just under 18,000 in 1990 to 63,000 by August 1994 when the Interior Minister announced that there would be no further additions.[36]

The government has steadily increased its military presence in the provinces under the emergency rule. According to the International Institute for Strategic Studies, the normal level of Turkish troop deployments in the area was around 90,000. This number had risen to 160,000 by June 1994.[37] By the end of 1994, taking into account also the number of police, special forces and village guards, there were 300,000 security forces deployed in eastern and south-eastern Turkey.[38] The size of the security forces in the area remained roughly the same during 1995. Apparently, approximately one-quarter of the total manpower of NATO's second-largest army was deployed in the area against the PKK.[39] In contrast, according to government figures at the end of 1994 the PKK fighters numbered only 4,000 to 5,000.[40] After the intense military campaigns against the PKK during the course of 1995 the government revised its figures and noted that the number of PKK fighters in Turkey was down to between 2,600 to 2,800. This appears to have forced the PKK to move into northern Iraq where the size of its force has increased to 3,000 to 4,000.[41]

The trans-state nature of the ethnic conflict between the Turks and Kurds was clearly illustrated by the agreement signed in October 1984 between Turkey and Iraq which allowed the armed forces of both states to enter each other's territory in hot pursuit of rebel units. In practice, only Turkey chose to exercise this right, mounting four cross-border operations involving the army and the air force before the agreement was abrogated by Iraq in 1988 at the end of the Iran–Iraqi war. The defeat of Iraq following the Gulf War and the creation of a safe haven for Kurds in northern Iraq enabled the PKK to use the area. Since August 1991 the Turkish military has mounted several ground and air cross-border operations into northern Iraq. The government has also attempted, however, to develop better relations with the Kurdish leadership in northern Iraq to improve the security of the Turkish border. The failure of this policy and the growing influence of the PKK in northern Iraq led the government to mount two more cross-border operations in March and July 1995 involving 35,000 and 3,000 troops, respectively.

The mountainous nature of most of eastern and south-eastern Turkey has enabled the PKK to raid villages during night-time and retreat in the day. The PKK has attacked or used villages as a staging post near to Turkey's borders with Iran and Iraq. The military responded with a controversial village evacuation policy. Villages that the military were unable to protect were forcibly vacated and at times burned to prevent them from being used by the PKK for logistical purposes. These villages were mostly along the Iranian and the Iraqi border and in mountainous areas. According to a report on migration and village evacuation prepared by Mazlum-Der, a fundamentalist religious group, 'in mountainous areas not one village has been left, except the ones belonging to the village guards'.[42]

In autumn 1994 a government crisis erupted when the Minister responsible for Human Rights Azimet Köylüoğlu accused the military of burning villages in the province of Tunceli. Prime Minister Çiller attempted to deny these allegations by claiming that the villages had been burned by the PKK. The crisis reached comic proportions when she tried to convince villagers that helicopters that had attacked these villages belonged to the PKK.[43] Members of the main opposition party in the Parliament argued that 1,500 villages in the province of Tunceli had been forcibly evacuated and that 250,000 people had been displaced.[44] In August 1995 a similar crisis erupted when the security forces were accused of yet another round of forced evacuations in the province of Tunceli. The official figure for the number of villages and hamlets evacuated by the security forces was put at 2,253 in October 1995.[45] However, the numbers of villages evacuated and burned were probably much higher. The PKK, too, in accordance with its 'Decree on Village Raids' has attacked and burned 'non-revolutionary' villages that do not support 'the national struggle for liberation'.[46] There are also villages that have been burned or vacated by their inhabitants after having been caught in the cross-fire between the PKK and the security forces. Forests have also become a target as the security forces cleared wooded areas in eastern Turkey and the PKK retaliated by burning forests in western Turkey, especially around Istanbul during summer 1994. However, there were far fewer forest fires in 1995.

As part of their strategy the PKK has compelled many remote villages to provide food and shelter for its militants. In turn, these villages are harassed by security forces who often fail to distinguish between civilians and the PKK. The impossible situation that villagers often find themselves in was well captured by the words of a village headman (*muhtar*) who said that they were 'the slaves of the military during day time and the slaves of the PKK at night'.[47] Consequently, many villagers have chosen to migrate to urban centres.

A report prepared by a group of Turkish Parliamentary deputies concluded that the security operations and the practice of village burning was fuelling Kurdish nationalism and was forcing especially young people to join the ranks of the PKK.[48] *The Economist* too has noted that Turkey 'may be winning battles against guerrillas but it is losing the war for the support of ordinary Kurds'.[49] One of the most significant consequences of this escalating violence is that the Kurdish question has come to occupy a prominent place on the political agenda and has also increasingly attracted the attention of the West. The PKK leadership was correct to remark that violence made 'the world accept the existence of a Kurdish question'.[50] The government has suffered both politically and financially. Ankara's inability to halt the violence and resolve the Kurdish question has seriously affected Turkey's relations with the West.

The cost of maintaining security in the region under emergency rule was estimated to be around $11.1 billion for 1994 (over 400 trillion Turkish liras at the time).[51] For a country whose GNP for 1993 was approximately $173 billion this was a considerable sum. Many have argued that this high expenditure led to extensive domestic borrowing which resulted in an inflation rate of over 140 per cent during 1994.[52] Expenditure involved in the mounting of several cross-border operations into northern Iraq must also be taken into account. The operation in March 1995 alone cost $65 million according to military authorities.[53]

Government officials have attempted to justify these high costs by arguing that they are committed to 'breaking the back' of the PKK. Prime Minister Çiller introduced a new slogan into Turkish politics when early in 1994 she announced that terrorism would 'either end or end' ('ya bitecek ya bitecek'). The Chief of the General Staff Doğan Güreş, just before completing his term of office, stated that as a result of the campaign against the PKK terrorism had been brought under control.[54] Many commentators remained sceptical as the PKK continued to attack civilians and teachers. However, the number of acts of terrorism involving the PKK dropped significantly from 4,063 and 4,012 in 1993 and 1994 to 2,059 in 1995 according to government statistics.[55]

The previously mentioned report prepared by the Parliament on 'mystery killings' noted that many people had a vested interest in the continuation of emergency rule. Government security personnel employed in the region where emergency rule operated received extra pay. This additional money, which allowed the security people to enjoy a considerable increase in their living standards, has come to be referred to as the 'Apo raise', after the nickname of the PKK leader. The salaries of the village guards are often paid as a lump sum to tribal leaders who keep a large proportion for themselves. Dependence on these leaders has undermined the ability of the state to combat the drug trade in which these leaders are heavily implicated. The boom in the construction of apartment buildings in cities such as Van has been connected to drug trafficking. The high demand on land and housing caused by migration and higher salaries has significantly pushed up property prices and rents. These developments have created a group of people who have a stake in the continuation of the status quo.

Violence has also led to a certain degree of polarization in society. The funerals of victims of PKK attacks have become occasions for extreme Turkish nationalist demonstrations. There have also been reports of the mistreatment of Kurds in western Turkey. This has taken the form of the boycotting of Kurdish-owned shops, the denying of jobs to Kurds and the harassing of Kurdish immigrants in small towns. As Barkey has noted: 'The combination of army operations and societal polarization has raided the consciousness of even the most assimilated Kurd'.[56] Young men born in the eastern provinces of the country are sometimes discriminated against by officials who automatically suspect them of being PKK sympathizers. This situation has been aggravated by politicians who resort to thinly disguised populistic speeches.

Gençkaya has noted that as a result of polarization, 'Turkish and Kurdish public opinion can hardly understand each other'.[57] However, what is striking is that this polarization by and large has not been widespread and has not actually manifested itself in the form of violent confrontations between ordinary Kurds and Turks. This may be attributed in part to intermarriage and the fact that many Kurds now perceive themselves also as Turks. Furthermore, the Kurdish question is increasingly being discussed publicly. In late 1995 and early 1996 there were several meetings and conferences where the Kurdish question was openly debated.

As a result of violence, many Kurds are rediscovering their Kurdish origins. This seems also to have raised ethnic consciousness in Turkey among other groups. Thus Kurdish immigrants settling in small towns in Thrace and areas just east of Istanbul have made Circassians, Bulgarian Turks and Pomaks much more conscious of their identities.

Migration and the Kurdish Question in Turkey

Since 1950 many people have migrated from the less developed regions of Turkey to urban and industrial centres in the western parts of the country. Shorter noted that whereas in 1950 18.1 per cent of Turkey's population lived in urban centres, by 1970 this had risen to 35.8, and by 1990 56.3 per cent of the population lived in urban areas.[58] Many people migrated from eastern and south-eastern Anatolia and from the Black Sea region in the period between 1980 and 1990 (Table 5.7). An overwhelming proportion of these

TABLE 5.7

NET MIGRATION BY REGIONS BETWEEN 1980 AND 1990

	Rate of net migration in % for 1980–85	Rate of net migration in % for 1985–90
Aegean	1.4	2.7
Black Sea	−3.0	−6.6
Central Anatolia	−0.6	−1.7
Marmara	3.9	7.2
Mediterranean	1.6	0.9
Eastern	−5.0	−9.3
South-eastern	−2.3	−3.3

Source: *İl ve Bölge İstatistikleri 1993*, op. cit., p.45 and *Türkiye İstatistik Yıllığı 1994*, (Ankara: Devlet İstatistik Enstitüsü, [DIE] 1995) p.96

migrants have moved to the Marmara region, principally to industrial cities such as Istanbul, Bursa and İzmit. Ayata studied migration in five out of the eight provinces covered by GAP. The study, based on a survey of 887 people, noted that while socio-economic factors remained important, political and security considerations also were responsible for migration.[59]

The upsurge in PKK attacks since 1992 resulted in a significant increase in migration within as well as out of the eastern and the south-east.[60] Because of the general insecurity and instability in the area the poor mostly move out of rural communities into provincial urban centres. The relatively well off migrate from regional urban centres to cities in western Turkey.

The forced displacement of rural communities leads to another type of migration. Villagers may be ordered to evacuate their settlements. Much of this migration has been to urban areas in eastern and south-eastern Anatolia. An estimated 14,000 people have also sought asylum in northern Iraq. This is particularly striking given that in the past Turkey was traditionally a country of asylum for Kurdish refugees from Iraq.[61] There are no general and systematic studies of this forced migration. It is difficult to differentiate between forced and voluntary migration. Only extremely tentative figures with regard to the scale of migration that has taken place within eastern and south-eastern Turkey may be given (Table 5.8).

TABLE 5.8

POPULATION IN 1990 AND 1994 OF PRINCIPAL URBAN CENTRES IN THE EAST AND SOUTH-EAST AFFECTED BY MIGRATION

	1990 (000)	Estimated late 1994 (000)
Batman	148	260
Diyarbakır	380	950
Hakkari	38	100
Şanlıurfa	276	650
Van	153	300
Total	995	2,260

Source: A. Özer, 'Güneydoğu Anadolu Bölgesinde Göç: Sorumlar ve Çözümler', paper presented at the conference, *Düşünce Özgürlüğü ve Göç Sempozyumu*, 10–12 Dec. 1994, Ankara; and interviews and newspaper reports

According to official statistics, 307,000 people have been displaced as a result of the evacuation of rural communities.[62] However, the scale of migration within and out of Kurdish-populated areas is much higher than this figure and greater than that suggested by Table 5.8. There are smaller towns in the region that have also received migrants who are not included in this table. Furthermore, urban centres near to eastern and south-eastern Turkey, such as Adana, Gaziantep and Mersin, have also received large waves of migrants in addition to the more distant cities of Antalya, Ankara, Bursa, Istanbul, İzmir and İzmit. Özer has argued that this migration accounts for a third of Istanbul's total population of approximately 12 millions.[63] On the other hand, one report has put the estimated number that have had to migrate within or out of eastern and south-eastern Anatolia at 2.5 to 3 million.[64] Whatever the exact figure may be, given the short time span the migration that has taken place within the country is enormous in scale.

Mutlu argued that even after 25 years of migration more than 65 per cent of the Kurdish population still lived in traditionally Kurdish populated areas in 1990.[65] Although his figures may have been accurate for 1990, after a later massive population movement probably a majority of the Kurds lived outside the east and the south-east by 1996. The projection that 'in about two generations' time the Kurds will 'replace the Turks as the largest ethnic group in Turkey'[66] may thus not materialize. Urbanization will slow the Kurdish population growth rate. Intermarriage may also weaken a sense of Kurdish ethnicity. The affect of assimilation or integration on people's identities also must be considered.

One solution to the Kurdish question in Turkey that has been advocated involves the establishment of a separate state for the Kurds. As regards the Kurds in Turkey alone, such a solution short of a massive transfer of population seems to be fast becoming impracticable. This may be one reason why Abdullah Öcalan has at times questioned the viability of establishing a separate state.[67] This reality was also recognized by the late President Özal who had contended that the best solution to the Kurdish problem was to encourage the Kurds to migrate to the western parts of the country. Özal had believed that this would weaken separatist demands as most Kurds would reap the benefits of a more prosperous life there.

However, the short-term economic consequences of migration have been negative. A depressed regional economy has become further impoverished. The cities have become overwhelmed with people who have swelled the ranks of the unemployed. Living standards for many have dipped appreciably as a result of migration. The lack of security in rural areas, government restrictions on grazing at high altitudes and the evacuation of many villages have undermined the once thriving husbandry sector. Villagers have been forced to slaughter their herds to finance their move to urban areas. Once constituting an important source of income for certain areas, the tourist industry has virtually disappeared. There has also been a flight of capital from these areas as the more prosperous have closed their businesses and small factories before moving to western Turkey.

As a result of this massive migration squatter areas in cities such as Adana have become a target for PKK recruiters. A report submitted to the Prime Minister's Office noted that the PKK, weakened in south-eastern Turkey, had changed tactics and started to move its recruitment and terrorist activities into urban areas with high concentrations of Kurdish immigrants.[68] This migration could create security problems along the Mediterranean coast and thereby damage tourism. In addition to providing a major source of foreign currency for the government, the tourist industry also offers employment for many including Kurdish immigrants.

Recent massive migration into urban centres has resulted in a housing shortage and in a steep rise in unemployment. Immediately after the major riots that occurred in Istanbul in March 1995, the President of the Turkish Grand National Assembly Hüsamettin Cindoruk noted that explosive situations existed in at least nine urban centres around the country.[69] Frustration with the economic situation has led some Kurds to participate in the lucrative, illegal drug business. Some of the village guards are involved with narcotics. The PKK also uses revenue from drug trafficking to finance its operations.[70]

There has been no serious study of the political consequences of Kurdish migration in Turkey. However, a number of general observations may be made. Through migration, more Kurds have become aware of the socio-economic disparities within the country. This has made some Kurds, particularly the young, more conscious of their separate identity and also more vulnerable to the propaganda of the PKK. On the other hand, immigrants are often absorbed in the day-to-day difficulties of starting up a new life in the cities. Once settled, many seem to develop a vested interest in becoming integrated into a society that still provides considerable opportunities for upward social mobility. It should be noted that the security forces have had greater success in apprehending PKK activists in the large urban areas than elsewhere and have been able to pre-empt terrorist attacks. The security forces attribute this to the co-operation they have received from Kurdish immigrants.

The Role of the Turkish Government and the Kurdish Question

The impact of the late President Turgut Özal in reversing Turkey's traditional policy of denying the existence of the Kurds has been described. In March 1991 Özal had set a precedent by holding talks with Kurdish leaders from northern Iraq. Özal had encouraged an open discussion of the Kurdish issue in Turkey. In April 1992 he had even suggested that the allowing of radio and television broadcasting in Kurdish and the teaching of Kurdish as a second language at school could help the government to deal with the question more effectively.

The formation of a coalition government in November 1991 between the True Path Party (DYP) and the SHP had initially raised hopes that Özal's plans might actually materialize. The government protocol had promised a series of liberal reforms. Although there was no direct reference to the Kurdish question, the protocol mentioned that in Turkey there were different ethnic groups which should be able to express and develop their cultural identities. It was argued that this would actually strengthen not weaken the unity of the state.[71]

The protocol was in part the outcome of an alliance that the SHP had formed with the HEP prior to the October 1991 elections. This alliance had boosted the SHP's electoral performance and had also opened the way for 22 Kurdish deputies with more radical views to be elected to Parliament. There had always been deputies of Kurdish origin in Parliament.[72] However, this was the first occasion on which a group had entered Parliament with a definite Kurdish agenda. Although the protocol was the product of political compromise, it was thought to have been worded in a manner that could possibly have resulted in legislation allowing broadcasting and education in Kurdish. However, almost immediately problems arose.

During the Parliamentary oath-taking ceremony on 6 November 1991, some of the newly-elected radical Kurdish deputies refused to repeat parts of the oath which committed deputies to preserve 'the indivisible integrity of the country and the Nation'. This created considerable commotion. Gençkaya noted that: 'This accelerated the tension between hardliners from both sides from the very outset, decreasing the possibility of dialogue'.[73]

In March 1992 14 of the HEP deputies that had entered Parliament on a SHP ticket resigned and rejoined their party. The split came shortly after the SHP went along with its coalition partner the DYP and renewed an extension of the emergency rule in the Kurdish-populated provinces of eastern and south-eastern Turkey. The SHP election programme had promised to end emergency rule and the village-guard system. A few days after the authorization was granted to extend emergency rule for another four months, *Newroz* celebrations (tradititional festivities to welcome spring) in Kurdish-populated areas were violently repressed by the security forces. These events led to the resignation of the 14 HEP deputies from the SHP. According to Robins, this was the end of the 'emerging relationship between moderate Kurdish nationalism and liberal Turkish thinking'.[74]

Polarization within Parliament culminated in the closure of the HEP in July 1993. Before this happened some members of the HEP formed the Freedom and Democracy Party (ÖZDEP). However, ÖZDEP was promptly shut down by the Constitutional Court. Similarly, the DEP, the successor to the HEP, was closed in June 1994. Anticipating the closure of the DEP, HADEP in effect another Kurdish political party, was formed in May 1994 and participated in the December 1995 national elections. Before the closure of the DEP the immunities of 13 of its Parliamentarians were lifted in March 1994 and a prosecution process started which led in December 1994 to the sentencing and imprisonment of seven DEP and one independent deputy. Four of these would be released following later court rulings. Then, in October 1995, the High Appeals Court confirmed the sentences of four of the deputies and called for the retrial of those who had been released.[75] Six other DEP deputies who had fled abroad played a leading role in the setting up of a 'Kurdish parliament-in-exile' in the Netherlands on 12 April 1995. One exiled DEP official Yaşar Kaya became the chairman of the parliament while the former deputy chairman of the DEP Remzi Kartal became the head of its executive council. The executive council committed itself to realize the Kurds' 'right to self-determination'.[76]

Under pressure from hardliners within his party, it seems that the then Prime Minister Demirel lost interest in finding a political solution to the Kurdish question. Instead he became absorbed in constitutional battles with President Özal concerning the sharing of executive powers. Demirel also appeared to give greater attention to foreign policy issues in the Balkans, Transcaucasus and Central Asia. The National Security Council (NSC), an influential body set up in 1960 to advise the government on defence and security issues and composed of the President, the Prime Minister, some members of the Cabinet, the Chief of the General Staff and the serving force commanders, acquired a growing say on the Kurdish question.[77]

At the time there was a marked increase in violence as the PKK began to mount more raids into Turkey from northern Iraq. The NSC saw the situation in south-eastern Turkey as a product of separatist terrorism which required a military rather than a political solution. President Özal's death in April 1993 led to a general deterioration of the situation. Özal had to some extent been able to balance the influence of the military in the NSC. The late President had been held in high esteem by the Kurds in Turkey and in northern Iraq. It was believed that Özal had helped to engineer the PKK's unilateral declaration of a ceasefire in March 1993. He had apparently been pursuing a political solution.[78] After his death officials were unsure how to deal with the ceasefire.

Demirel worked to be elected President. The main coalition partner, the DYP, was thus absorbed in efforts to find a new party leader and Prime Minister. Military officials exploited this opportunity. The military looked upon the PKK's ceasefire declaration as a sign of weakness and proof of the value of pursuing a military solution. Soon after her election Prime Minister Tansu Çiller briefly considered the possibility of allowing education and broadcasting in Kurdish. However, these ideas were subsequently dropped when she encountered opposition from hardliners in her party and the military. The new President, Demirel, also argued that 'unless terrorism is solved, cultural issues cannot be debated'.[79]

Barkey has noted that Çiller's election as Prime Minister 'strengthened the position of hardliners in Ankara. Her inexperience in security and foreign policy matters, the expectation that her primary focus ought to be the economy and the possibility of a serious challenge to her leadership of the party during its annual convention ... deterred her ... from challenging Demirel and the military on Kurdish issues'.[80] As indicated earlier, early in October 1993 Çiller fleetingly toyed with the idea of a Basque model, but quickly denied having entertained the idea when she faced strong criticism from her party as well as the military.

Through 1994 Çiller continued to oscillate. In preparation for the local elections in March 1994 she embarked on a policy to get 'the PKK out of the Parliament'. This culminated in the lifting of the immunities of the DEP deputies. This populistic approach did help Çiller's party to receive the most votes in the local election. The Welfare Party (RP) considerably increased its votes in Kurdish-populated parts through a campaign that stressed Islamic brotherhood and promised a more 'just' world. Alarmed at the success of the RP, Çiller once more referred to the possibility of allowing private education and broadcasting in Kurdish in order to win more votes in south-eastern Turkey.[81] Again, the Prime Minister encountered opposition from the President who a few months earlier had declared that instruction in Kurdish was not possible. Demirel had alleged that if Kurdish-language instruction were permitted there would then be demands for schooling in other languages too. This, the President argued, would undermine the unity of the country.[82] For Demirel any concessions would be considered as a concession to terrorism and were unacceptable.[83] All the promises the DYP had made to the junior coalition partner, the SHP, about the implementation of a democratization package agreed upon in July 1993 were placed on hold until the PKK had been crushed.

The SHP was badly weakened by the DEP crisis and performed poorly in the March 1994 local elections. SHP members of the Cabinet and Parliamentary deputies have frequently called for the introduction of some form of education in Kurdish that would not undermine the official status of Turkish as the country's official language. They have also advocated radio and television broadcasting in Kurdish. But the DYP refused to take up a 'democracy package' that the SHP had prepared in May 1994 which had included these provisions.[84] In December 1994, Murat Karayalçın of the SHP, the then Deputy Prime Minister, even advocated the need to 'discuss and debate the idea of a federation for the South-East' and argued that 'Özal's approach was right'.[85]

After the merger between the SHP and the CHP on 18 February 1995 a new government protocol was negotiated between Tansu Çiller and Hikmet Çetin, then leader of the enlarged CHP. This stressed the need to amend the infamous Article 8 of the Anti-terror Law. The protocol also called for several constitutional amendments but did not refer direct to the Kurdish question. Instead, in an uneasy understanding, it was agreed that democratization would help to improve the situation in eastern and south-eastern Turkey.

In July 1995 the government succeeded in getting through Parliament for the first time a package of amendments to the 1980 Constitution. Most significantly, the amendments have made it more difficult to lift the immunities of Parliamentary deputies and have possibly opened the way to a more open civil society by facilitating the formation of associations and political parties.[86] As previously noted, in October 1995 Parliament amended the notorious Article 8 of the Anti-terror Law. It appears that an attempt was made to provide a tighter definition of 'separatist' propaganda. This was particularly important because anybody calling for a political solution to the Kurdish issue had run the risk of punishment. The amendments were also made to apply retroactively, allowing the courts to free some of the previous offenders. Though many critics found the amendments somewhat cosmetic it did appear that they opened the way to a relatively freer discussion of the Kurdish question.

National elections were held in December 1995. There was little discussion of substantive issues such as the Kurdish question during the election campaign which centred mostly around criticisms of particular personalities. The elections failed to produce a clear winner. Instead the votes were divided between the RP, the Islamic party, and the two conservative parties, the DYP and ANAP. The two social democrat parties, the CHP and the Democratic Left Party (DSP) trailed behind. HADEP and the right-wing Nationalist Action Party (MHP) failed to win any seats because their votes did not exceed the national threshold of ten per cent.

After more than two months of political bargaining an ANAP–DYP coalition government was formed in March 1996 headed by the ANAP leader Mesut Yılmaz. The government programme did not make any direct references to the Kurdish issue but promised to phase out emergency rule gradually in south-eastern Turkey and mobilize funds to rebuild and develop the economy of the area.[87]

The Role of Political Parties in Turkey and the Kurdish Question

Some political parties in Turkey believe that there is no Kurdish question but, instead, refer to a problem of terrorism. There are radical Kurdish political parties which are illegal in the country which advocate ideas ranging from cultural autonomy to the establishment of an independent Kurdish state.

Other parties refer both to the Kurdish question and a terrorism problem and believe that the two are related. These parties are prepared to accept new arrangements that could allow the Kurds to express their identity provided that this would not jeopardize the unity and integrity of the Turkish state. However, political parties are not monolithic entities. Groups of deputies and individuals within a party may hold different views.

The MHP and the DSP, and also the DYP, which in early 1996 seemed to be dominated by hardliners, have been referring solely to a terrorism problem in Turkey. The most uncompromising position has been held by the MHP and their leader Alparslan Türkeş. The MHP leader has often argued that the problem in south-eastern Turkey stems from the support that foreign governments are giving to terrorism. Türkeş has been critical of those who talk about recognizing a Kurdish reality and who advocate the need to search for political solutions. According to him, these were either ploys to divide Turkey or ideas that would precipitate a process leading to the disintegration of the country.[88]

An ardent Turkish nationalist, according to Türkeş the Kurds were 'overwhelmingly of Turkish descent'.[89] Türkeş has been lobbying for the formation of an organization dedicated to fighting the PKK. This organization would employ 100,000 people including within its ranks experts in sociology, psychology, economics and intelligence.[90] Even though Türkeş has vehemently opposed education and broadcasting in Kurdish, the MHP is quite popular among Kurdish tribes that have supported the village-guard system. In September 1994 seven tribes joined the MHP and the leader of the Alan tribe Hamo Meral proudly stated in Kurdish that 'we are pure Oğuz Turks'.[91] The MHP entered the 1991 national elections together with the RP in an electoral pact. Hence there are no separate statistics for the number of votes the MHP received. The MHP received around five per cent of the votes in the Kurdish-populated areas in the 1994 local and the 1995 national elections (Table 5.9). In the 1995 elections the party performed well in small towns along the Mediterranean and the Aegean coast but failed to exceed the ten per cent national threshold in order to gain Parliamentary representation. Before the 1995 national elections the party had 17 seats.

The DSP led by Bülent Ecevit has continued to adhere to the traditional nationalist and centralist policies of the pre-1980 CHP – the party Ecevit had led for many years. According to Ecevit, the problem in south-eastern Turkey was a socio-economic and not an ethnic one. To him, terrorism was a product of unemployment and external interference by Western powers which were aiming to set up a separate Kurdish state. He has called for land reforms to end feudalism in the region and pressed for the development of industry to alleviate unemployment. Ecevit was opposed to the village-guard system. He was also against separate education in Kurdish and has criticized those who advocate any form of autonomy.[92] The DSP's traditional support of

TABLE 5.9

AVERAGE PARTICIPATION RATES AND DISTRIBUTION OF
VOTES BY POLITICAL PARTIES FOR RECENT ELECTIONS
FOR COUNTRY AND PROVINCES WHERE MORE THAN
15% OF THE POPULATION DECLARED THEIR MOTHER
TONGUE AS KURDISH DURING THE
1965 NATIONAL CENSUS[93]

| Parties | Election: Average Participation (%) | | | | | |
| | 1991 National | | 1994 Local | | 1995 National | |
	Turkey %	17 Provinces %	Turkey %	18 Provinces %	Turkey %	18 Provinces %
ANAP	24.0	22.5	21.0	19.0	19.7	16.3
CHP	–	–	4.6	2.8	10.7	5.7
DSP	10.8	2.8	8.8	0.9	14.6	3.2
DYP	27.0	20.8	21.4	22.1	19.2	16.2
HADEP	–	–	–	–	4.2	19.5
MHP	–	–	8.0	5.3	8.2	5.8
RP	16.9	16.6	19.1	27.3	21.4	27.2
SHP	20.8	33.7	13.6	14.2	–	–
Others	0.4	0.6	3.2	6.0	1.6	2.6
Independent	0.1	1.5	0.3	2.5	0.5	3.4
Participation	83.9	80.2	92.2	87.1	85.2	79.9

secularism, inherited from the old CHP, has also led Ecevit to become the most vocal critic of the RP's policies which advocated religious brotherhood between Kurds and Turks. He has accused the RP of being even more divisive than the PKK.[94]

In contrast to the electoral success of the old CHP in eastern and south-eastern Turkey in the 1970s, the DSP performed very poorly in those parts of the country in the national and local elections held in 1991, 1994 and 1995 (Table 5.9). However, after the 1995 national elections the DSP emerged as the fourth party ahead of the CHP with 76 seats. Before the elections the DSP had only ten Parliamentary deputies. After the formation of the ANAP–DYP coalition government in March 1996 the DSP was set to play an influential role as a power broker. The new government did not command a majority of seats in the Parliament and was dependent on Ecevit's support to secure a vote of confidence in the new coalition.

With regard to the DYP, except for a brief period after the 1991 national elections, the views of hardliners in the party such as Coşkun Kırca, İsmail Köse, Yaşar Topçu and Baki Tuğ have tended to dominate. Çiller was forced to retreat from her relatively more liberal views on the Kurdish question. The veteran party member Abdülmelik Fırat, the grandson of Shaikh Said, has also clashed with the hardliners and with President Demirel.

After having worked with Demirel for 37 years, Fırat resigned from the DYP in February 1994 over his differences with the hardliners and Demirel on the Kurdish question.[95] In September 1994 Fırat led 33 deputies from several parties and signed a document calling on the need to discuss the Kurdish question in Parliament. The document declared that the problem could be resolved without threatening the unity and integrity of Turkey. Subsequently he was harassed by the police and prevented from travelling abroad. He entered the 1995 national elections as a candidate of HADEP and failed to be re-elected when HADEP could not meet the ten per cent threshold. Early in 1996 he was detained and held under custody while the authorities brought a case against him under the Anti-terror Law. Owing to his poor health and considerable public pressure in March 1996 he was released from detention pending his trial.

The DYP has continued to harbour many prominent Kurdish deputies under its roof, and as the successor of the AP which was active in the 1960s and 1970s, it enjoys considerable influence especially among conservative Kurds. Hence the hardening of the DYP's position on the Kurdish question and its preference for a military approach did not seem to have cost the DYP votes in the 1994 local elections. However, in the 1995 national elections the DYP vote in Kurdish-populated provinces fell to just over 16 per cent. This was in part due to the decision of the party leadership to replace some of the traditional Kurdish candidates with individuals from outside the Kurdish-populated provinces who were not of Kurdish origin. The general deterioration in the economic performance of the country and the inability of the party, as the senior coalition partner in government, to address effectively the problem of migration resulting from the forced evacuation of villages were other important factors which accounted for the party's poor performance.

Originally founded by Turgut Özal, ANAP has now retreated from Özal's earlier position on the Kurdish question. A growing number of ANAP deputies had become critical of Özal's radical position on the Kurdish issue. In the face of this criticism, Özal had even considered setting up a new party that 'would embrace the Kurds'.[96] Under the leadership of Mesut Yılmaz, ANAP has begun to follow a line somewhat similar to the DYP's. However, Yılmaz has noted that 'the party recognizes the social and cultural dimensions of the Kurdish problem and it is in favor of discussing the issue freely'.[97] His position has tended to fluctuate between one supportive of Kurdish cultural rights and one in line with the official state position. In July 1994, soon after Çiller spoke of the possibility of education and broadcasting in Kurdish, Yılmaz had complained about her ideas to President Demirel.[98] However, when visiting the United States in March 1995 Yılmaz himself supported the teaching of Kurdish as an optional lesson in schools and backed the introduction of private Kurdish television.[99] During the 1995 national election campaign he scarcely referred to the Kurdish issue. He had forcefully opposed a report published in August 1995 by the Turkish Chamber of Commerce and Commodity Exchanges (TOBB). The report was critical of current policies on the Kurdish question and called for liberal reforms. Yılmaz charged that the report read like a document produced by the CIA.[100] Once Prime Minister though of a new coalition government, Yılmaz surprised many in March 1996 by announcing that the Kurdish question required a political and not a military solution. He referred to the need to introduce administrative, social and economic reforms.[101]

There were a number of prominent deputies of Kurdish origin in ANAP, some of whom came from influential tribes. Kamran İnan, deputy for Bitlis, had served on several occasions as a Cabinet Minister. However, he has spoken little in public about his personal views on the Kurdish question. Şerif Bedirhanoğlu, the deputy for Van, was a descendant of the famous Bedirhans who played a central role in the Kurdish nationalist movements of the 1920s. He has favoured cultural rights for the Kurds, including the possibility of education in Kurdish.[102] During Özal's leadership ANAP was very popular among the Kurds. However, as may be seen from its electoral performance in March 1994, it lost some of these votes. In the province of Malatya, the birthplace of Özal, the votes of ANAP went down almost by half from 41.1 per cent in 1991 to 23.1 in 1994 and 23 in 1995. The electoral performance of ANAP in the eastern and the south-eastern provinces of Turkey has steadily declined (Table 5.9).

The SHP and the CHP held almost identical positions on the Kurdish problem before their merger in February 1995 when they took the name of the CHP. Both had opposed a military solution. Deniz Baykal, the leader of the CHP before and then after the merger, had taken pride in the fact that his party was the first to refer to the Kurdish problem in its party pro- gramme.[103] The SHP and the CHP supported cultural rights for Kurds, including broadcasting and schooling in Kurdish. However, they both also emphasized that Turkish would remain the only official language and the public language of instruction throughout the country. Both parties had also opposed emergency rule and the village-guard system for eastern and south- eastern Turkey. In June 1995 some CHP members of the DYP–CHP coalition government caused a crisis by refusing to sign Cabinet recommendations to Parliament to extend emergency rule for another four months.[104] CHP ministers and deputies were outspoken about human rights abuses and about the village evacuation and burning practices of the military.

However, the SHP in the past and the CHP since the merger have failed to change significantly the course of the government on the Kurdish question.

After the HEP deputies split from the original SHP the number of SHP seats in Parliament was reduced to 65 out of 450 – too small a number to make an impact on the legislative process. Nonetheless, the CHP may be credited for keeping the democratization process alive by ensuring that the issue remained on the Parliamentary agenda. In July 1995 it played an active role in getting Parliament to adopt a series of amendments to the Constitution. They also lobbied for the revision of Article 8 of the Anti-terror Law. However, the inability of the SHP to deliver on its 1991 electoral promises and its failure to prevent the closure of the DEP resulted in the SHP becoming the party which lost the highest proportion of the votes in the Kurdish-populated provinces in the period between 1991 and 1994. In the 1995 national elections the performance of the Social Democrats within the enlarged CHP went from bad to worse as the percentage of votes they won in the Kurdish-populated provinces plummeted to just under six per cent. At the national level the CHP barely made it over the threshold with 10.7 per cent of the votes, obtaining only 49 deputies in Parliament (Table 5.9).

The RP has become one of the most outspoken critics of government policies towards the Kurds. According to it, Kurds and Turks are part of the Islamic nation (*ümmet*). RP members believe that appeals to Islamic brother-hood could solve the Kurdish question. In autumn 1993, when the PKK threatened to attack all political parties active in south-eastern Turkey, the RP was the only major party which maintained most of its operations in the region. In July 1994 the RP formed a committee to monitor government practices in south-eastern Turkey.[105] The following month, after touring the area Şevket Kazan, the deputy chairman of the RP, prepared a critical report on government practices there. This included a long list of recommendations for solving the Kurdish question and the terrorism problem.[106]

The RP is in favour of lifting emergency rule, abolishing the village guards and finding a 'just' solution to the Kurdish question. However, the ambiguous 'just' solution slogan is one that the RP has used extensively across the country for a wide range of problems. The RP has been supportive of broadcasting and education in Kurdish. Its appeal to the common bonds of Islam has attracted those who have shied away from politicizing their Arab, Kurdish or Turkish ethnic identities. The use of religion and its organizational skills have made the RP the most popular party in the Kurdish-populated provinces and the RP has steadily increased its votes there. In an electoral pact with the MHP the RP had received only 16.6 per cent of the vote in the region in 1991. In the face of strong competition from HADEP, the 1995 electoral per-formance of the RP in Kurdish-populated areas was particularly impressive (Table 5.9). HADEP's inability to pass the ten per cent national threshold meant that the RP swept most of the seats available in the Kurdish-populated provinces. The RP increased its number of seats in Parliament from 38 to 158 and took 38 of the 84 seats available in the Kurdish-populated provinces.

Before the 1995 national elections there were four small parties in the Turkish Grand National Assembly. The views of the New Democracy Movement (YDH), led by Cem Boyner, on the Kurdish question attracted much attention. The YDH was only officially registered as a political party in December 1994. In July of that year Boyner had spoken of the need to separate the Kurdish question from the problem of terrorism. He argued that, although violence had to be met by violence, the Kurdish question itself required a political solution.[107] He was soon declaring, though, that the approach of the military was making a solution to the Kurdish question much less likely. Boyner became famous for his assertion that there was no Kurdish problem but rather a Turkish problem because Turks for a long time had failed to accept Kurdish ethnicity. According to Boyner, a solution would have been found when the phrase 'Happy is one who can say one is a Turk' is replaced by 'Happy is one who can say I am a citizen of Turkey'.[108] But, as noted earlier, Prime Minister Çiller would refer to the latter wording in a speech in Karabük in January 1995.

Boyner's thoughts on the Kurdish question were considered to be close to those of late President Özal. Boyner himself actually declared that he would try to carry out what Özal had attempted to achieve.[109] Boyner has demanded the recognition of the cultural rights of the Kurds. He has favoured strengthening local authorities and devolving powers to them on issues concerning education, culture and health. In line with the earlier views of Murat Karayalçın, the former leader of the SHP, and Özal, Boyner argued that it should be possible to discuss the notion of a federation as one possible solution. However, Boyner himself believed that Turkey should remain a unitary state.[110] Although he claimed that in eastern Turkey he was winning the political battle while the state was winning the war,[111] the YDH performed poorly in the national elections in 1995, receiving only 0.5 per cent of the total votes and 1 per cent of the votes in the Kurdish-populated provinces.

The HEP was founded in June 1990. As noted earlier, 22 of its members were elected when the HEP formed an electoral alliance with the SHP for the 1991 national elections. The SHP won 26 out of the 34 seats for the eight eastern and south-eastern provinces where the HEP had candidates. However, many of these deputies would quit the SHP and reform the HEP in 1992. After the HEP was closed down in July 1993 these deputies eventually established the DEP which held its first congress in January 1994. However, as described earlier, the DEP was also closed down by the Constitutional Court and seven of its deputies were sentenced to prison terms while six fled the country.

Both the HEP and the DEP stressed that the Kurdish question should be solved by democratic and peaceful means. But the exact nature of the solution was never clearly defined. Both parties gave the impression that the minimum they would settle for would be cultural concessions to Kurdish ethnicity. However, the deputies from both parties also seemed to allude to 'a binational state' as they emphasized a 'Turkish and Kurdish ethnic equality based on law'. Yaşar Kaya, one of the ex-DEP activists in exile in Europe, interpreted this to mean a solution based on what he called the model of the former Czechoslovakia, adding that 'if the parties wanted to divorce later on, they could do that, too, as did the Czechs and Slovaks a few years ago'. Kaya considered this to be the DEP line and also the 'softest approach'.[112] The former Czechoslovakia, of course, had not exactly been a shining example of a so-called 'binational state', bearing in mind the Czech domination of the federation in the Communist era. One can only assume that Kaya probably had more in mind the nature of the eventual peaceful 'velvet divorce' between the Czechs and the Slovaks.

At the oath-taking ceremony at the newly-elected Parliament in November 1991, the HEP deputies had spoken in Kurdish and displayed colours associated with the PKK. During the DEP congress in January 1994 PKK flags were displayed and Turkey was depicted as an occupying and enemy country. The DEP was accused of being, in effect, the extension of the PKK in the Turkish Parliament. The tensions increased when a group of young military cadets were killed by a PKK bomb at a railway station near Istanbul in February 1994. The newly-elected leader of the DEP Hatip Dicle declared that in a war everyone in a uniform was a target.[113] This precipitated a political and legal process that then led to the expulsion of 13 DEP deputies from Parliament and the closure of the DEP.

Although the DEP had called for more democracy and for a peaceful solution to the Kurdish question some of the former DEP deputies were very intolerant of Kurds in other political parties. According to Yaşar Kaya, many prominent deputies of Kurdish origin serving in other parties, such as Hikmet Çetin, Kamran İnan, and Fehmi Işıklar, a former deputy speaker of the Parliament, were traitors who had betrayed the Kurdish cause.[114] Remzi Kartal, one of the ex-DEP deputies in exile, was critical of the attempts of Şeraffetin Elçi, the ex-CHP deputy, to form a moderate Kurdish party. Kartal complained that Elçi was aiming to divide Kurdish political opinion. Kartal's remarks came only days after the the PKK leader Öcalan had made a similar statement.[115]

After the DEP's closure HADEP took up the Kurdish cause in Turkey. In contrast to the DEP, the HADEP leadership has consciously followed a more moderate line on the Kurdish question. HADEP has maintained a distance from the PKK and has avoided any discourse that could be construed as separatist. According to Kemal Parlak, the chairman of HADEP in Istanbul, HADEP advocated a peaceful solution to the Kurdish question and was also a party which was interested in the problems of Turkey as a whole.[116] Thus it was not surprising that HADEP would decide to run in the December 1995 elections in alliance with several small, socialist political parties.

HADEP received more than 20 per cent of the votes in eight of the 18 Kurdish-populated provinces. In Diyarbakır and Hakkari it received 46.3 and 54.2 per cent of the votes, respectively. However, HADEP performed poorly in major western cities with large Kurdish immigrant populations. As a result it failed to get over the national threshold and did not secure representation in Parliament. This generated considerable disappointment within the party and among many commentators in the media who argued that the national threshold had been unfairly high. Fears were also expressed that the exclusion of HADEP from Parliament might lead to its radicalization. However, the party leadership turned down a call by Öcalan to join the pro-PKK 'parliament-in-exile' in Europe. HADEP officials also declared that they would continue their alliance with socialist parties and work for a political solution to the Kurdish question from outside Parliament. In the words of these officials: 'The Kurds have given us full support. Now we must face the people with the kind of programmes and propaganda which could secure the support of the Turks too'.[117]

A large number of Kurdish groups operate outside Turkey. These include the PKK and the Kurdistan Communist Party (KKP) which advocate the use of violence. The Kurdistan Socialist Party (KSP) prefers political means to achieve its aims. The leader of the KSP Kemal Burkay, in exile in Europe, is in favour of a federal solution to the Kurdish question. At the end of its fourth congress in February 1995 the KSP called, *inter alia*, for the replacement of the present Turkish Constitution with one which guaranteed the rights and liberties of the Kurds.[118] The KSP objected to the operations of the Kurdish 'parliament-in-exile' and has declined to participate in it, arguing that the parliament had been formed by the PKK and the DEP without adequate consultations with other Kurdish groups.[119]

As discussed earlier, the PKK aims to set up a united and socialist 'Kurdistan' after a secessionist armed struggle. However, at the fourth congress of the PKK in 1990 a possible federal solution to the Kurdish question was discussed. It was argued that independence for the Kurds did not have to mean the creation of a separate state.[120] This development, and Özal's readiness to talk about a federation as a potential solution, may explain why Öcalan backed a ceasefire in 1993. This was followed early in March 1994 by Öcalan's announcement that the PKK was open to all solutions and that it did not intend to divide up Turkey.[121] He expressed similar views in an interview with the BBC. Öcalan argued that what the PKK wanted was a democratic union within Turkey, as the Kurds alone could not survive economically.[122] In November 1995 Öcalan declared a truce and announced that the idea of a federation 'should not necessarily imply separatism'.[123] Shortly before, in what appeared to be an amazing volte-face, Öcalan had declared: 'I am in love with Turkey. I am not a Kurdish nationalist.'[124] To some, these were possible indications that the PKK was increasingly moving towards a political solution. Others argued that within the PKK there were hardliners who were against any compromise. Turkish officials considered the PKK truce as a political move to gain European goodwill. The PKK could also use the winter respite to reinforce its armed ranks.

It is quite possible that these fluctuations in the PKK's stated policy are no more than pragmatic deviations from a long-term objective to set up a united, socialist, Kurdish state. Öcalan's views on religion appear to have varied too. The PKK's party programme of 1977 which had appealed to Kurdish nationalism and Marxism-Leninism had been highly critical of religion.[125] However, the conservative and traditional nature of many Kurds forced the PKK to moderate its position on religion. The PKK even attempted to manipulate Islam for its political propaganda.[126] The impressive performance of the RP in south-eastern Turkey during the local elections in 1994 also seems to have affected the PKK. A few months after the elections Öcalan argued that the struggle mounted by the PKK was in harmony with the essence of Islam. Öcalan declared that 'what is being repressed in Turkey is the Kurdish identity as well as Islam'. According to Öcalan, the PKK freedom struggle would liberate Islam and the Kurds by weakening the Kemalist hold on Turkey.[127] The PKK's influence will largely depend on the policies that the government adopts towards the Kurdish question as well as on the effectiveness of HADEP.

It is important to note that throughout 1995 the Kurdish question was being debated much more extensively in the Turkish media. A growing number of interest groups were also becoming involved. In August 1995 a report on the Kurdish question prepared by an academic Doğu Ergil was published.[128] This was commissioned by TOBB under the leadership of Yalım Erez, himself an ethnic Kurd. The close relations Erez enjoyed with the government and Prime Minister Çiller led many to argue that the report had been actually requested by the Prime Minister. Erez was later elected as a member of Parliament for the DYP in December 1995 and was then appointed to serve in the ANAP–DYP coalition cabinet.

The TOBB report was based on a field survey of 1267 subjects, most of whom were Kurds. The report took a critical view of government policies and argued that it was not correct to define the Kurdish problem as simply one of terrorism. It was stressed that a large majority of the people surveyed wished to remain within Turkey; but many also called for a new political and administrative structure for the state. However, the report noted that only 4.2 per cent of those surveyed were in favour of holding talks with the PKK. Thus, in the words of the report: 'The solution does not lie with the PKK. An agreement should be reached with the people of the area.'[129] The report triggered a lively debate. The decision of the authorities first to open an investigation into the report and then their decision in December 1995 to drop the case has been interpreted as evidence of a relative liberalization of political life in Turkey following the amendments introduced to the Constitution and to Article 8 of the Anti-terror Law.

Prominent businessmen in Turkey have also started to express their opinions publicly. In November 1995 Sakıp Sabancı announced his report on the problems of eastern Turkey. This came soon after allegations that he had recommended the 'Basque model' as a solution to the Kurdish question. The MHP leader Türkeş had complained that 'he [Sabancı] should mind his own business and not interfere with the business of politicians.'[130] In his report Sabancı underlined that there was a need for the private and public sectors to co-operate to help to develop the economy of the region. However, he added that building factories in the area would not help 'without recognizing the cultural rights of Kurds'.[131] The prominent Jewish businessman and industrialist İshak Alaton and Halis Komili, the chairman of the influential Turkish Industrialists' and Businessmen's Association, in interviews they gave to the media in December 1995 recognized the need to extend cultural rights to the Kurds. Alaton stated: 'I am saying it very openly: there is a Kurdish problem in Turkey. There is a problem of Kurdish identity ... Terrorism is one thing, and finding a solution to Kurdish identity is a totally different thing.'[132]

Two non-governmental organizations, the IHV and the IHD, have been monitoring human rights abuses in eastern and south-eastern Turkey. They publish regular reports with detailed statistics on these. Another non-governmental organization the Turkish branch of the Helsinki Citizens Assembly (HCA) has also become active on the Kurdish problem. It organized a conference in Istanbul in January 1995 where the Kurdish question was extensively discussed. Subsequently, the HCA launched a project in which representatives from several cities and towns were to participate. This was intended to be an exercise in bridge-building between the Turks and the Kurds by encouraging civic participation.

Two large conferences were held in Istanbul in February 1996 where participants from several non-governmental organizations, together with politicians and intellectuals, debated the Kurdish problem. One of these conferences entitled 'The Kurdish Problem and Democratic Solution Symposium' was organized by the Kurdish Institute. This had been set up in 1992 but had for long remained inactive owing to state harassment. The other meeting, announced as a 'Gathering for Peace' conference, called upon the government to accept the PKK's offer of a unilateral ceasefire and to open discussions to end the conflict.[133] The increasing interest of non-governmental organizations, businessmen and academics in the Kurdish question may well open new avenues in the search for a political solution.

As described earlier, several political parties in Turkey have also recently taken up what is in effect the issue of 'minority rights', with particular reference to the case of the Kurds. Among all of the legally-operating parties in Turkey there is a definite consensus that the territorial integrity and sovereignty of the state should not come into question. The granting of what would amount to 'minority rights' in matters such as education and broadcasting would have to be realized in a manner which would not be perceived as threatening to the unity of the Turkish Republic. Only limited forms of self-determination short of territorial self-determination could, in practice, be accepted by a future government.

It is generally accepted that the PKK is far from representing the views of the majority of the Kurds in Turkey. The number of PKK supporters has not been more than a few hundred thousand.[134] Many Kurds throughout Turkey appear to favour a solution that would allow them to express their identity within Turkey rather than outside the country. This has been reflected in Kurdish participation in national and local elections, in the work of Parliament and in the government, as well as in political parties. The fact that participation rates in elections in Kurdish-populated areas have rarely fallen below the average for the rest of Turkey suggest that the Kurds largely remain integrated in national political life.

The Kurds in Turkey are represented in political parties and organizations which range from ones promoting Turkish nationalism to other illegal ones which advocate a separate Kurdish state. The Kurdish question is clearly a complex one. The Kurds in the country hold a wide diversity of views. However, the establishment of 'Kurdish' political parties – i.e., political parties based solely on ethnicity – is not permitted. The problems associated with the right of freedom of association with reference to minority groups will be discussed later. The Kurds, though, are not excluded from participation in the political system in Turkey. But, in spite of developments in 1995 and early 1996 in particular which have created an environment somewhat more conducive to open discussion, not all opinions and ideas with regard to the Kurdish question can be openly and freely discussed. The continuation of this state of affairs would only benefit the hardliners, both Turkish and Kurdish. However, an increasingly more active and aware civil society in Turkey might well encourage moderate Kurdish groups to prevail and in this way break the dominance that both the hardline Turkish and Kurdish nationalists have enjoyed.

Notes

1. P. Andrews (ed.), *Ethnic Groups in the Republic of Turkey* (Wiesbaden: Reichert, 1989).
2. These figures were cited during a television debate in the programme, *Siyaset Meydanı*, on ATV, 24 Dec. 1994.
3. M. Van Bruinessen, *Agha, Shaikh and State* (London: Zed, 1992) pp.14–15.
4. M. Izady, *The Kurds: a Concise Handbook* (Washington DC: Taylor & Francis, 1992) p.119.

5. S. Mutlu, 'The Population of Turkey by Ethnic Groups and Provinces', *New Perspectives on Turkey*, 12, (Spring 1995) p.45.
6. A. E. Özsoy, I. Koç and A. Toros, 'Türkiye'nin Etnik Yapısının Ana Dil Sorularına Göre Analizi' *Nüfusbilim Dergisi/Turkish Journal of Population Studies*, 14, (1992) pp.112–13.
7. S. Mutlu, op. cit., p.35.
8. M. Van Bruinessen, op. cit., p.22.
9. R. Ballı, *Kürt Dosyası* (Istanbul: Cem Yayınevi, 1992) p.235.
10. *İller İtibariyle Çeşitli Göstergeler* (Ankara: Devlet Planlama Teşkilatı, 1993) p.1. The figures cited in million TL are fixed at 1993 prices.
11. For a detailed technical study of the project see J. Kolars and W. Mitchell, *The Euphrates and the Southeast Anatolian Development Project* (Carbondale: Southern Illinois Press, 1991). For an analysis of the future economic potentials of this project see K. İnan, 'The South-East Anatolia Project "A Perspective for Future Investors"' *Turkish Review Quarterly Digest*, Spring 1989.
12. *Milliyet*, 31 Oct. 1994. For a similar report see also *Evrensel Ekonomi*, 8 June 1995.
13. *Cumhuriyet*, 14 May 1994.
14. P. Robins, 'The Overlord State: Turkish Policy and the Kurdish Issue', *International Affairs*, 69, 4, (Oct. 1993) p.663.
15. Noted by *Milliyet*, 23 Dec. 1994. According to one report, in the mid-1990s the GNP per capita for south-eastern Turkey was $500 compared with a national average of $2000. See C. Chesnot, *Le Monde Diplomatique*, Oct. 1994.
16. A. Aygan, 'PKK Yapısı ve İşleyişi' *Yeni Forum*, 190, (1 Aug. 1987) p.22; I. İmset, *The PKK: A Report on Separatist Violence in Turkey* (Ankara: Turkish Daily News Publication, 1, 1992) p.16. For an account of the use of violence by the PKK from the perspective of the PKK see A. Öcalan, *Kurdistan Halk Savaşı ve Gerilla*, (Köln: Wesanen Serxwebun Publications, 1991).
17. US Department of State, *Patterns of Global Terrorism, 1993*, (Washington DC: 1994) p.9; and *Patterns of Global Terrorism, 1994* (Washington DC, 1995) p.8.
18. I. İmset, *PKK, Ayrılıkçı Şiddetin 20 Yılı (1973–1993)* (Ankara: Turkish Daily News Yayınları, 1993) pp.125–31.
19. *Turkish Daily News (TDN)*, 6 Oct. 1993. On 24 May 1993 the PKK broke the ceasefire it had declared in March by stopping a bus near Bingöl and killing 35 conscripts who had just been discharged from the army.
20. For the details of this rule, which banned the sale of Turkish newspapers, forbade the operation of Turkish political parties and courts, and prevented the collection of taxes, etc., see ibid., 27 Oct. 1993 and *Nokta*, 24–30 Oct. 1993.
21. These journalists were Mehmet Ali Birand, Hasan Cemal, Cengiz Çandar, Salih Memecan and Ramazan Öztürk, all with a reputation for objective reporting. For their account see *Sabah* 13 May 1994.
22. *TDN*, 8 Jan. 1996.
23. Türkiye İnsan Haklarıları Vakfı, *Olağanüstü Hal Bölgesi'inde Eğitim Raporu* (Ankara: 1994).
24. *Yeni Yüzyıl*, 20 Dec. 1994; and *Milliyet* 3 Jan. 1995.
25. I. İmset (note 16) p.82.
26. *Özgür Ülke*, 13 Sep. 1994.
27. US Department of State, *Country Reports on Human Rights Practices for 1991* (Washington DC: 1992) p.1247. Law 2935 on the State of Emergency was adopted on 25 Oct. 1983, *T.C. Resmi Gazete*, 27 Oct. 1983, No. 18204.

28. P. Robins, op. cit., p.664.
29. *TDN*, 26 Dec. 1994.
30. *Yeni Yüzyıl*, 25 Nov. 1995
31. Supplement on 'Human Rights and Justice' in *TDN*, 6 Jan. 1996.
32. Ibid., 3 March 1995; 6 Jan. 1996.
33. *Yeni Yüzyıl*, 19 April 1995 and *TDN*, 18 April 1995. The report was not actually officially released as some of the members of the Commission refused to sign the report unless certain sections of the report were reworded in a manner less critical of the security authorities. See *Yeni Yüzyıl*, 17 April 1995.
34. İ. Imset (note 16) p.105.
35. *Cumhuriyet*, 12 May 1994.
36. *Özgür Ülke*, 1 Aug. 1994.
37. International Institute for Strategic Studies, *The Military Balance 1994–1995* (London: IISS, 1995) p.36.
38. *Yeni Yüzyıl*, 23 Dec. 1994.
39. *TDN*, 10 Oct. 1995.
40. *Yeni Yüzyıl*, 23 Dec. 1994. The PKK put the number of its fighters at 30,000 while local people put their numbers at 15,000. According to a US report, the PKK forces numbered between 5,000–6,000. See *Patterns of Global Terrorism, 1994*, op. cit., p.47.
41. *Yeni Yüzyıl*, 24 July 1995. In autumn 1995 the governor for the Emergency Rule Region put the number of the PKK fighters at 6,000 including those in northern Iraq. See *TDN*, 10 Oct. 1995.
42. *TDN*, 14 Dec. 1994.
43. *Hürriyet*, 28 Oct. 1994.
44. *Cumhuriyet*, 12 Oct. 1994.
45. This figure was cited by President Demirel during an interview with *TDN*, 2 Oct. 1995.
46. I. İmset, 'Fighting Separatist Terrorism', *Turkish Probe*, 4 Nov. 1993, p.6.
47. Interview by the authors with the *muhtar* of a village in the province of Hakkari, June 1995.
48. For a brief summary of the report see *Cumhuriyet*, 11 Oct. 1994.
49. *Economist*, 17 Dec. 1994.
50. Quoted in I. İmset (note 16) p.78.
51. *Özgür Ülke*, 1 Jan. 1995.
52. For the thesis that the security expenditures fuel domestic borrowing and hence inflation see R. Kayalı, 'İç Borçların Sorumlusu: Güneydoğu' *Yeni Yüzyıl*, 29 Dec. 1994.
53. *TDN*, 3 May 1995.
54. *Sabah*, 19 Aug. 1994.
55. *TDN*, 8 Jan. 1996.
56. H.J. Barkey, 'Turkey's Kurdish Dilemma', *Survival*, 35, 4, (Winter 1993–94) p.58.
57. Ö.F. Gençkaya, 'The Kurdish Issue in Turkish Politics' in J. Calleja, H. Wiberg and S. Busuttil (eds.), *The Search for Peace in the Mediterranean Region* (Malta: Mireva Publications, 1994) p.211.
58. F. Shorter, 'The Crisis of Population Knowledge in Turkey' *New Perspectives on Turkey*, 12, (Spring 1995) p.18.
59. S. Ayata, *GAP Bölgesi Nüfus Hareketleri Araştırması*, (Ankara: T.C. Başbakanlık GAP Bölge Kalkınma İdaresi Başkanlığı, 1994).
60. This section is mostly based on interviews held with officials as well as local people

and press reports. Also see S. Ayata, op. cit. and A. Özer, 'Güneydoğu Anadolu Bölgesinde Göç: Sorunlar ve Çözümler', paper presented at the conference, *Düşünce Özgürlüğü ve Göç Sempozyumu*, 10–12 Dec. 1994, Ankara.

61. For Turkey as a country of asylum for Kurds see K. Kirişci, 'Refugee Movements and Turkey', *International Migration*, 29, 4, (Dec. 1991) pp.545–59.

62. This figure was cited by President Demirel during an interview. See *TDN*, 2 Oct. 1995.

63. A. Özer, 'Güneydoğu'da göç ve yarattiği sorunlar',*Yeni Yüzyıl*, 13 March 1995.

64. *Courrier International*, 121, 26 Jan.–1 Feb. 1995. A leading Kurdish politician, Murat Bozlak, has put the figure at 3.5 million. See *Yeni Yüzyıl*, 17 Dec. 1995.

65. S. Mutlu, op. cit., p.50.

66. M. Izady, op. cit. p. 119.

67. R. Ballı, op. cit., pp.230–7.

68. For a summary of the report see *Yeni Yüzyıl*, 12 June 1995.

69. Ibid., 21 March 1995.

70. N.B. Criss, 'The Nature of PKK Terrorism in Turkey', *Studies in Conflict and Terrorism*, 18, (1995) p.29; and Y. Alexander, 'Narco-Terrorism: Future Threats', *Intersec*, 10, 11/12, (Nov.–Dec. 1995) pp.430–1.

71. *Doğruyol Partisi ile Sosyaldemokrat Halkçı Parti Arasında İmzalanan Ortak Hükümet Protokolü ve Ekleri*, 19 Nov. 1991, pp.15, 55.

72. As information on the ethnic origins of the deputies in the Turkish Grand National Assembly is not publicly available scholars have made use of the listed places of birth of these deputies. For this information with regard to the first ten Turkish Grand National Assemblies see, F.W. Frey, *The Turkish Political Elite* (Cambridge MA: MIT Press, 1965). Gençkaya Ö.F., in J. Calleja *et al.* (eds.), op. cit., p.197, calculated that 23, 24 and 23 per cent of the 450 deputies in the 17th, 18th and 19th Grand National Assemblies were born in the mostly Kurdish-populated areas of Turkey. For 1995, the number of Kurdish deputies in the Parliament was between 100–125 according to J. Brown, 'The Turkish Imbroglio: Its Kurds' *ANNALS, AAPSS*, 541, (Sep. 1995), p.117.

73. Ö.F. Gençkaya in J. Calleja *et al.* (eds.), op. cit., p.196.

74. P. Robins, op. cit., p.667.

75. *Yeni Yüzyıl*, 27 Oct. 1995.

76. *TDN*, 19 April 1995.

77. For an analysis of the formation and the role of the NSC in Turkish politics in the 1980s and 1990s see W. Hale, *Turkish Politics and the Military* (London: Routledge, 1994) pp.138, 290–1.

78. *Turkish Probe*, 31 Aug. 1993.

79. *TDN*, 15 July 1993.

80. H.J. Barkey, op. cit., p.57.

81. *Cumhuriyet*, 7 July 1994.

82. Ibid., 3 April 1994.

83. *Hürriyet*, 9 July 1994.

84. *Sabah*, 16 May 1994.

85. *Milliyet*, 6 Dec. 1994.

86. *TDN*, 26 July 1995.

87. *Yeni Yüzyıl*, 7 March 1996.

88. *Sabah*, 2 Aug. 1994; and *Milliyet*, 26 Dec. 1994.

89. *Yeni Yüzyıl*, 26 Dec. 1995.

90. *Cumhuriyet*, 1 July 1994; and *Sabah*, 1 Jan. 1995.
91. Quoted in *Hürriyet*, 24 Sep. 1994. For a report on the Kurdish supporters of the MHP see *Aktüel*, 12–18 Oct. 1995. Oğuz Turks are considered to be one of the first Turkish tribes to arrive in Anatolia from Central Asia.
92. He articulated these views in a very forceful manner during a debate on the Turkish television channel *TRT-1*, 9 June 1994.
93. The list of provinces is from *1965 Genel Nüfus Sayımı* (Ankara: Devlet İstatistik Enstitüsü [DIE, 1969]). The original list on the basis of the 1965 census has 15 provinces out of a total of 67 with a population where more than 15 per cent used Kurdish as their mother tongue. The government increased the number of provinces in Turkey to 71 in 1989, 73 in 1990, 76 in 1992 and 79 in 1995. Those new provinces that incorporated parts of provinces in the original list of 15 with a Kurdish mother tongue population of more than 15 per cent were added to the list for 1991, 1994 and 1995. Hence the list for 1991 has 17 provinces, with Batman and Şırnak added, and for 1994 and 1995 18 provinces, with the inclusion of Iğdır.
94. *Cumhuriyet*, 27 June 1994.
95. See interview with Abdülmelik Fırat in *TDN*, 4 Nov. 1994.
96. *Hürriyet*, 27 Sep. 1992.
97. *Cumhuriyet*, 20 Aug. 1994.
98. Ibid., 13 July 1994.
99. *TDN*, 22 March 1995.
100. *Yeni Yüzyıl*, 7 Aug. 1995.
101. Ibid., 15 March 1996.
102. *Özgür Ülke*, 14 March 1994.
103. *Cumhuriyet*, 24 March 1994.
104. *Yeni Yüzyıl*, 20 June 1995.
105. *Özgür Ülke*, 24 July 1994.
106. *TDN*, 25 Aug. 1994.
107. *Sabah*, 7 July 1994.
108. Ibid., 30 Aug. 1994; and *Cumhuriyet*, 27 Nov. 1994.
109. *Cumhuriyet*, 20 Sep. 1994.
110. *Yeni Yüzyıl*, 25 Dec. 1994.
111. Ibid., 27 April 1995.
112. *TDN*, 14 April 1995.
113. *Sabah*, 17 Feb. 1994.
114. Interview with Yaşar Kaya published in *TDN*, 4 April 1995.
115. *Özgur Ülke*, 2 and 5 May 1994.
116. *TDN*, 20 Dec. 1995.
117. Ibid., 28 Dec. 1995.
118. Ibid., 11 March 1995.
119. Ibid., 17 April 1995.
120. I. İmset (note 18) p.231.
121. *Özgür Ülke*, 14 March 1995.
122. *Milliyet*, 29 Sep. 1994.
123. *TDN*, 21 Nov. 1995.
124. Ibid., 13 Oct. 1995.
125. *PKK, Kürdistan Devriminin Yolu, Program*, (Köln: Serxwebun Yayınları, 1983) p.201.
126. I. İmset (note 18) p.137.
127. *Özgür Ülke*, 13 July 1994.

128. Türkiye Odalar ve Borsalar Birliği (TOBB), *Doğu Sorunu: Teşhisler ve Tespitler*, (Ankara: TOBB, 1995).
129. Ibid., p.25.
130. *Yeni Yüzyıl*, 6 Oct. 1995.
131. Ibid., 21 Nov. 1995.
132. Ibid., 12 Dec. 1995.
133. *TDN*, 9 Feb. 1996.
134. The highest figure quoted in the media so far was actually by the Turkish military during the height of the PKK's popularity in 1993. At the time the Chief of Staff Second Commander, General Ahmet Çörekçi, had put the number of PKK sympathizers at 375,000. See ibid., 12 Oct. 1993.

6

The International Dimension of the Kurdish Question

DEVELOPMENTS beyond Turkey have had a significant impact on the Kurdish question in the country. The trans-state nature of the Kurdish question must be taken into account. The massive exodus of refugees from northern Iraq in 1991 at the end of the Gulf War forced the world to focus its attention on the Kurds. This mass movement compelled Turkish decision-makers to deal with the Kurds in northern Iraq. Officials in Ankara had previously been ignoring these people. The Kurdish question has complicated Turkey's relations with Iraq, Iran and Syria. The collapse of the Soviet Union and the end of the Cold War signalled the beginning of a new era in international politics. In stark contrast with the past Western governments began to take a growing interest in Turkey's human rights performance at a time when violence between the Turkish security forces and the PKK escalated.

The Launching of Operation PROVIDE COMFORT

The defeat of the Iraqi military by the UN coalition forces encouraged the Shia Moslems in southern Iraq and the Kurds in northern Iraq to rebel. The Kurdish nationalist uprising seemed to be successful until the Iraqi military turned against the Kurds after having crushed the Shiite revolt. By the end of March 1991 the Kurdish rebellion was about to collapse. The Kurds had mistakenly believed that the United States would enforce a no-fly zone over northern Iraq which would cover Iraqi helicopters and gunships as well as fixed-wing aircraft. The collapse of the Kurdish uprising was sudden and complete. Thousands of northern Iraqi Kurds were forced to flee from their homes ahead of the advancing Iraqi army. Military and civilian reports from the border began to pour in about Iraqi shelling. A flood of refugees retreated up the mountains along the Iraqi–Turkish border. In these circumstances the Turkish NSC convened an emergency meeting on 2 April.

The NSC decided to keep the border closed until the Security Council passed judgement. A letter was immediately sent to the Council calling for a meeting and noting that 'the Iraqi Government forces are deliberately pressing these people [refugees] towards the Turkish border in order to drive them out of their country. These actions violate all norms of behaviour towards civilian populations and constitute an excessive use of force and a threat to the region's peace and security.'[1]

Those attending the NSC meeting acknowledged that most of these refugees were the kin of Kurds in Turkey, and that it was essential to come to their help for political if not humanitarian reasons. The then opposition leader Demirel and several Kurdish deputies called for the opening of the Turkish–Iraqi border.[2] However, there was the fear that allowing the refugees in the mountains to come down might have a snowball effect, attracting even larger numbers. Many Turks were also concerned that the presence of Iraqi Kurdish refugees on Turkish soil would intensify feelings of nationalism and separatism among Kurds in Turkey. The immediate concern, however, was to ensure that the problems caused by an earlier influx of over 50,000 Kurdish refugees in 1988 would not be repeated. On that occasion Western European officials had complained of the way in which the Turkish authorities had provided the refugees with inadequate facilities and had refused to allow more outside assistance and support.[3] In turn, the Turkish government and most of the media had accused the West of employing double standards, demanding from Turkey a treatment they were themselves unwilling to extend to these refugees. Turkish officials were particularly critical of Western Europe's reluctance to accept any refugees for resettlement. They were also angry that the West did not acknowledge that Turkey was channelling a considerable portion of its scarce resources to maintain the refugees. As Minister of State Kamran İnan noted: 'The world did nothing then to help us house and feed the refugees.' Hence, 'at the outset of the 1991 crisis, in April, the Turkish government decided not to repeat what they saw as their mistake in 1988.'[4]

Officials in Ankara were also much concerned that Turkey should not become a buffer zone to hold back refugees from reaching the rest of Europe. Turkey is the only country among the European parties to the 1951 Convention Relating to the Status of Refugees which borders a non-European geographical area and which has experienced large movements of refugees in the recent past. The Turkish authorities are well aware of the potential problems relating to forced migration into Turkey. The efforts of the EU to create a 'fortress Europe' with regard to the admission of refugees have strengthened the Turkish conviction that most European governments wanted to keep refugee problems regionalized.

In the 1991 crisis, the Turkish military penetrated Iraqi territory in an effort to keep the refugees out of Turkey. However, the armed forces also brought humanitarian assistance.[5] The NSC decision to keep the borders closed seemed to be a calculated move aimed at provoking an unprecedented international response to the crisis. The rough outlines of a response began to emerge immediately after the adoption of Security Council Resolution 688.

The Turkish military had been instructed to keep the refugees out at all costs, short of firing at them.[6] However, the military failed to implement the decision as a growing number of refugees poured into Turkey. The area along the Iraqi frontier was 'inhabited by a population that through ethnic and family ties was strongly sympathetic to the plight of the refugees' and this created mounting domestic pressure.[7] The Turkish decision to deny the refugees asylum also sparked international criticism.

The French government responded swiftly to the crisis. The then Foreign Minister Roland Dumas declared that: 'Just as Germany's murder of Europe's Jews brought about the concept of a "crime against humanity", so Mr Hussein's mistreatment of the Kurds argued for recognition of a "duty to intervene" to prevent gross violations of human rights.'[8] It was this attitude that led the French government to call for amendments to the ceasefire resolution which was being negotiated in the Security Council.

The failure of France to secure these amendments and the fact that Security Council Resolution 687 establishing a ceasefire between Iraq and the UN coalition did not make any reference to the refugee crisis developing in northern Iraq forced Turkish diplomats to take matters into their own hands. On the morning of 5 April 1991, Turkish diplomats held a critical meeting with their West European counterparts in Ankara. A draft version of the eventual Security Council Resolution 688 was apparently agreed upon.[9] Later in the day the French submitted this to the Security Council where it was adopted by a majority vote.

From the Turkish government's point of view this resolution was important for two reasons. The situation resulting from the refugee crisis was defined as a threat to international peace and security. This made it likely that a need would eventually arise for Turkey and its allies to establish a safe haven and create a military force to protect it. The resolution also insisted that Iraq should allow immediate access to humanitarian assistance to those in need. This would enable the Turkish government to argue that the refugees should be brought down from the mountains to the Iraqi side of the border to allow relief assistance to be extended to them more easily.

President Özal played a central role in the introduction of the idea of a safe haven. To President Bush he made it clear that Turkey was being overwhelmed, and that he expected to see the United States come to the support of a NATO ally that had proved its loyalty during the Gulf War.[10] Özal knew that to ensure the return of the refugees and extend assistance there was an immediate need to stop Iraqi aggression and create a secure environment. What he seemed to have in mind was the creation of a safe zone along the Iraqi border.

President Bush responded to Özal's calls by ordering military air-drops and by despatching Secretary of State James Baker to Turkey. Baker's visit to the border area on 8 April lasted only seven minutes. What he observed convinced him that something urgent and out of the ordinary had to be done. In the meantime, the idea for a safe zone was taken by the British Prime Minister to an EU meeting in Brussels specially convened to discuss the crisis. Özal's initial idea of a safe zone along the border to provide easier delivery of humanitarian aid was found to be somewhat problematic. Western officials feared that this might create a 'Gaza Strip'-type situation. Major pushed for an 'enclave' (later changed to a 'safe haven') large enough to ensure the return of the refugees to their villages and towns whence they had fled.[11]

President Bush warned Iraq not to fly any aircraft or engage in any military operation above the 36th parallel. When European efforts to create a UN-sanctioned safe haven failed as a result of Soviet, Chinese and Indian objections, Bush announced on 16 April that US troops would enter northern Iraq to create a 'safe area' in the plains around Zakhu.[12] A safe haven in northern Iraq was thus created independently of the UN and in a form considerably different than that envisaged by Özal. In the words of *The Economist,* the Turks had 'decided that the emergence of some sort of a Kurdish enclave in Iraq would be a little less dangerous than the arrival of millions of Kurds inside Turkey itself.'[13]

This led to the despatch of an international force to the region to be involved in an operation which became known as Operation PROVIDE COMFORT. This distributed massive amounts of humanitarian assistance to the refugees and helped to prepare the refugees for repatriation. With the size and complexity of the task, the military wing of Operation PROVIDE COMFORT had expanded by the end of May 1991 to more than 20,000 troops from 11 countries. The operation was also strengthened by an air attachment deployed in Turkey near the Iraqi border to provide military cover for the operation and to deter Iraq from attacking the safe haven. Operation PROVIDE COMFORT, with the accompanying safe haven, provided the security and protection that was needed to ensure voluntary repatriation. Initially, refugees were brought down from the mountains to about 20 camps along the border. 'The first wave of voluntary repatriation to Iraq from Turkey started in the last week of April 1991 ... Within five weeks, 95 per cent of Dohuk's more than 400,000 former residents had returned, as had another 60,000 persons who lived beyond its borders in [Iraqi] government-controlled territory, but who were unwilling to proceed there.'[14]

By early June the last of the border camps was closed and the remaining 13,000 refugees were moved to a special camp in Silopi in Turkey. Subsequently, in July, the military wing of Operation PROVIDE COMFORT was scaled down. Troops were withdrawn from northern Iraq and redeployed in south-eastern Turkey. The purpose of this allied, multinational, rapid-reaction force (briefly referred to as Operation POISED HAMMER before being called Operation PROVIDE COMFORT II) was to deter incursions by the Iraqi army into northern Iraq. In September 1991 the ground troops were removed and the air wing of this multinational rapid-reaction force was redeployed to a NATO base in southern Turkey. In 1992 a small Military Co-ordination Center was opened under the co-command of a US and a Turkish colonel to oversee military developments as well as supervise the work of non-governmental organizations.

Many in Turkey believed that Operation PROVIDE COMFORT was paving the way for the establishment of a Kurdish state. Some argued that the Operation enabled the PKK to mount raids more easily into Turkey. Opposition to and suspicion of the activities of Operation PROVIDE COMFORT led to the Turkish government's decision in October 1995 to limit the future renewal of the operation's mandate to three months. On eight previous occasions the Parliament had renewed the operation's mandate for six-monthly periods. In March 1996 the new ANAP–DYP government was involved in intense negotiations with the United States to revise the command structure and rules of engagement for Operation PROVIDE COMFORT.

The Operation, while alleviating one major security concern for Turkey, triggered the emergence of another. The Iraqi loss of sovereignty above the 36th parallel culminated in the establishment of what one analyst has called Kurdish 'statehood by stealth'.[15] This development would have significant repercussions for Turkish policy-makers with regard to the Kurdish question.

Turkey and the Situation in Northern Iraq

There are some Kurdish tribes which straddle the Turkish and Iraqi borders. Before the Iraqi invasion of Kuwait these groups were able to maintain regular contacts with little difficulty across the frontier. In spite of a number of ethnic affinity links between these Kurdish tribes in south-eastern Turkey and northern Iraq, trans-state ethnic co-operation between the Kurds was not always smooth. With regard to northern Iraq, however, the Kurdish supporters of the Patriotic Union of Kurdistan (PUK) led by Jallal Talabani, and especially the Kurdish followers of the Kurdistan Democratic Party (KDP) led by Massoud Barzani, have more recently clashed with PKK forces which have sought refuge in territories controlled by the northern Iraqi Kurds. But since the death of President Özal, with the deterioration of relations between the PUK and the Turkish government, Talabani's supporters have become more tolerant of PKK activities in Iraq. The PKK has been able to extend its influence in northern Iraq as tensions between the KDP and the PUK have increased since 1994.

Officials in Ankara are mindful of the processes of 'diffusion' and 'contagion' in relation to Kurdish groups in Turkey and in northern Iraq. As regards diffusion, conflict in both Turkey and Iraq involving the Kurds has directly affected policy-making in each. In effect, 'spillover' has worked in both directions. The PKK has found sanctuary in northern Iraq, and northern Iraqi Kurds have sought refuge in Turkey to the alarm of the authorities in Ankara. Turkish officials are also particularly concerned about a possible contagion effect where the activities of the northern Iraqi Kurds may provide inspiration and guidance for the PKK in Turkey. Specifically, the government is apprehensive about the prospects of the possible establishing of an independent Kurdish state in northern Iraq or, owing to pressure from the northern Iraqi Kurds, the creation of a real federal structure in Iraq. Kurds in Turkey could then be encouraged to lobby more vigorously for independence or the formation of a federal system for Turkey. At most, Turkish officials are prepared to support real autonomy for the northern Iraqi Kurds within a unitary Iraqi state. However, even that arrangement would set a precedent. Some Kurds in Turkey may then press to emulate the northern Iraqi model of autonomy within Turkey itself.

Turkish officials have been determined to ensure that northern Iraq would not be used by the PKK as a base for launching armed operations into Turkey. At the same time, Ankara has been concerned not to undermine Iraq's territorial integrity. The Turkish government is also keen not to upset its relations with Iran and Syria. The authorities have been eager to make use of Turkey's role in Operation PROVIDE COMFORT to mobilize inter-national support against the PKK.

The Iraqi Kurds had been hostile to Iraqi–Turkish security co-operation between 1984 and 1988. After 1988 there were no Turkish operations in Iraq until the conclusion of the Gulf War when between August 1991 and May 1992 nine took place. Ankara perceived the Kurdish insurgency in northern Iraq as a major source of instability in the area. The Kurds in northern Iraq had maintained close relations with the PKK. Barzani of the KDP and Talabani of the PUK had often accused Turkey of inflicting damage on Kurdish villages in northern Iraq when Turkish armed forces mounted cross-border operations in pursuit of PKK militants.

Özal, with the support of senior diplomats from the Foreign Ministry, had taken the first step in establishing relations with the Kurds of Iraq in March 1991.[16] Kurdish representatives were invited to Ankara to hold talks with officials including Özal himself. These contacts developed to the extent that Ankara issued Turkish diplomatic passports to Talabani and Barzani to enable them to travel abroad. At one point these relations became so warm that Talabani toyed with the idea of 'joining democratic Turkey'.[17]

Negotiations in 1991 between the Iraqi government, the KDP and the PUK concerning the status of the Kurdish safe haven failed to produce satisfactory results. This led to the KDP and the PUK's agreeing to hold elections in May 1992 for a regional parliament in northern Iraq. The outcome was a power-sharing arrangement between the the two Kurdish groups. In October 1992 this parliament decided that its objective was a 'federation [al-ittihad al-fidirali] within a democratic parliamentary Iraq'.[18]

When Turkish officials had given their support for Operation PROVIDE COMFORT and the accompanying establishment of a safe haven, they had not imagined that this would lead to these developments. However, in spite of the threat to Iraq's territorial integrity, relations between Turkey and the Kurdish leadership in northern Iraq remained positive. The Iraqi Kurds seemed determined to protect their administration by ensuring that the PKK could not use the safe haven for mounting raids into Turkey. The Iraqi Kurds supported the Turkish military operation to uproot PKK bases in northern Iraq in autumn 1992. Ankara and the Kurdish leadership in northern Iraq had become dependent on each other with regard to their security interests.[19]

Military and political co-operation with the Turkish government was recognized by many northern Iraqi Kurds as essential in order to deter a possible Iraqi assault. These Kurds also acknowledged their economic dependence on Turkey. All international humanitarian assistance passed through Turkey. After the visit of a Turkish delegation to the area in autumn 1993, Ankara launched a $13.5-million assistance programme of its own. This was completed in late 1994 and a new $12.0-million package was introduced in March 1995.[20] Turkey has also allowed many trucks to ferry food to northern Iraq in return for small quantities of oil. The scale of this trade was put at $200 million a year,[21] and it has, to some extent, alleviated the economic problems for the northern Iraqi Kurds who have suffered from the UN trade embargo on Iraq and the internal embargo imposed on northern Iraq by Baghdad.

Massoud Barzani noted that since 1991 Turkey 'has become our only window to the outside world. We consider our relations with Turkey to be extremely vital.'[22] Barzani also emphasized that Operation PROVIDE COMFORT was his only security guarantee and spoke of Turkey's critical role in the area.[23] This relationship also benefited Turkey. Trade with northern Iraq has become a useful source of income for south-eastern Turkey's otherwise depressed economy. But in no way could this compensate for the loss of the substantial trade turnover between Turkey and Iraq caused by the imposition of sanctions.

Turkish officials have realized that co-operation with the northern Iraqi Kurds could enable Turkey to combat the PKK more effectively. However, there have been problems. The PKK has still been able to use northern Iraq as a logistical base to launch attacks against Turkey. The security arrangement reached between Turkey and the Kurdish leadership after the 1992 operation soon became ineffective. Turkey failed to support a revillagization programme along the Iraqi side of the border. Many villages along the frontier had been forcibly evacuated by Iraq officials in 1975. The revillagization programme was supposed to assist the repopulation of the area and make easier the policing of the territory against the PKK. But the PUK leadership lost interest in policing the border outside its traditional areas of support. This enabled the PKK to return to the border area, especially after the unilaterally-declared ceasefire of spring 1993 ended in June of that year. Numerous Turkish air force raids followed creating tension and resentment among the local population in northern Iraq.

Armed clashes also broke out during 1994 between KDP and PUK forces. The two groups were in dispute over the allocation of revenues collected from border trade. The decision of the PUK to occupy the city of Arbil, the seat of the Kurdish administration, was another source of friction. However, as the American political analyst Prados has noted: 'Root causes of the conflict stem from fundamental differences of ideology and leadership between the more conservative, tribal KDP and the more secular, leftist PUK.'[24]

Turkish officials were apprehensive about this conflict as it provided an opportunity for the PKK to extend its influence in northern Iraq. In June 1994 the tension between the KDP and the PUK was temporarily defused when the Turkish authorities succeeded in bringing together the two parties.[25] However, hostilities flared up again in December when PUK forces occupied Arbil. Turkish and American efforts to mediate failed. Ankara's concern that the PKK should not exploit these divisions led to the massive Turkish intervention in northern Iraq in March 1995.[26]

Unlike the situation in 1992, much to their annoyance the KDP and PUK leadership were not informed about the March 1995 operation. However, when the operation was being wound down in late April 1995 the KDP seemed much more willing to help the Turkish government to improve the security of the border area. The KDP appeared interested in reaching an agreement similar to the one of October 1992 which had referred to the need to repopulate the border area with the support of the government.[27] The KDP's willingness to co-operate with Turkey against the PKK drew criticisms from the PUK leadership.[28]

The Turkish intervention in northern Iraq opened the way to the KDP and the PUK's agreeing to a three-month ceasefire brokered by the US. With American mediation the KDP and PUK leaderships held two rounds of inconclusive talks in Dublin in August and September 1995. On the ground in northern Iraq PKK units began to attack the KDP while the PUK took a position supportive of the PKK. Although in December 1995 the PKK and the KDP agreed to a ceasefire, tensions between the two and between the KDP and the PUK persisted.

Turkish officials have also been suspicious of those occasions when the KDP and PUK enjoyed close relations with one another. In July 1994, when the leaders of the northern Iraqi Kurds met in Paris in the presence of Western observers and declared their intention to hold an election and merge their military forces, Turkish decision-makers were alarmed. The Turkish officials perceived that the territorial integrity of Iraq was being threatened. In reaction, the then newly-appointed Foreign Minister Mümtaz Soysal announced new principles to restrict access from Turkey to northern Iraq for Western non-governmental organizations.[29] The Turkish government suspected that many of these organizations were engaged in activities which put into question the territorial integrity of Iraq. Together with the French government, Ankara also intervened to prevent the northern Iraqi Kurds from holding a second Paris-type meeting.[30] Turkish officials regarded the Iraqi Kurds' efforts to seal the decisions adopted at the previous meeting in July as an attempt to form 'the embryo of an independent Kurdish state'.[31]

It would seem that Turkish officials were in favour of continued tensions between the KDP and the PUK in order for the Kurdish parliament and administration in northern Iraq to remain paralysed. However, at the same time Ankara did not want the conflict between the KDP and the PUK to escalate to a level which the PKK in northern Iraq could then exploit.

The Turkish authorities seemed to prefer an outcome where the northern Iraqi Kurds would have extended autonomy within a territorially-intact Iraq, but Ankara was opposed to Kurdish demands for a federal structure in Iraq. Turkish officials have called on the northern Iraqi Kurds to begin a dialogue with the Iraqi authorities. The PUK leadership in particular objected to this Turkish pressure. The PUK announced that it was only in favour of holding talks with a more democratic regime in Baghdad.[32] Likewise, Sami Abdurrahman, a KDP official, noted: 'We see the solution of the Kurdish problem within the framework of Iraq, naturally a democratic Iraq, and on the basis of federation. Not autonomy.'[33] This conflicted with the Turkish government's position. Although officials from the Foreign Ministry have usually preferred to take a more pragmatic approach to the situation in northern Iraq, they have been constrained particularly by hardliners, both inside and outside the government.

Relations between Turkey and the KDP, which has traditionally controlled the areas of northern Iraq bordering Turkey, have tended to be positive. Barzani's greater willingness to co-operate with Turkey and his readiness to be pragmatic with respect to Kurdish aspirations in northern Iraq appeared to have gained to some extent the trust of many Turkish decision-makers. Ankara has tended to be suspicious of Talabani's commitment to respect Iraq's territorial integrity and keep the PKK out of northern Iraq.

Relations between the PUK leadership and Turkey cooled particularly after the death of Özal in April 1993. He had seemed more willing to take risks and had shared Talabani's opinion that Saddam Hussein should be removed from power. Since Özal's death the Turkish government has come to base its policies on an acceptance that Saddam will not be removed and that Turkey would have to co-exist with a Saddam-led Iraq as its neighbour. Increasingly critical of Ankara's policies, as of March 1996 Talabani had not visited Turkey since the death of Özal.

The PKK has advocated the establishment of a united, independent, Kurdish state and has supported the use of terrorism to achieve this end. An independent 'Kurdistan', according to the PKK leadership, could embrace parts of Turkey and Iraq. Both the KDP and the PUK have been opposed to the use of terrorism and have preferred to limit their political demands and call only for a democratic and federal Iraq. The northern Iraqi Kurds have condemned PKK violence and the KDP has regularly warned the PKK not to mount military operations against Turkey from northern Iraq. In March 1995, though, Talabani announced that his organization would use diplomacy rather than force to prevent the PKK from attacking Turkey. Talabani added: 'We do not view the PKK as a terrorist organization but as a political organization.'[34] This was in stark contrast to the statement of Nechirwan Barzani, a nephew of Massoud Barzani, who had said that the 'PKK constituted a threat not only for Turkey but also to us'.[35] In March 1996, seeking to consolidate its presence along the Iraqi–Turkish border, the PKK forcibly evacuated villages in northern Iraq which were inhabited by tribes closely associated with the KDP.[36]

Most of the Turkish media and many politicians in Ankara were disturbed by developments in northern Iraq and looked upon the safe haven there as a threat to Turkey. In Parliamentary debates over whether the mandate of Operation PROVIDE COMFORT should be extended, many deputies denounced the Operation and claimed that it was a Western ploy which had as its aim the establishment of an independent Kurdish state in northern Iraq. The most outspoken opponents of the Operation have been the leaders of the DSP and the RP, Bülent Ecevit and Necmettin Erbakan, respectively.[37]

Concern about the situation in northern Iraq and the role of Operation PROVIDE COMFORT seemed to be widely shared by the Turkish public. A public opinion survey taken in June 1995 indicated that 67.2 per cent of those who were polled wanted those non-Turkish military units involved in the Operation to withdraw from Turkey.[38] Many in the country feared that Kurdish independence in northern Iraq could encourage the Kurds in Turkey to seek their own independence with external assistance. Richard Naab, a retired colonel who served with Operation PROVIDE COMFORT, has referred to the curious situation where Kurds in northern Iraq 'need the PKK because it makes the area attractive to Turkey. Both the KDP and PUK are afraid that if the PKK did not exist, Turkey would lose interest in helping the Kurds.'[39]

It may be argued, however, that Turkish foreign policy-makers seem to have been relatively successful in adapting themselves to the new circumstances resulting from the emergence of a Kurdish safe haven in Iraq. They have been able to develop reasonably co-operative relations with the local Kurdish leadership. The KDP official Sami Abdurrahman has remarked: 'If we look back ten years ago, who on earth could imagine such relations between Turkey and the Kurds of Iraq?'[40] It is worth noting in passing that in October 1984 the then Turkish Foreign Minister, Vahit Halefoğlu, had been despatched to Baghdad to persuade the government not to go ahead with its plans to reach a compromise agreement with the PUK in the north.[41] However, by the mid-1990s, in the eyes of most politicians and the public in general in Turkey, the emergence of what was perceived as a quasi-Kurdish state under Western protection was seen as threatening to Turkey's unity and territorial integrity.[42] In March 1995, immediately after the completion of the Turkish military intervention in northern Iraq, Mehmet Gölhan, then Defence Minister in Ankara, remarked that Turkey's security could only be guaranteed if Baghdad could reinstate its control over the north.[43] It appeared that many in Turkey at the time shared Gölhan's sentiment.

The Kurdish Question and Turkey's Relations with its Middle East Neighbours

The emergence of a quasi-Kurdish state in northern Iraq put the issue of Iraq's territorial integrity high on the Turkish foreign policy agenda. Turkish decision-makers have become concerned that the establishment of a Kurdish state and the breakup of Iraq could precipitate major interstate rivalry in the region. President Demirel stated that the 'disintegration of Iraq would cause such problems that 50 years would not be enough to resolve them'.[44] Turkey was thus instrumental in organizing periodic, trilateral, consultative meetings of Iranian, Syrian and Turkish officials.

At the first of these in November 1992 Turkey set out to assure Iran and Syria that the then on-going Turkish military operation in northern Iraq was limited to uprooting the PKK. Turkey did not intend to stay and create a buffer zone in northern Iraq. The Iranians in particular suspected that Turkey intended to stay on. Indeed, there was a brief period, soon after the Kurdish refugee crisis in 1991, when Turkish officials took up the argument that the Kirkuk–Mosul area in northern Iraq had been unfairly taken away from Turkey in 1925.[45] The Mosul question was revived. At the height of the military intervention in northern Iraq in March 1995 President Demirel argued that the border was badly demarcated and needed to be revised in order to make it more defensible. Demirel added that Mosul and Kirkuk had been taken away from Turkey unjustly.[46] In July 1995 Ecevit declared that Turkey should create a 'provisional security border' inside northern Iraq.[47]

The trilateral meetings not only emphasized a regional commitment to Iraq's territorial integrity. They also became an additional forum in which Turkey could press Iran and Syria to co-operate against the PKK. After the commencement of work on GAP in 1983, there were regular Turkish reports of how Syria was supporting the PKK in order to apply pressure on Turkey over the management of the waters of the Euphrates.[48] Turkish and Syrian officials have held regular bilateral meetings on this problem. The meeting held in April 1992 led to Syrian dismantling of PKK training camps in the Bekaa Valley. But other meetings were less successful. Officials in Ankara and the Turkish public believed that Syria still actively supported the PKK. Öcalan's ability to operate in Syria with impunity met fierce criticism in Turkey.

Tensions between Turkey and Syria increased after reports appeared that Öcalan had fled to Syria immediately before Turkish forces entered northern Iraq in March 1995. Öcalan's presence in Syria was denied by officials in Damascus. Turkey has sought US support against Syrian-inspired terrorism. But by early 1996 Syria appeared to have maintained its contacts with the PKK.

Relations between secular Turkey and theocratic Iran have been strained. In the context of the Kurdish question, officials in Ankara have frequently accused Iran of allowing the PKK to maintain bases on the Iranian side of the frontier. Many Turkish citizens also suspected that Iran supported Islamic fundamentalist terrorism in Turkey in order to weaken Turkey's secular regime. Iran, in turn, has often accused Turkey of allowing the Iranian opposition to operate there freely. Tehran has looked upon Ankara as a stooge of the West.

Nevertheless, there have been positive developments in Turkish–Iranian relations. In October 1992 regular, low-level meetings of Turkish and Iranian security experts began. The Interior Ministers of both countries hold talks occasionally. President Demirel's visit to Tehran in July 1994 paved the way for Turkey and Iran to sign an agreement in September 1995 promising co-operation against terrorism. It should be noted in passing that Turkey and Iran are important trading partners.

The Turkish military intervention in northern Iraq in March 1995 met only mild Iranian criticism. President Hashemi Rafsanjani accepted Demirel's assurances that the operation would be of a limited duration and that the military build-up was not in any way directed towards Iran.[49] At the time Iran, which had itself intervened in northern Iraq on a number of occasions and has had to confront a Kurdish armed opposition of its own, declared that its borders had been closed to Kurds from Iraq or Turkey. The Iranian Interior Minister, clearly referring to the PKK, announced that 'Iran does not allow any activity by Turkish opposition groups in the border region.'[50] Turkey and Iran have frequently reiterated their commitment to the territorial integrity of Iraq and have opposed the establishment of a Kurdish state in northern Iraq. Both Turkish and Iranian officials share the fear that the disintegration of Iraq could adversely affect regional security and complicate the Kurdish question in their own countries. However, Iranian officials were opposed to Operation PROVIDE COMFORT, viewing it as a vehicle through which the United States was able to maintain a military presence close to Iran's borders.

Seeking to counter Turkish–US influence in the area, Iran was actively involved in attempting to reconcile the warring KDP and PUK. Barzani and Talabani held discussions in Tehran in October 1995. As a result, Iranian military units entered parts of northern Iraq in November to help to maintain the ceasefire that was agreed upon by the KDP and the PUK. Rafsanjani assured Demirel that the Iranian presence was only a token one.[51] Nevertheless, Turkish officials were seriously concerned at Iran's growing influence among Kurdish groups in northern Iraq.

Turkish–Iraqi relations were the most affected by the creation of a safe haven in Iraq. Previously, in support of UN sanctions against Iraq, Turkey had closed the oil pipeline which ran from Iraq to the Turkish Mediterranean coast. The Turkish army was deployed along the Iraqi border in the Gulf War, thereby pinning down an important section of the Iraqi army in the north and relieving some of the pressure on the allies in the south. The launching of Operation PROVIDE COMFORT would lead to a further deterioration in Turkish–Iraqi relations.

As noted already, Turkey was opposed to any developments which would threaten the territorial integrity of Iraq. Thus in autumn 1992 the then Turkish Foreign Minister Hikmet Çetin noted that Turkey could accept autonomy for the Kurds only with the prior consent of the central authorities in Iraq.[52] However, this did not go far enough to improve relations with Iraq. Although, in general, the international community was determined to keep Iraq isolated, Turkish officials had to co-exist with it as a neighbour. The Iraqi Foreign Minister Muhammed Sayyid al-Sahaff during a visit to Turkey in February 1995 argued that the Kurdish problem in Iraq was Iraq's internal problem just as the Kurdish problem in Turkey was Turkey's. The Minister noted that 'Turkey and Iraq will always be here. Thus the two countries must solve their own problems.'[53] Sayyid al-Sahaff appeared to imply that Turkey should no longer support Operation PROVIDE COMFORT.

Turkey's foreign policy towards Iraq was also influenced by other considerations. Suffering economically from the UN embargo against Iraq, Turkey has actively explored the possibility of reopening the Kirkuk–Yumurtalık oil pipeline. Many in Ankara perceived that Iraq's inability to exercise its sovereignty over northern Iraq threatened Turkey's security. Turkish decision-makers faced a paradoxical situation. On the one hand, fearful of a possible new flood of refugees, Turkey continued to support Operation PROVIDE COMFORT. On the other, the authorities preferred that Baghdad should re-establish control over northern Iraq.

In January 1994 Turkey proposed to co-operate with Iraq to rescue the

Kirkuk–Yumurtalık pipeline which was beginning to show signs of severe corrosion. Oil needed to be flushed out of the pipeline and replaced by fresh oil after the completion of maintenance work. The oil in the pipeline, jointly owned by both countries, would be sold through the UN and the revenues would be used to cover Iraqi debts to Turkey and finance UN humanitarian assistance to Iraq.[54]

Baghdad did not react favourably to these proposals, although Turkey secured the support of the US and other Security Council permanent members. In October the Iraqi government hardened its position and linked the implementation of the rescue project to the complete lifting of the UN sanctions.[55] Hopes were again momentarily raised in Turkey when the Security Council adopted resolution 986 in April 1995 which, in effect, would have amounted to a partial lifting of the economic embargo on Iraq. This would have permitted the sale of a certain amount of Iraqi oil in return for the purchase of food and medicine. The resolution allowed the sale of the oil through Turkey. It would have helped to restore the pipeline and would have revived the economy of the region. However, Iraq rejected the resolution and again demanded that all the sanctions against Iraq should be lifted first.

In January 1996 the project was reactivated when the UN began negotiations with Iraq for the implementation of resolution 986. Iraqi–Turkish technical talks concerning the possible opening of the pipeline also commenced. In March the Iraqi Oil Minister Amir Mohammed Rasheed visited Ankara. A memorandum of understanding was agreed between Turkey and Iraq concerning the terms for the use of the pipeline if Iraq and the UN could reach an agreement on the implementation of resolution 986.[56] The Oil Minister had travelled to Turkey by land, crossing territory under the control of the KDP. This led to speculations that a *rapprochement* was taking place between the Iraqi government and Barzani.[57] The implementation of the plan would require the co-operation of the KDP and the PUK and, in practice, the PKK as well. Turkish officials were aware that the PKK could derive financial benefits because resolution 986 required that a proportion of the oil revenues should also go to northern Iraq.

The future reopening of the pipeline was also very much tied up with the eventual re-establishment of Iraq's sovereignty over northern Iraq. Many in Turkey seemed to believe that this eventuality would enhance Turkey's security. However, in order to maintain good relations with the West, Turkish officials would have to ensure that Baghdad's authority in northern Iraq would be established in a manner that would meet the approval of the Iraqi Kurds. The demand of these Kurds for a federal arrangement was opposed by both Turkey and Iraq. Baghdad appeared to favour a form of autonomy similar to previous arrangements, when, in practice, the Kurds had enjoyed little or no autonomy.

The trans-state nature of the Kurdish question has deeply affected Turkey's relations with its Middle Eastern neighbours. The non-democratic governments in the region remain determined to protect the territorial integrity of their countries while the Kurds in these states are still divided. Turkish officials seem to be involved in an impossible exercise of attempting to balance the country's domestic and external security concerns against the need to maintain reasonably harmonious relations with neighbouring states, with the West and with Kurdish groups in northern Iraq.

The Kurdish Question and Turkey's Relations with the West

Although the West has repeatedly stressed its commitment to preserve the territorial integrity of Iraq, many Turkish officials feared that Operation PROVIDE COMFORT was being used by Western governments as a means to secure the emergence of a Kurdish state in northern Iraq. Harsh Western criticisms concerning Ankara's handling of the Kurdish question also led many Turks to believe that the West was aiming to divide up their country.

During the Cold War, the West had remained relatively silent with respect to the Kurdish question in Turkey. The April 1991 refugee crisis and its aftermath and the increase of violence and human rights abuses in south-eastern Turkey forced a reassessment. Numerous political forums in Europe attributed the upsurge of violence in Turkey to the government's repression of the Kurds. These groups pressed for the Kurds in Turkey to be granted 'minority rights'. Such ideas have in general been received negatively by the Turkish public. Hikmet Çetin, himself of Kurdish origin, when Turkish Foreign Minister declared to the European Parliament in May 1992 that the Kurds were not a minority. He argued that the Kurds enjoyed equal rights with all other citizens in Turkey.[58]

The diplomatic offensive initiated by the Turkish government in 1992 led to some changes in the European position towards the Kurdish question. Jas Gawronski, who wrote a report on the Kurdish 'people' and their rights, objected to some left-wing members of the European Parliament who were seeking to introduce amendments to his report. These deputies were calling for a recognition of the right to 'self-determination' including the right to independence. The report was finally adopted in June 1992 without these amendments.[59] While criticizing the Turkish government for excessive use of force against the PKK and its supporters, the European Parliament came to acknowledge that the PKK was a terrorist organization. The right of Turkey to defend itself against terrorism was also recognized.

In spite of intensive efforts on the part of the Turkish government, it was not until November 1993 that Germany and France banned the PKK from operating in their countries. The PKK had mounted attacks on Turkish targets in Europe in June and November 1993. In January 1994, during a tripartite meeting of Foreign Ministers in Ankara, both Britain and Germany stressed the importance of guaranteeing Turkey's security and stability. However, this was accompanied by a warning that Turkey had to fight terrorism without compromising respect for human rights and freedom of expression.[60]

The lifting of the immunities of the radical DEP members of the Turkish Parliament in March 1994 and then the abolishing of the DEP in June were seen in the West as clear violations of the freedom of expression. Western officials believed that these actions could only worsen the Kurdish problem. Germany temporarily suspended military assistance to Turkey.[61] After visiting Ankara in September 1994 Miguel Martinez, the President of the Parliamentary Assembly of the Council of Europe, prepared a report which expressed support for Turkey's fight against terrorism. The report recommended the need to protect Turkey's territorial integrity but criticized it for human rights violations and restrictions on freedom of expression. As noted in a previous chapter, the report recommended changes to a number of articles of the Turkish Constitution and called for the release of the Kurdish deputies from custody.

The situation went from bad to worse when Kurdish deputies were sentenced to serve prison terms in December 1994. The EU postponed its decision on the signing of a Customs Union Treaty with Turkey. The Council of Europe threatened to consider the suspension of Turkey's membership if the Constitution were not reformed. But on 6 March an agreement to activate a customs union between the EU and Turkey was signed. The agreement was ratified by the European Parliament in December 1995 with a vote of 343 in favour, 149 against, with 36 abstentions.[62]

Russia's decision to use force in Chechnya had reminded Western officials of the significance of Turkey's geostrategic position. The US administration had thus pushed hard for Turkey to be included in a customs union with the EU to strengthen the country's stability and security. Both the United States and the EU have given importance to the prospects of participating in a dynamic Turkish economy which commanded more than 60 million consumers and which was expanding economic ties with Central Asian countries.

The PKK was starting to pose a threat to domestic security in Western Europe. In Germany over half a million Kurds lived side by side with one million Turks. Attacks on Turks and Turkish-owned businesses, violent demonstrations and the PKK's involvement in drug trafficking led to an important loss of support for the cause of the Kurds in Germany. The Bundestag adopted a law which allowed for the deportation of Kurdish asylum seekers implicated in violence.[63] In Western Europe in general there was a fear that escalating violence between Turks and Kurds in Turkey could lead to similar acts of violence in Europe.

Growing calls for democratization from within Turkey itself also led to an improvement in relations between Turkey and Western Europe. After the closing of the DEP, the President of the Turkish Grand National Assembly Hüsamettin Cindoruk argued that the West had lost confidence in Turkish democracy. He added that it was not surprising that Europe had difficulty in understanding why a democracy would banish certain political expressions from the Parliament. He called for urgent efforts to bring about greater democratization within Turkey.[64] This line of thinking was also reflected in the media, which by and large spoke of the need for greater freedom of expression. As described previously, in July 1995 certain constitutional amendments were passed and in October Article 8 of the Anti-terror Law was revised.

However, the massive Turkish military operation in northern Iraq in March 1995 provoked harsh international criticism and led to calls for an immediate withdrawal. The Foreign Ministers of Germany, France and Spain, representing the EU, who were in Turkey to discuss the customs union accord, inevitably focused on the operation.[65] The Turkish government despatched Erdal İnönü, the newly appointed Foreign Minister, to the major European capitals to explain the purpose of the intervention. İnönü stressed that Turkey was determined to pull out the forces within a short period. However, on 5 April 1995 the European Parliament condemned both PKK terrorism and the Turkish military intervention and called on member governments to impose a military embargo on Turkey. The European Parliament also urged Turkey to find a political solution to the Kurdish question.[66] But as we have seen, the European Parliament would in December 1995 eventually agree to ratify the customs union between the EU and Turkey.

The Parliamentary Assembly of the Council of Europe on 26 April 1995 passed a resolution which recommended that Turkey be suspended from the Council if within two months it failed to harmonize its laws and Constitution with the principles of the Council. The resolution also demanded an improvement in Turkey's human rights record, especially with regard to the Kurds.[67] European governments softened their position to some extent once the Turkish military withdrew from Iraq early in May. The Secretary General of the Council of Europe Daniel Tarcys admitted that the recent decision of the Council had included some mistakes. He emphasized that the Council's intention was not to isolate Turkey but to encourage it to democratize.[68]

These unusually strong European criticisms seemed to have had an unintendedly adverse affect on the Turkish leadership. In particular, the threat to suspend Turkey from the Council of Europe when it aspired to join the EU rekindled the belief that Europe did not want a Moslem Turkey in Europe. Europe's insistence on the need to find a political solution to the Kurdish question has led many in Turkey to conclude that Europe was seeking the fragmentation of the country. President Demirel himself articulated this viewpoint in a forceful manner in a widely watched talk show on a private Turkish television channel.[69] During the interview the President quoted statements from the meeting he had with the French Foreign Minister Alain

Juppe in late March 1995. Juppe had remarked: 'We believe that the [Kurdish] problem is not just a military one, at the same time it also has political characteristics.' He had also stated: 'Among the public opinion of France, Germany, Spain and other European countries, there are people who believe that PKK terrorists are struggling for the social and political rights of Kurds.' These assertions were interpreted by Demirel as clear evidence of European plans to partition Turkey.[70] The President argued that European demands for a 'political solution' were in reality calls for the granting of autonomy for the Kurds which he insisted would lead the country into a state of anarchy.

The Turkish public also reacted negatively when the British government in March 1995 allowed MED-TV – a pro-PKK television channel – to broadcast its programmes to Turkey from the UK. The following month the Dutch government allowed the Kurdish 'parliament-in-exile' to hold its first meeting in The Hague in spite of Turkish government protests. Reacting to these developments, hardliners in and out of the Turkish Parliament argued that easing restrictions on freedom of expression would assist the spreading of propaganda aimed at dividing the Turkish state. However, some reforms to the legal system in Turkey would eventually be agreed upon in 1995 as a result of domestic pressure. The need to secure the the ratification of the customs union agreement with the EU was another important factor.

European governments have been urging Turkey to improve its human rights record and change its policy toward the Kurds. On the other hand, they have acknowledged that the PKK was a terrorist group which seriously threatened Turkey's stability and security. Officials in the West were aware that a destabilized Turkey could become more vulnerable to extremist politics which could in turn endanger Western interests in what was an unstable region.

The US administration has on many occasions expressed its support for Turkey's right to combat PKK terrorism. In Washington the PKK was regarded as a terrorist organization. The Acting Director of the Central Intelligence Agency Admiral William Studeman argued during his address to the US House Judiciary Committee that the PKK was a threat not only to Turkey but to the United States too.[71] In particular, the PKK's growing involvement in drug trafficking was seen as an important threat to US interests. Robert Gelbard, Assistant Secretary of State for International Narcotics and Law Enforcement Affairs, noted American concern on this topic during a press conference at the Foreign Press Center in Washington in October 1995.[72] The administration has also been critical of the Kurdish 'parliament-in-exile', considering it a PKK-financed operation which lacked popular basis and legitimacy.[73]

However, the administration has been critical of Turkish anti-terrorism policies. A number of American officials and members of Congress have visited Ankara to express their displeasure with the government's human rights performance in its fight against terrorism. The conviction and sentencing of the DEP deputies in December 1994 to prison terms drew particular criticisms from both the Congress and the administration. The Assistant Secretary of State for Democracy, Human Rights and Labor John Shattuck was despatched to Turkey twice within six months. He noted that the United States was becoming increasingly concerned about internationally-recognized freedoms of speech being curtailed in Turkey through prosecutions.[74]

Growing allegations in Congressional and human rights circles that Turkey was using cluster bombs against civilians in south-eastern Anatolia led to efforts to prevent the transfer of these weapons to Turkey. Many in Turkey had believed that an arms embargo was on the cards when in December 1994 Joseph Nye, an Assistant Secretary of Defense, visited Ankara.

In May 1994 the House Appropriations Committee drafted legislation which would not only reduce the amount of assistance available to Turkey, but would also make 25 per cent of this aid conditional on an improvement in Turkey's human rights performance. In July amendments in the Senate also introduced restrictions on the use of any American military equipment acquired through the assistance programme for internal security purposes. Turkish officials responded by arguing that these restrictions would benefit the PKK and would have the effect of destabilizing Turkey. These sharp criticisms along with Prime Minister Çiller's personal appeal to President Clinton seem to have led to the lifting of the restriction on the use of the military assistance for internal security purposes. However, the final version of the legislation nevertheless made the last ten per cent of the aid conditional on an improvement in Turkey's policies on the Kurdish issue.

The US administration's reaction to the news of the Turkish military intervention in northern Iraq in March 1995 was much milder than the response of European governments had been. President Clinton declared that the operation had been necessitated by the PKK's threat to Turkey's security but stressed that the utmost care should be given to protect the civilian population.[75] The United States was also concerned that the cross-border operation should be of short duration.

The reaction of the public opinion and the press in the United States to the cross-border operation was much harsher. The columnist William Safire wrote that Turkey was aiming to control petroleum facilities and occupy northern Iraq until Saddam Hussein's forces could return to the area.[76] The American press also alleged that innocent civilians were suffering as a result of the operation.[77] The harshest criticism came from John Edmund Porter, a Republican Representative for Illinois. At a meeting of the House Foreign Operations Subcommittee, Porter alleged that Turkey was committing a genocide in northern Iraq.[78]

On a visit to the United States in April 1995 Prime Minister Çiller stressed that Turkey was 'the only secular democracy among 52 Muslim states' and added that the states in the Middle East had either 'the Iranian model' or 'the Turkish model' to choose from. The Prime Minister went on to argue that Turkey needed to fight terrorism to protect the secular Turkish model from fundamentalism. The fact that she was talking almost at the very moment when news arrived about the bomb explosion in Oklahoma City led Çiller to argue convincingly that 'the massive effort now to find the culprits of Oklahoma justifies sending 35,000 troops into northern Iraq.' She promised that the cross-border operation would end very soon and pledged that her government was committed to continue with democratization programmes. She also added that the air corridor to Armenia, a highly sensitive issue in the United States, would be opened.[79]

When the cross-border operation ended in May 1995 the US State Department spokesman reflected the administration's relief when he announced that: 'Prime Minister Çiller had assured President Clinton and Secretary of State Christopher that the operation would be of limited scope and duration. She kept her word.'[80] Nevertheless, the administration and the Turkish government continued to view the future of northern Iraq differently. The United States favoured a solution that would allow the Kurds in northern Iraq to enjoy autonomy in a federally restructured Iraq. The continuation of Operation PROVIDE COMFORT was viewed by American officials as essential in order to deter Saddam Hussein's forces from attacking the Kurdish safe haven. Turkish officials would seem to prefer to see northern Iraq eventually coming under the control of Baghdad. It would appear that the Turkish government has been viewing Operation PROVIDE COMFORT as a temporary arrangement to prevent the Iraqi authorities from precipitating another flood of refugees into Turkey. Officials in Ankara seem to have reconciled themselves to the idea of the northern Iraqi Kurds enjoying autonomy within a unitary Iraqi state. But the Turkish authorities remain opposed to the formation of a federation in Iraq. In the short run, as Marc Grossman, the US Ambassador in Turkey, has noted, both the American and the Turkish government were eager for Talabani and Barzani 'to end fighting and to focus on their responsibilities for peace and security in the area'.[81] The failure of the United States to work out an agreement with the KDP and PUK in two meetings in Dublin in August and September 1995 has been indicated earlier.

In spite of the infighting between the KDP and the PUK, the United States remained committed to maintaining a safe haven for Kurds in northern Iraq. The United States was thus dependent on Turkey's goodwill and co-operation in order to maintain Operation PROVIDE COMFORT. Robert H. Pelletreau, Assistant Secretary of State for Near Eastern Affairs, and Joseph Nye, Assistant Secretary of Defense for International Security Affairs, when addressing the Senate Foreign Relations Committee in March 1995 stated: 'It would be very difficult to sustain the operation without Turkey'.[82] As we have seen, far from happy with the continuation of Operation PROVIDE

COMFORT in its current form, the new ANAP–DYP coalition government began talks in March 1996 with US officials with regard to the future of the Operation.

For some time American–Turkish relations were strained by Turkish efforts to seek compensation for the losses it had incurred as a result of economic sanctions against Iraq. According to President Demirel speaking in June 1994, the loss of trade with Iraq and the closure of the oil pipeline had cost Turkey between $15 and $20 billion.[83] Turkish officials have also lobbied for a partial lifting of the sanctions on Iraq. Prime Minister Çiller during her visit to the United States in October 1993 had appealed for the partial lifting of the UN embargo.[84]

Intensive lobbying on the part of the Turkish government throughout 1994 did lead the United States eventually to support a Turkish plan to rescue the Kirkuk–Yumurtalìk pipeline. This plan encountered difficulties when Iraq opposed the terms offered by the UN with regard to a possible partial lifting of the economic embargo. Strobe Talbot, Deputy US Secretary of State, acknowledged in his visit to Turkey in April 1995 that: 'Turkey has, of course, had to pay a price for its critically important role in the implementation of the will of the international community, and in continuing impositions of the sanctions against the Iraqi regime.'[85] Hopes of a partial lifting of the embargo were revived when in early 1996 the UN and Iraq were engaged in talks over a possible oil for food deal. In the meantime, the US administration allowed the economic embargo to be eroded by not objecting to the border trade between Turkey and Iraq.

The US administration still regards Turkey as a country of considerable strategic importance. American officials view Turkey as a relatively stable, pro-Western state which could offer itself as a useful model for others to emulate, particularly the Turkic states of the former Soviet Union. Hence the US administration has supported a number of economic initiatives favouring Turkey. The Department of Commerce has identified Turkey as one of the ten big emerging markets of close interest to the United States.[86] Richard Holbrooke, the former Assistant Secretary of State for European and Canadian Affairs, has gone on record as saying: 'As a democratic Muslim nation, a committed member of NATO, and a moderate, secular, pro-Western country in a politically unstable region, our support for Turkey's economic program will be critical in safeguarding important on-going US interests at the critical intersections of Europe, Asia and the Middle East.'[87]

Most importantly, the United States has supported Turkey's efforts to join the EU. The administration used its influence with the EU to obtain the ratification of the customs union accord with Turkey. In this context amendments to the Turkish Constitution and the Anti-terror Law were welcomed in the United States as important steps in Turkey's democratization process.

Clearly, the relationship between Turkey and the United States is a multifaceted one. Congress has focused on Turkey's human rights violations and has been critical of Turkey's attempts to respond to the Kurdish insurgency by military means. The United States has been advocating a solution to the Kurdish question that would allow the Kurds to express their ethnic and cultural identity. The State Department spokesman noted that the United States wanted the Turkish government to ensure 'that the human and civil rights of the Kurds are protected, and indeed advanced'. He added: 'We do not support autonomy for Turkish Kurds within Turkey.'[88] At the same time, the administration has emphasized Turkey's strategic importance and has attempted to bridge relations between Turkey and the Congress.

In Turkey, on the other hand, there was a growing feeling that Ankara was making important sacrifices by maintaining sanctions against Iraq and supporting Operation PROVIDE COMFORT without receiving adequate recognition. Many among the Turkish public fear that the United States supports the establishment of a Kurdish state at the eventual expense of Turkey's territorial integrity. This fear is so deeply embedded that even the Turkish military regards the US with suspicion, in spite of the fact that the US and Turkey have been allies for almost 50 years. In a book authorized and published by the Turkish General Staff, Colonel Kocaoğlu observed that: 'The US, under the pretext of protecting human rights, is assisting the formation of a Kurdish state in northern Iraq which eventually will demand land from Turkey.' Kocaoğlu added that it was difficult to defeat the PKK because the PKK received support from the US.[89]

In order to maintain good relations with the West, and particularly with the United States, Turkey must remain favourably disposed toward the Kurds in northern Iraq. At the same time, Turkish officials have tried to dissuade the Kurdish leadership there from supporting the PKK. There has also been an intense diplomatic effort on Ankara's part to ensure a regional and Western commitment to the territorial integrity of Iraq.

In the context of Turkey's involvement in Iraq, the reconciling of Turkish interests with those of Iran, Iraq and Syria has met some success. All these states oppose the emergence of an independent Kurdish state. Turkey seems to have found some modest, though fragile, grounds for co-operation with Iran on security and economic issues. On the other hand, relations with Syria do not seem to show any signs of improvement. Syria's continued support for the PKK and Turkey's reluctance to discuss the water problem remain major stumbling blocks. Difficulties concerning the plan to rescue the Kirkuk–Yumurtalık pipeline and Iraq's belligerent posture towards Kuwait and the international community in October 1994 have reminded Turkish decision-makers of the difficulties of co-operating with the present regime. This, inevitably, has reinforced the importance of Operation PROVIDE COMFORT which serves as an effective deterrent force against Iraq.

During the Cold War Turkey had been regarded by the West as a reliable and valuable ally. With the end of the Cold War some Turkish and Western statesmen began to portray Turkey as an island of stability and a model for many countries to follow. Turkey became a sought-after partner as attempts were made to resolve the numerous ethnic conflicts in territories near to Turkey's borders.[90] But the country's inability to solve the Kurdish question is beginning to undermine this image. Western governments have become increasingly critical of Turkey's policies with regard to the Kurds. Amendments to the Constitution and to the Anti-terror Law in 1995 did lead to the ratification of the customs union treaty between Turkey and the European Union. However, Turkey's participation in the European integration process was still open to question. The government has come under pressure from Europe and the US to work out a political solution to the Kurdish question. However, an increasing number of politicians and officials in Turkey believe that the West aims to partition Turkey. This makes it much more difficult for moderates in Turkey to steer through Parliament further packages of measures on political liberalization and democratization. With regard to the Kurdish question, on the one hand international pressure may encourage further democratization in Turkey. But on the other, this pressure also seems to generate a conservative backlash in Turkey.

Notes

1. *UN Security Council Document S/22435*, 3 April 1991.
2. *Milliyet*, 4 April 1991.
3. Two examples of such criticisms may be found in *Parliamentary Assembly Council of Europe Doc. 5995*, 17 Jan. 1989 and *Doc. 6267*, 18 Jan. 1991.
4. *World Refugee Survey 1992* (Washington, DC: US Committee for Refugees, 1992) p.82.
5. *Milliyet*, 4 April 1994.
6. Ibid.
7. *Asylum Under Attack* (a Report of the Lawyers' Committee for Human Rights, 1992) p.36.
8. *Economist*, 13 April 1991, p.53.
9. *Turkish Daily News (TDN)*, 6/7 April 1991.
10. *Newsweek*, 29 April 1991.
11. *Time*, 22 April 1991; and *Economist*, 13 April 1991, p.14.
12. 'Update on Iraqi Refugees and Displaced Persons' – statement by N. Lyman, Director of the Bureau for Refugee Programs, *Dispatch*, 27 May 1991, p.379.
13. *Economist*, 13 April 1991, p.53.
14. *UNHCR Report on Northern Iraq: April 1991–May 1992*, (Geneva: UN High Commissioner for Refugees, 1992) p.5.
15. F. Cuny, *Northern Iraq: One Year Later* (Washington, DC: Carnegie Endowment, 1992) p.15.
16. M.A. Birand, *Apo ve PKK* (Istanbul: Milliyet Yayınları, 1992) p.265.

17. G. Fuller, 'The Fate of Kurds', *Foreign Affairs*, 72, 2, (Spring 1993) p.114.
18. O. Bengio, 'The Challenge to the Territorial Integrity of Iraq' *Survival*, 37, 2, (Summer 1995) p.80. For an analysis of the emergence of the Kurdish federated state see also M. Gunter, 'A de facto Kurdish State in Northern Iraq', *Third World Quarterly*, 14, 2, (1993).
19. This interdependence was also noted in, W. Hale, 'Turkey's Time: Turkey, the Middle East and the Gulf Crisis', *International Affairs*, 68, 4, (Oct. 1992) p.690.
20. *TDN*, 25 March 1995.
21. *Yeni Yüzyıl* and *TDN*, 27 Dec. 1994. It was reported that approximately 1,500 trucks were crossing the border each day.
22. Interview published in *Al-Safir*, 2 Aug. 1994 as reported by *Middle East Intelligence Review*, 11 Aug. 1994 (via Internet Wire Service).
23. *Yeni Yüzyıl*, 10 April 1995.
24. A.B. Prados, 'The Kurds: Stalemate in Iraq', *Congressional Research Service Report for Congress*, 95-397F, (Nov. 1995) p.4.
25. *Reuters*, 13 June 1994 (via Internet Wire Service).
26. For details of US and Turkish mediation efforts see *TDN*, 10 and 13 March 1995.
27. Ibid., 31 March 1995 and 8 May 1995.
28. Reported from the German magazine *Focus* in *Yeni Yüzyıl*, 16 May 1995.
29. *TDN*, 11 and 13 Sep. 1994.
30. Ibid., 19 Sep. 1994.
31. Ibid., 12 Oct. 1994.
32. *Yeni Yüzyıl*, 23 March 1995.
33. Quoted in *TDN*, 8 May 1995.
34. Ibid., 5 May 1995.
35. *Yeni Yüzyıl*, 6 May 1995.
36. *TDN*, 14 March 1996.
37. A brief summary of their views before the debate in Dec. 1994 may be found in ibid., 29 Dec. 1994. For an analysis of the growing opposition among deputies against Operation PROVIDE COMFORT and Turkey's policies in northern Iraq based on parliamentary debates see B. Oran, *'Kalkık Horoz': Çekiç Güç ve Kürt Devleti*, (Ankara: Bilgi Yayınevi, 1996) pp.99–144.
38. *TDN*, 12 June 1995. A public opinion survey taken in 1992 had indicated a similar result with almost 70 per cent of those polled saying 'No' to the presence of Operation PROVIDE COMFORT in Turkey. See ibid., 19 Nov. 1992.
39. Ibid., 13 March 1995.
40. Ibid., 8 May 1995.
41. N. Entessar, *Kurdish Ethnonationalism* (Boulder CO: Lynne Rienner, 1992) p. 133.
42. For a forceful presentation of this thesis see M. Kocaoğlu, *Uluslararası İlişkiler Işığında Ortadoğu* (Ankara: Gnkur. Basımevi, 1995) pp.289–400. This book, written by a colonel, was authorized for circulation by the Turkish General Staff as a reference work.
43. *TDN*, 5 May 1995.
44. *Hürriyet*, 4 June 1994.
45. G. Fuller, *Iraq in the Next Decade: Will Iraq Survive Until 2002?* (Santa Monica CA: RAND Corporation, 1992).
46. *Yeni Yüzyıl*, 29 April and 2 May 1995.
47. *TDN*, 7 Sep. 1995.
48. For an analysis of the water issue in Turkey's relations with Iraq and Syria, see G.

Kut, 'Burning Waters: the Hydropolitics of the Euphrates and Tigris', *New Perspectives on Turkey*, 9, (Fall 1993).

49. *Yeni Yüzyıl*, 30 March 1995.
50. *TDN*, 17 April 1995.
51. Ibid., 27 Dec. 1995.
52. Ibid., 8 Nov. 1992.
53. Ibid., 12 Feb. 1995.
54. Ibid., 12 Jan. 1994.
55. Ibid., 4 Oct. 1994.
56. Ibid., 6 and 11 March 1996.
57. *Yeni Yüzyıl*, 6 March 1996. KDP officials were willing to co-operate to open and ensure the operation of the pipeline, but they added that this did not mean that the KDP had altered its position regarding its relations with Baghdad. See *TDN*, 13 March 1996.
58. Information provided by a Turkish diplomat present at Çetin's presentation.
59. *Cumhuriyet*, 10 June 1992.
60. *TDN*, 21 Jan. 1994.
61. *Hürriyet*, 8 April 1994. The suspension was subsequently lifted. See *Milliyet*, 2 May 1994.
62. *TDN*, 14 Dec. 1995.
63. *Yeni Yüzyıl*, 18 March 1995.
64. *Milliyet*, 29 June 1994.
65. *TDN*, 24 March 1995.
66. *Yeni Yüzyıl*, 7 April 1995.
67. Ibid., 27 April 1995.
68. *TDN*, 8 May 1995.
69. *32. Gün*, TV programme, 8 May 1995. Subsequently the interview was covered in *Yeni Yüzyıl*, 10 May 1995 and *TDN*, 10 May 1995.
70. The French Foreign Ministry insisted that Alain Juppe had never said anything that threatened the unity of the Turkish state. See *Yeni Yüzyıl*, 4 May 1995.
71. Reported in ibid., 8 April 1995 and *TDN*, 9 May 1995.
72. *TDN*, 1 Nov. 1995.
73. Ibid., 2 Nov. 1995.
74. Ibid., 14 Dec. 1994.
75. *Yeni Yüzyıl*, 21 March 1995.
76. Article in the *New York Times* reported in *Yeni Yüzyıl*, 31 March 1995.
77. For a survey and summary of the American press on this issue see ibid., 1 April 1995.
78. *TDN*, 8 April 1995.
79. Ibid., 21 April 1995.
80. Quoted in *Yeni Yüzyıl*, 7 May 1995.
81. Quoted in *TDN*, 13 April 1995.
82. Quoted in ibid., 6 March 1995.
83. *New York Times*, 5 June 1994.
84. For a fierce criticism of Çiller for making this proposal see the article by *New York Times* columnist William Safire in 'Here's a Better Road for Turkey to Travel', *International Herald Tribune*, 29 Oct. 1993.
85. *TDN*, 13 April 1995.
86. Interview with Marc Grossman in ibid., 1 Feb. 1995.
87. Ibid., 6 March 1995.

182   THE KURDISH QUESTION AND TURKEY

88.   Ibid., 13 April 1995.
89.   M. Kocaoğlu, op. cit., pp.327, 352.
90.   K. Kirişci, 'New Patterns of Turkish Foreign Policy Behaviour' in C.Balım, E.Kalayçıoğlu, C. Karataş G. Winrow, and F. Yasamee (eds.), *Turkey: Economic, Social and Foreign Policy Challenges for the 1990s* (Leiden: Brill, 1995).

7

Possible Solutions to the Kurdish Question

OBVIOUSLY TO talk of a possible solution to the Kurdish question one needs to be clear what the question actually involves. However, as shown earlier, many in the Turkish armed forces and in the Grand National Assembly believe that there is no Kurdish question or minority problem in Turkey. The problem is one of terror according to their perceptions. In order to stamp out this terror perpetuated by the PKK, Turkish officials have hitherto opted to resort to a military solution. Such a policy is unlikely to reap benefits in the longer term. It appears that unless there is a dramatic turnabout in the politics of the region, PKK units will always be able to evade the Turkish armed forces by finding sanctuary in the remote mountains of the east or in the territory of neighbouring states. Undoubtedly, the terrorism problem is a serious issue which requires to be addressed. The trans-state dimension of this particular problem should always be borne in mind. Nevertheless, the Kurdish question in Turkey is also fundamentally concerned with the need for the authorities to address more seriously what has become an increasing recognition among official Turkish circles of the so-called 'Kurdish reality'.

The politicized elements of the Kurds in Turkey who have become more conscious of what they believe to be a separate identity are clearly frustrated. They are not officially recognized as a nation, ethnic group or ethnic minority by the authorities in Ankara. Continued frustration could well turn to desperation and play into the hands of the PKK radicals. Talk of the recognition of a 'Kurdish reality' by prominent Turkish politicians does not go far enough. What do they mean by granting this recognition? Should it not be acknowledged that the Kurds as a distinct group or people are entitled to certain rights (minority rights) in addition to the rights they should already possess as Turkish citizens? Should not the recognition of a separate identity and culture be adopted as a policy instead of possible further attempts to assimilate Kurds who do not wish to be assimilated? Such official recognition certainly need not result in the fragmentation of the state, although clearly certain officials in Ankara are fearful of such a prospect. However, there is a danger that this official recognition could leave an impression that the Kurds as a group enjoy more privileges than the rest of the population.

Ultimately, it will be up to key Turkish politicians to take a lead and seriously tackle the Kurdish question. The international community should not attempt to compel the Turkish authorities to adopt particular policies. That would only prove counterproductive as Turkish officials will not take kindly to outside duress and a xenophobic backlash could also be possible. Such a reaction could feed upon the so-called 'Sèvres syndrome' which, as noted earlier, became an issue on the Turkish political agenda in spring 1995. While not refraining from criticism, the international community should show patience and understanding and at the same time offer encouragement to the government in Ankara. In the wider regional context the immediate prospects are not propitious although the international community could provide a useful stabilizing influence in the longer term. Given past history and current realities, there is not going to be a quick or simple solution to the Kurdish question in Turkey and in the region as a whole. The resolution of what is, after all, a trans-state ethnic conflict will take time, but the Turkish authorities could start to initiate what could become a resolution process.

Ethnic conflicts need to be resolved rather than merely settled. The needs of all relevant parties must therefore be satisfied. In particular, the existence of different groups and respect for the identity of each must be guaranteed and recognized by other actors involved in the conflict. Because of the highly sensitive nature of the issues involved in an ethnic conflict, solutions cannot be imposed by outside parties. It has been suggested that when a protracted conflict reaches the stage of a 'hurting stalemate', the time is ripe for the intervention of a third party to help to achieve a resolution.[1] However, ripeness may not be perceived by the key actors involved in the conflict. Contending parties in an ethnic conflict are not monolithic entities. Hence certain factions, for instance, in a particular ethnic group may disagree with their co-ethnics and continue the armed struggle.[2] These factions may even violently turn against and repress their co-ethnics, accusing them of acting too moderately or of even being in league with their ethnic rivals.

In practice, to resolve any ethnic conflict many factors need to be taken into account. Each such conflict is unique and merits detailed individual examination. The history of relations between the ethnic groups within the territory of a state, the political culture of that state, the levels of consciousness of the leaders and masses of the groups, the similarities and differences between the ethnic groups, the size and geographical distribution of these groups, the intensity and duration of the conflict, the regional context and the general nature of international relations are among some of the factors that might require consideration.

The addressing of economic problems in eastern and south-eastern Anatolia could help to produce a more conducive environment in which the Kurdish question could be more effectively tackled. As noted previously, the influential Turkish businessman Sakıp Sabancı in a report published in late 1995 appealed for new investment in these regions. Sabancı proposed the establishment in Istanbul of a centre, the Eastern Anatolian Union for Economic and Social Development, which could supervise new investments in co-ordination with an Eastern Anatolian Development Unit based in Erzurum and with eight Regional Economic and Social Development Units distributed throughout eastern and south-eastern Anatolia.[3] But, as we have discussed earlier, new investments in these areas will not be forthcoming until violence ceases and stability is restored. One must therefore return to question whether ethnic conflicts should be resolved by 'political' rather than 'military' means. Many commentators would prefer a 'political solution'. However, what would constitute a political solution in the case of Turkey and the 'Kurds'?

Secession

The linkage between secession and territorial forms of self-determination was discussed earlier. In today's predominantly state-centric world the issue of secession is undoubtedly a highly problematic one. In the debate on self-determination, the UN General Assembly resolution 2625 of October 1970 alluded to the possible right of secession against a discriminatory and unrepresentative government. The General Assembly Declaration of December 1960 on the Granting of Independence to Colonial Countries and Peoples had noted that the authorities of a state should not use force to prevent self-determination in connection with a 'people's' right to complete independence. However, first a 'people' would need to demonstrate to the international community that it is one entitled to independence. A people could then justifiably wage a war of national liberation against the central authorities of a state. But terrorist organizations could also claim that their resort to violence has part of a liberation war. Counter-acts of violence on the part of the state authorities could lead to escalation and to the outside world a civil war might then indeed appear to be in progress. One could argue that the PKK is employing this strategy and the Turkish authorities may be unwittingly enacting their role. What is a war of national liberation is clearly another controversial issue. One should note here though that talk of liberation wars does at least open up the possibility of 'qualified intervention' by outside parties to support the 'peoples' involved.[4]

    Turkish officials would definitely oppose any possible 'qualified intervention'. In spite of this line of argument, the general prevailing view currently remains one at odds with the opinion that there is a right to secession and territorial self-determination. Nevertheless, the issue is one which is under increasing discussion. Secession has been defined as:

A kind of collective action, whereby a group (whether officially recognized as a legitimate political subunit or not) attempts to become independent from the state that presently claims jurisdiction over it and, in doing so, seeks to remove part of the territory from the existing state.[5]

As a result of a successfully completed secession a new state could be formed or a group could take the territory which they inhabit and separate from one state and attach their territory to another, already existing state. In both instances the partition of the original state is involved.

Secession is not identical to irredentism, but the two are closely related. Irredentism is concerned with any territorial claim made by the authorities of one state to territory within another. These claims are generally supported on the grounds of history or common ethnicity.[6] Irredentism is often then a trans-state ethnic phenomenon. It is the government of a state which makes these claims. On the other hand, secession depends more on group sentiment and loyalty. Chazan has argued that there are two forms of irredentism. The common variant described above involves demands made by governments. Another more ambiguous form, proposed by Chazan, concerns an ethnic group which is a minority in two or more states. This group may seek union with a state or call for independent statehood.[7] The Kurds in Turkey, Iran, Iraq and Syria would be a case in point here. However, this would actually be a form of secession as explained above although Chazan was attempting to stress the importance of the common trans-state ethnic linkage, i.e., not just any territory was being united or partitioned.[8]

Buchanan has argued that a 'group' has a right to secede only if it is a victim of 'discriminatory redistribution'. This would usually involve three types of case. The first would involve the systematic application of economic policies or taxation schemes by the authorities of a state which would seriously disadvantage a particular group. Alternatively, the distinctive culture or form of communal life of a group could face extinction – perhaps owing to the forced assimilation policies pursued by the state authorities – and thus the group would have a legitimate right to secede to preserve its way of life – with the proviso that its culture met certain standards of decency, whatever these might be. Thirdly, secession could be justified if a group must defend itself against threats to the survival of its members by third-party aggressors when the authorities of the state in which the group lives are not offering protection to the threatened group.[9] Secession against a particularly repressive regime hence could be included within these criteria. Buchanan was opposed to the 'historical entitlement' argument in connection with the claim to territory by a secessionist group. This was because of the question of how far one should go back in history in order to substantiate a claim on the grounds of historical entitlement.[10] Such an argument could be of relevance only in the case of territory recently seized by an occupying state which did not originally have an obvious legitimate claim to the territory. The Soviet annexation of the Baltic states was one example.

Other scholars are willing to adopt a more permissive approach to the right of secession. According to their arguments, secession may be possible but would be dependent on such factors as the degree of distinctiveness of the secessionist group, the viability of its potential state, the degree of world harmony as opposed to disruption that could ensue from the secession, and the need for the overwhelming majority of the inhabitants of a particular region, preferably inhabiting an area on the borders of the state, to be in favour of secession.[11]

According to Horowitz, usually backward peoples in backward regions of a state aim to secede as they have little to gain by remaining within the state. Horowitz has claimed that advanced ethnic groups in backward regions are more reluctant to secede, as it would be more profitable for them to remain where they were.[12] But what of an ethnic group widely scattered geographically and lacking unity, such as the Kurds in Turkey? Many of them now inhabit the urban areas of western Turkey. Horowitz has contended that backward peoples in advanced regions rarely aim to secede as it would not be to their economic benefit. Certainly, in spite of the number of active secessionist movements in the world there have been few successful secessions since 1945. Secession is actually a final, desperate attempt to 'exit' the state when a group's efforts to secure 'access' or express its 'voice' have been frustrated. Exit in this instance is a high-risk policy because often it will not be achieved peacefully but rather at the cost of much suffering and many lives.

Given their concern for the need to maintain territorial integrity and state unity, no Turkish government will voluntarily allow any group to secede and thereby partition Turkish territory. Many officials would argue that the Kurds in Turkey do not need to secede as they are well-treated as first-class citizens who are not in need of minority rights, and whose culture is not in danger of extinction. Nevertheless, a number of politicized Kurdish groups have advocated the right of secession from Turkey. The PKK leadership has demanded this right; but at other times the PKK has also been seemingly prepared to accept many other possible solutions to the Kurdish question in Turkey. Other Kurdish groups have recommended armed struggle – although they themselves are not necessarily involved in this struggle to secure a unified and independent 'Kurdistan'. For example, the ex-Marxist and now Socialist KAWA-Unity of the Proletariat of Kurdistan, and other socialist Kurdish bodies such as the Kurdistan Liberation Party and YEKBUN (Unity) have advocated such a policy. However, secession does not appear to be a realistic option for the Kurds for the foreseeable future. No international organization or state is pressing Turkey to allow the Kurds to secede. On the contrary, the need to protect the territorial integrity of the country is stressed. A successful

Kurdish secession could have dire consequences for the stability of the whole region. In one possible scenario the spillover affect of secession could even prompt secessionist campaigns further afield. Examples could be the Turks in Bulgaria and Greece, the Azeris in Iran, and the Abkhazians and South Ossetians in Georgia. The conflict within Turkey is not perceived at present by the international community as a war of national liberation in which the Kurds could then perhaps be entitled to support. The PKK and other Kurdish groups are hence pursuing other possible alternatives.

Consociationalism

Consociationalism or power-sharing is associated with the works of Lijphart. His studies originally focused on examples of power-sharing in states such as the Netherlands, Belgium, Austria and Switzerland, although later he considered the relevance of consociationalism for the South African polity.[13] The aim of consociationalism is to ensure a form of democracy where the views of ethnic, linguistic or religious minorities could always be taken into account, in addition to the needs and wants of the majority. Minorities would thus not become alienated from the state in question. The emphasis is on consensus and equality rather than majority rule. One important aim is to prevent forceful or involuntary assimilation. Consociationalism may embrace different types of power-sharing arrangement at the level of the state or within regions or other sub-units of it. It may also vary in extensiveness from merely applying to a sharing of positions within the cabinet, to a more wide-spread allocation of positions within the legislature and across several public sectors. Forms of consociationalism have been evident outside Europe in, for example, Malaysia (1955–69), Lebanon (1943–75) and Fiji (1970–87). Another example of consociationalism was attempted in Cyprus (1960–63).

There are four basic features of fully-fledged forms of consociationalism. First, the elites of the political parties of the main groups (or 'segments') within the society need to establish a grand coalition government. The elites of these groups should share out proportionally public service appointments and the allocation of public funds. These groups should be granted autonomy or be part of a federal arrangement of government. These specific features will be examined individually on their own merits later in this chapter. Suffice it to say here that where groups are territorially concentrated federalism is a viable option, and where groups are widely distributed or are intermixed then non-territorial, cultural forms of autonomy are possible. The final basic feature of consociationalism is the minority veto, which should be an available option for minority groups when their vital interests may be affected by a decision made by the majority. The aim of the minority veto is to ensure that decisions are agreed upon by consensus. However, this mechanism should be used sparingly, otherwise the entire system could be undermined.

In his writings Lijphart has identified a number of factors that favour power-sharing arrangements with regard to different ethnic groups within the same state. The two most important are the absence of a majority ethnic group and the absence of large socio-economic differences among the groups. Preferably ethnic groups should be roughly the same in size so that there is a balance of power among them. There should not be too many groups so that negotiations between them will be less difficult. The total population of the state should be relatively small so that decision-making is less complex. Overarching loyalties that reduce the strength of particularistic ethnic loyalties would be helpful. Perceived external dangers would promote internal unity. The geographic concentration of ethnic groups would make federalism a more attractive option. Existing traditions of compromise and accommodation between the ethnic groups would also be of help. It would be better for the groups to be united rather than internally divided and geographically scattered. The existence of cross-cutting divisions such as class, religion and language overspreading the groups would also be beneficial.

Consociationalism has come under fire for several reasons. One criticism is its inflexibility. Change is difficult to accommodate as segments or groups tend to be regarded as fixed entities. A traditionally more dominant ethnic group within a state is also unlikely to concede more power-sharing responsibilities to a usually less influential ethnic group on account of demographic changes for instance. In any case, is consociationalism a form of democracy since it remains highly dependent on secret bargaining between elites with the exclusion of more general debate among the population?[14]

The emphasis on inter-elite co-operation has been criticized for a variety of other reasons. Would bargaining between elites of different ethnic groups really work in practice, as it has been argued that rival counter-elites are likely to emerge to denounce this co-operation? Hence leaders of ethnic groups, in order not to be undercut or outflanked by challengers from within their ranks, must invariably be seen to take a more extreme position to defend their group's interests. This would not be conducive to inter-elite bargaining and compromise.[15] Moreover, for consociationalism to continue to work, successive generations of political leaders would need to support it: 'The moment rival elites believe that the benefits of war exceed the costs of peace a consociational system is doomed.'[16] Elites of different groups may rather pursue policies to suit their own selfish interests and gain control of certain resources.[17] The rank and file members of certain ethnic groups may not be under the control of their elites and, for example, may choose to riot or initiate pogroms.[18] Or perhaps co-operation may actually develop between non-elites of different ethnic groups, especially if they are able to participate in an open and competitive political system.[19]

An ethnic group or segment may not be clearly defined. As previously discussed, the boundaries between ethnic groups may fluctuate. Consociationalism may work better in societies divided along class or linguistic lines among industrialized states rather than in ethnically-divided societies in the developing world where groups are less homogeneous and the issues are more emotive. Power-sharing arrangements may be more suitable for moderately rather than deeply divided societies. The classic examples of Belgium, Austria, the Netherlands and Switzerland referred to societies with religious and linguistic divisions, although in the successful case of Lebanon until 1975 religious and ethnic cleavages overlapped.[20] Also consociationalism may perhaps only be suitable for small states.

In the light of this discussion it should be apparent that consociationalism is not readily applicable in Turkey, a large, developing country confronted with an ethnic conflict of a trans-state dimension, and where since 1923 inter-elite co-operation between Turks and Kurds has been sporadic and confined to agreements struck with individual Kurdish chiefs and tribes. Very few of the favourable factors conducive to power-sharing apply to Turkey. Certainly, the two most important conditions are not present. At least the problem between the Turks and the Kurds is currently the only ethnic issue of real concern for the authorities in Ankara. Cross-cutting cleavages such as religion and class exist. But it has been pointed out earlier that the Turks and the Kurds in general belong to the separate Sunni and Alevi divisions of Islam. Also the common Marxist views held by Turkish and Kurdish youth in the 1960s, which resulted in a form of violent, non-elite co-operation against the state authorities, had by the 1970s and the 1980s become of secondary importance in the face of a growing upsurge in Kurdish nationalism.

The four basic features of consociationalism do not appear to be realizable in Turkey for the foreseeable future with regard to the Turks and the Kurds. A dramatic turnabout in thinking among official circles in Ankara would be required. Kurdish political parties are not officially permitted, although there are Kurdish deputies within the ranks of the major political parties. The significance of this will be discussed later. Federalism and autonomy are also problematic issues for the government as will also be examined later. The concept of 'proportionality' and the mechanism of the 'minority veto' run counter to the official Turkish line that the Kurds are already first class citizens and thus do not require additional privileges.

No political group within or outside Turkey appears to have considered seriously the possibility of adopting the consociational model. It would seem to create divisions artificially in Turkish society where previously divisions may not have existed. One should recall that through integration and assimilation some 'Kurds' in Turkey, who may even hold important positions in government, may now not want to be separated from 'Turks' since they may perceive themselves to be Turks themselves. Some individuals may perceive themselves to be both Turks and Kurds, and so 'Turks' too cannot be thought of as a homogeneous ethnic group. It is suggested later that 'multiculturalism' rather than consociationalism offers better prospects for a long-term and peaceful solution to the Kurdish question in Turkey.

Forms of Autonomy

What is meant by autonomy? The term is vague and open to varying interpretation. In practice there are several forms of autonomy which differ in their nature and extensiveness. According to Connor, autonomy is an 'amorphous concept' which ranges from very limited options to complete control over all matters except foreign policy: 'It can therefore incorporate all situations between total subordination to the centre and total independence.'[21] Most scholars would rather argue that autonomy falls short of independence. Autonomy may be based on territory where ethnic groups are geographically concentrated. Non-territorial, cultural forms of autonomy are also possible where ethnic groups are widely scattered and intermixed. In the latter case, groups are able to control the cultural aspects of their life. With territorial autonomy, groups may be able to establish more control over cultural, political, social and economic issues by making use of their geographic concentration. Home rule is also a possibility where an ethnic group may just concede decision-making powers in the areas of defence and foreign policy to the central government.

  According to Hannum, a 'fully autonomous' territory would possess most of the following features: there would be a locally-elected legislature having some independent legislative authority, limited by the constitution, over matters such as education, the use of language, the structure of local government, land use and planning. There would be a locally-selected chief executive who may be subject to approval by the central government. This executive may have the responsibility to administer and enforce national and local laws. There would be an independent local judiciary given full responsibility to interpret local laws. Disputes over the extent of local authority or about the relationship between the autonomous and the central government could be decided by a state judiciary or a joint dispute-settling body. There could also be power-sharing arrangements between the autonomous and the central government in areas of joint concern such as the police, exploitation of natural resources, and the operations of ports and communications facilities.[22]

  As noted above, autonomy may be one of the basic features of consociationalism. The CSCE Copenhagen Declaration of June 1990 referred to the rights of minorities to establish possible 'local or autonomous administrations'. Prime Minister Tansu Çiller has herself it seems at least momentarily considered the applicabilty of the Basque model of territorial autonomy in the case of Turkey. The workings of the Basque model have been discussed earlier.

The example of the Basques may be used as evidence that the granting of territorial autonomy to an ethnic group need not necessarily lead to the disintegration of the state. However, critics and sceptics may argue that regionalism was introduced in Spain only in the early 1980s and that the ETA-Militar hardliners are still willing to use violence to bring about the secession of the Basque provinces. One must always bear in mind that in contrast to Turkey, Spain is not situated in a highly unstable and volatile region. The example of the Sikhs in India is employed by some to illustrate how the bestowal of territorial autonomy on a particular ethnic group may actually exacerbate the situation within a state. Thus, in spite of the decision of the Indian government in New Delhi to grant autonomy to Punjab, the demands of militant Sikhs for complete independence and the establishment of 'Khalistan' have intensified and violence in the region has escalated.[23]

If ethnic groups do not have a specific regional base, cultural autonomy is a possible alternative to territorial autonomy. In this instance the representatives of an ethnic group would have full control over aspects of their cultural life including matters of education and language. Autonomous cultural communities may be governed by cultural councils. In Estonia, for example, the Cultural Autonomy Law of 1925 allowed self-defined minorities to apply for the right to establish cultural councils. These bodies had modest revenue-sharing powers and exercised control in areas such as education and other matters relating to culture. The dispersed German and Jewish minorities made use of these cultural councils to obtain a measure of self-government.[24] In Belgium today the members of Parliament are divided into Dutch, French and German-speaking councils which have authority over cultural issues. Having also territorially-based regional institutions, Belgium is an example of a state where a combination of both territorial and non-territorial forms of autonomy is in operation.[25]

Gottlieb's proposed 'states-plus-nations' approach is a variant of autonomy for ethnic groups distributed across the boundaries of a state.[26] Hence this approach may be applicable in the case of a trans-state ethnic conflict. It allows for so-called 'soft forms of unions' between national communities divided by frontiers. According to Gottlieb, these groups, while keeping the citizenship of the state in which they reside, should be allowed their national identity and should be able to co-operate and work together with their co-nationals or co-ethnics in neighbouring states. Here recognized functional spaces or special functional zones across borders could be created where some form of local governance should be allowed and national traditions and cultural rights should be respected – on the condition that these privileges do not run counter to the policies of the central governments of the states concerned.

What are the possibilities of granting the Kurds a measure of autonomy in Turkey? According to the TOBB Report, 13 per cent of those polled were in favour of some form of autonomy and another 13 per cent supported the establishment of a separate Kurdish state.[27] Apart from Çiller's passing mention, no other prominent Turkish politician has been prepared to entertain the idea of granting the Kurds autonomy in Turkey. Autonomy is associated with the much-despised Treaty of Sèvres. The Sèvres syndrome is a crucially important factor. In the face of increasing Western pressure to make concessions to the Kurds, as described previously President Demirel referred in a television interview in May 1995 to the existence of a supposed Western 'conspiracy' against Turkey which aimed to create a situation even worse than that envisaged by the Sèvres Treaty. It seems, however, that Turkish decision-makers appear to overlook the fact that for many years the Ottoman Empire had flourished by using a form of cultural and territorial autonomy embodied in the *millet* system. Gottlieb's state-plus-nations approach is not really applicable to the Kurdish case given the regional context and the nature of the regimes in Iran and Iraq in particular.

If autonomy were ever to be granted to the Kurds in Turkey a mixed form of territorial and cultural autonomy would be preferable given the geographical distribution of the Kurdish population. A considerable degree of autonomy may have to be offered given that politicized Kurdish groups will probably not be content with the granting of cultural rights alone. One should take note of Hannum's point: that within a minority group many may wish only to participate on an equal basis in a state without being forced to abandon their own identity and without being compelled to become a member of a segregated 'autonomous' community.[28]

Federal Schemes

Federal arrangements may also facilitate the resolution of ethnic conflicts. Federalism and territorial forms of autonomy may be closely interconnected. In unitary states all powers are reserved to the central government which may choose to devolve powers to sub-units of government. Powers devolved to these sub-units may easily be transferred back to the central government. The removal of previously devolved powers is much more difficult in federations where devolution is prescribed in a constitution, reserving powers to sub-units of government on certain issues. In genuine federations the central government and local sub-units have separate domains of power and there may also be concurrent jurisdiction in particular matters. Constitutional amendments should require the consent of both levels of government. The legislature should be bicameral with one of the chambers handling issues of importance to the sub-units and where the smallest of these units would usually be overrepresented. There are different types of federalism. Germany and the United States are classic examples of administrative federalism. Federations may be based on ethnic lines as in the past cases of the Soviet Union, Yugoslavia and Czechoslovakia. Canada is an example of a type of federalism which is based both on administrative and ethnic lines. Some federations, such as the former Soviet Union, were federations in name only with most powers actually reserved for the central (federal) government. Federations could allow for substantial powers to be devolved to the sub-units, including even the right to secede (which should not be a mere right on paper as was the case in the Soviet Union).

What of confederations? In these instances the sub-units are reserved extensive powers and given considerable autonomy. Only issues related to foreign policy and defence may remain under the control of the central government. Confederations are actually thus merely a particular form of federation. To argue differently would be, as Zartman has noted, a 'figment of a legal imagination': 'The stark necessity of locating sovereignty some-where and respecting its overwhelming exercise means that a confederation is really a federation, as in Switzerland, or else it is only an alliance of sovereign states, as in Senegambia.'[29]

Horowitz has provided a number of reasons why federations may facilitate the resolution of an ethnic conflict.[30] Government is brought closer to the population with the establishment of 'proliferating points of power' which may take a considerable load off the government at the centre. Within certain limits, therefore, the more sub-units there are, the possibly more effective is the federation. Adjustment of territories covered by the sub-units could be carried out as a type of electoral reform where legislative majorities and minorities based on particular ethnic groups in the sub-units may be made and remade. Horowitz has assumed here that there are ethnically-based political parties within the sub-units. In ethnically-homogeneous sub-units or provinces the focus of attention would shift away from wider inter-ethnic tensions toward more local intra-ethnic disputes. This could even have an impact on the notion of self-determination because it would become more difficult to determine what the 'self' actually consisted of. In ethnically-heterogeneous provinces ethnic conflict at the centre could also be reduced. There could instead be incentives for inter-ethnic co-operation in those cases where a majority ethnic group in the province may be a minority in the country as a whole, and the minority ethnic group in that province may be the majority group in the state overall. Hence federalism could even be effective when ethnic groups are not territorially compact. Finally, the need for bureaucracies at the provincial level provides new career opportunities for ethnic groups who may not be well-represented in government at the centre.

Many of Horowitz's points of argument in favour of federalism as a means of resolving ethnic conflicts within a state (ignoring for now the more complicated problem of a trans-state ethnic conflict) are open to question. At present ethnically-based federations are disintegrating. The Soviet and the Czechoslovak model dissolved peacefully unlike the violent unravelling of Yugoslavia. Even Canada is confronting serious problems with its French-speaking minority and the increasingly more vocal demands of its indigenous peoples. May federalism encourage ethnic groups to attempt to secede eventually because of possible frustration with the policies of the central government? A minority ethnic group would always be outnumbered and probably thus outvoted at the level of central government. In general, federations may encounter difficulties in distributing powers between the centre and the subunits of government and this could generate hostility particularly in the case of ethnically-based federations. In Yugoslavia, for example, the Croatian and the Slovene republics were opposed to providing increasingly larger amounts of money to the federal fund to subsidize the poorer republics inhabited by other ethnic groups. Inter-ethnic conflict could continue to prevail within ethnically-heterogeneous provinces in a federation. This may be especially problematic if the victimized minority ethnic group within the province actually constitutes the majority and the dominant ethnic group within the country as a whole.[31] Even the allocation of jobs within a provincial bureaucracy could lead to new problems. Horowitz himself has noted that there may develop an assumption that members of an ethnic group with 'their own' regions have no right to work in central government or anywhere outside their region.[32]

McGarry and O'Leary have argued a case for the implementation of a scheme of 'cantonization' in order to faciltate the resolution of ethnic conflict.[33] In practice, this may also be regarded as a special form of federalism. Political power is devolved to very small, ethnically-homogeneous units or cantons. This scheme allows for asymmetrical relations between different cantons and the central government. Following on Horowitz's line of argument, cantonization has the advantage of decompressing the area of ethnic conflict and competition into more manageable units. Policing and judicial powers may be gradually devolved to these areas. McGarry and O'Leary admit that the arrangement is not foolproof. Problems may arise on the drawing-up and the policing of the units of government. Cantonization is much more difficult to realize if the ethnic groups are intermixed. Importantly, there is always the danger that policing and judicial powers might be used by paramilitary organizations to seize control of at least parts of the cantons and then declare them liberated zones. The likelihood that the PKK would resort to such tactics means that cantonization will not be introduced in Turkey for the foreseeable future.

The general problems concerning federalism discussed here could be applied to the case of Turkey if a federation were to be established there.

Given the distribution of the Kurds in Turkey, a mixed form of administrative and ethnic federalism along the lines of the Canadian example would perhaps be more appropriate. One possible advantage over territorial autonomy with regard to the example of Turkey is that under federalism powers would be devolved to provinces or sub-units throughout the whole of the country rather than, for instance, only in south-eastern Turkey. One commentator has suggested that the Turkish political system could do with a measure of decentralization, arguing that this could be a good pretext to facilitate the resolution of the Kurdish question.[34] Along these lines, Ahmet Özer, General Secretary of the GAP Municipalities Association, proposed in December 1994 the creation of locally-elected executives and legislatures throughout the country which could benefit from a Development Fund. These new bodies could have their own tax-raising powers and control over matters related to education, health and culture among others.[35] However, just as autonomy is likely to be seen as the start of the slippery slope to secession and the dis-integration of the Turkish state, officials in Ankara are likely to perceive federalism – of whatever type – as equally destructive. As noted previously, even politicians such as Boyner, Özal and Karayalçın have spoken out against a federal solution for Turkey although the three believed that the issue should at least be discussed.

According to the findings of the TOBB Report as many as 42.5 per cent of those polled were in favour of the formation of a federal Turkey. However, the author of the report himself has admitted that many of these people were not sure what a federation actually entailed.[36] In February 1995 in the final communique of the fourth congress of the KSP the party's leader Kemal Burkay appealed for the formation of a Kurdish–Turkish federation.[37] It was not clear what type of federalism Burkay had in mind. In remarks made in the United States in April 1994 the then DEP deputy Mahmut Kılınç spoke of his liking for the American and the German model of federalism.[38] Why he should have preferred an administrative form of federalism as opposed to an ethnically-based model is not clear. The Democratic Party of Kurdistan-Unity, which calls itself a broad-based national party, while declaring that its ultimate goal is an independent Kurdistan, is also evidently open to other solutions such as autonomy or devolution. In March 1994 the PKK leader Öcalan, in his letter addressed to the International Conference on 'North West Kurdistan', argued that he was prepared to discuss any alternatives including the formation of a federation in order to reach an agreement with the government.[39] As we saw earlier, previously, the fourth congress of the PKK in 1990 had earlier taken up the idea of a federal system for Turkey. The fact that the PKK would appear to be in favour of federalism – although its real objective looks to be the establishment of an independent state – seems to make it exceedingly unlikely that any Turkish government would agree to such an arrangement in the foreseeable future.

Provision of Special Rights

A previous chapter has discussed in detail the rights of minorities, the problems associated with their recognition, and whether certain minority ethnic groups should be accorded special rights in addition to those they should already enjoy as individual citizens. With reference to the Kurds in Turkey, the possible 'minority' rights which are often referred to concern the use of Kurdish in schools and in television and radio broadcasts. In theory, the Kurdish language could be used in classes in private schools, and on private radio and television channels without putting into question the status of Turkish as the only official language of the country. The establishing of private schools and universities in Turkey using Kurdish as the medium of instruction would probably be more difficult for Turkish officials to accept even though there are schools and in some instances universities where the language of instruction is French, German, English or Italian. Some Kurds in Turkey with satellite dishes are able to receive broadcasts of the pro-PKK MED TV which is transmitted from London.

Another 'minority right' which could be relevant to the Kurds in Turkey is the right to maintain contacts and ties with fellow kin groups across state frontiers. This was discussed earlier with reference to the applicability of self-determination for a trans-state ethnic problem. Gottlieb's states-plus-nations approach also would accommodate such a right. The CSCE Copenhagen Declaration of June 1990, the UN General Assembly Declaration on the Rights of Persons Belonging to National or Ethnic, Religious and Linguistic Minorities of December 1992, and the Council of Europe's Framework Convention for the Protection of National Minorities of February 1995 all refer to this specific right. In practice, the Turkish government and governments of other states in the region would probably be reluctant to allow this to be applied generously out of concern that a Pan-Kurdish movement could be promoted as a consequence. Unofficial contacts between Kurdish groups across state borders have been noted earlier.

The right of freedom of association for a minority is particularly problematic. Would a Turkish government agree to the formation of Kurdish political parties? There are ways around this difficulty. In effect, a political party could be formed which is Kurdish in all but name. The status of HADEP in Turkey is a case in point. In another example, the Movement for Rights and Freedoms in Bulgaria is to all intents a political party for the Turks. Token representation of non-Kurdish figures in a party could help to mask what may be in effect an ethnically-homogeneous political party. However, taking into account the fate of the DEP deputies, it is obvious that any political party, Kurdish or otherwise, should aim to avoid any contact with the PKK. There are nevertheless positive indicators concerning the current state of Turkish party politics. This will be examined below. The question of whether ethnically-homogeneous political parties are actually useful for ethnic conflict resolution will also be discussed.

When prominent Turkish politicians talk of recognizing the Kurdish reality do they have in mind granting certain rights to the Kurds which may be, in effect, minority rights, even if the Kurds, in theory at least, may still not be officially recognized as a minority? Özal's past call for a 'political solution' may have been intended to accommodate such rights. In April 1993 the SHP's congress promulgated a list of Primary Objectives which advocated, *inter alia*, education in Kurdish, Kurdish-language radio and television, and the right of freedom of expression for citizens of Kurdish origin. In the summer of 1993 and 1994 Çiller also briefly referred to such rights. The RP has also at times sounded sympathetic on these issues although ultimately its followers are of the opinion that a solution based on Islam will transcend ethnic differences.

Leading Turkish politicians tend to sound more positive with regard to rights for Kurds when making speeches outside Turkey. For example, as we noted earlier, the ANAP leader Mesut Yılmaz speaking in March 1995 in the United States surprisingly supported the idea of education and broadcasting in Kurdish. Upon his return, Yılmaz appeared immediately to lose interest in a political solution to the Kurdish question. In reality, in order to start education programmes and radio and television broadcasting in Kurdish constitutional amendments would need first to be approved by the slow-moving Turkish Grand National Assembly. However, the deputies are unlikely to introduce amendments to the Constitution concerning Kurdish rights if they perceive themselves to be subject to considerable international pressure.

Lord Avebury, when talking of the importance of language and cultural rights for the Kurds in Turkey, emphasized the need for the setting up of proper institutions to implement them. Thus he has argued that in place of officials based in Ankara, a separate education authority should be created in order to select Kurdish teachers. Similarly, according to Avebury, a regional administration for the Kurds would be in effect a vehicle of colonialism unless Kurds themselves were able to staff the regional body.[40]

The TOBB Report noted that 15 per cent of those polled called for the state to recognize a Kurdish identity, allow the Kurds cultural rights and provide an appropriate democratic environment where those rights could be enjoyed.[41] It would seem that most Kurdish political groups would be in favour of obtaining, in effect, minority rights, probably in the hope that more concessions might later ensue. For the same reason, many Turkish governments would be reluctant to accord such rights. In the short term the aims of YEKBUN appear to be: official acknowledgement of the existence of a Kurdish nation and the granting of political freedoms for the Kurds. Point Ten of the International Conference on 'North West Kurdistan' held in Brussels in March 1994 referred to the need to lift all bans on Kurdish organizations in Turkey, including the PKK, and demanded the legal recognition of the right to use the Kurdish language.[42]

Arguably, making some concessions on the use of Kurdish in education, radio and television could work to the advantage of the government. Turkey's image internationally would undoubtedly immediately improve. Such concessions could help to create a climate of trust between Turkish officials and some of the Kurdish political groups. In practice, in making these concessions Turkish officials would probably lose little and have much to gain. Many Kurds, including those with radical political views, are eager to ensure that their children learn Turkish and a foreign language as well as Kurdish at school.[43] A 'dialogue' could begin which would not have to lead to discussions about the break-up of Turkey. These policies could be tied in with moves towards more democratization within Turkey as part of a political solution.

Further Democratization

It is generally recognized that Turkey is one of the few states in the Middle East – acknowledging Turkey's Middle Eastern as well as European identity – which has a practising democratic regime. In spite of occasional military coups and periods of political instability, a multiparty system has been functioning reasonably effectively since the Second World War. Nevertheless, there is a widespread acknowledgement outside Turkey that further democratization within the country is required. Some politicians in Turkey also appear to share this view.

The human rights record in Turkey could improve considerably. For some observers Article 8 of the Anti-terror Law will have to be repealed rather than merely revised before genuine freedom of expression can exist in Turkey. Ironically, in early 1996 there were attempts to put on trial again, according to the terms of the amended Article 8, the four ex-DEP deputies who had been released after previous court rulings in 1994 and 1995. Originally eight deputies had been arrested, seven of whom had been DEP deputies.

The constitutional amendments finally approved by the Turkish Grand National Assembly in July 1995, *inter alia*, referred to the immunities of Parliamentary deputies and the right to set up associations and political parties. These provisions had no direct bearing on the fate of the ex-DEP deputies as the Constitutional Court quickly ruled that the amendments with regard to immunities could not be applied retroactively. Under the new amendments if a political party were closed the individual members of it would not automatically lose their Parliamentary immunities. According to the revised Article 84 of the Constitution, deputies could be imprisoned only if they were directly involved in incidents which led to the dissolution of their party. Previously, in theory all of the deputies of a party could be imprisoned following the closing of their party.[44]

Ethnically-based political parties were not legalized by the new constitutional amendments. In February 1996 the Constitutional Court appeared ready to ban the Democracy and Change Party (DDP) on the grounds that it was a threat to the unity of the state. Between 1991 and the end of 1995 the Court had closed down nine parties, seven of these because of their pro-Kurdish policies.[45] The arrest in January 1996 of the sick Abdülmelik Fırat once again placed Turkey's record on human rights under the spotlight, even though the arrest was criticized by many in Turkey.

Turkish officials should initiate a dialogue with moderate Kurdish political groups in an attempt to build an atmosphere of trust. The arrest of several of the DEP deputies and the fleeing abroad of a number of others because of alleged links with the PKK has created new obstacles in the path toward commencing such a dialogue. While not necessarily approving of their policies and methods, arguably many politicized Kurds have some form of relationship with the PKK. Officials in Ankara would have to tolerate or choose to disregard possible indirect links between Kurdish political groups and the PKK.

Pro-Kurdish sympathizers and various Kurdish groups have advocated that a dialogue should begin with the Turkish authorities. Speaking in the summer of 1994, Lord Avebury believed that serious talks should begin between the government and democratic representatives of the Kurds. He had in mind discussions with the DEP deputies but not with the PKK.[46] Other non-PKK politicized Kurdish groups believe that the PKK should be brought into the discussion to establish a democratic platform in order to halt the violence.[47] Point Ten of the International Conference on North West Kurdistan also referred to the need to start a 'democratic dialogue' after the establishment of a 'bilateral ceasefire under international supervision' and the lifting of all bans on Kurdish organizations in Turkey, including the PKK.[48] The 'democratic' credentials of many of the radical Kurds have been questioned earlier. Given their lack of experience in democracy, for many politicized Kurds it seems that democracy is to be pursued provided it coincides with their own political views. In November 1994 Öcalan talked of his readiness for a 'dialogue within a democratic framework' with the government and stated that the PKK was prepared not to violate the borders of Turkey.[49] Turkish officials interpreted Öcalan's remarks as a sign of increasing weakness. The Interior Minister Nahit Mentese declared that this was the clearest indication yet that the PKK was nearing its end and emphasized that the state never bargained with anyone.[50]

In November 1994 the Commission for Security and Co-operation in Europe (or the 'Helsinki Commission') released a report prepared by the American Senator Dennis DeConcini on Turkey and the Kurds. This included a series of non-binding recommendations which referred to the need for special rights to be granted to the Kurds and stressed the value of dialogue and further democratization. Measures to be taken to lessen tensions in south-eastern Turkey were also suggested. The DeConcini report recommended that all non-violent political parties should be allowed to participate in political life; all restrictions on the freedom of expression including those contained in the Anti-terror Law should be abolished; the state of emergency in the south-east should be repealed; the village-guard system in that part of the country should be dismantled; all restrictions on Kurdish linguistic and cultural expression should be lifted; the Kurdish language should be used on television, radio, in print, in music and other media; a government-sponsored Institute of Kurdish Studies should be opened and schools should be allowed to offer instruction in Kurdish; and a high-level conference should be convened to examine all aspects of Turkish–Kurdish relations.[51] Many of these points were covered in the final communique of the fourth congress of the KSP released in February 1995.[52] The Kurdish 'parliament-in-exile' presented a report to an OSCE-sponsored conference in Ottawa in July 1995 entitled 'The Present Situation in Kurdistan'. In addition to calling for the OSCE to appoint a mediator to end the conflict between the PKK and the Turkish armed forces, the report also appealed for the convening of an international conference to reach a negotiated solution to the Kurdish question along the lines of the successful Madrid Conference on the Israeli–Palestinian problem.[53]

One point to note here is that high-profile individuals in the West such as Senator DeConcini and Lord Avebury are seen by many in Turkey as suspicious because of their links with Kurdish radicals and their well-known anti-Turkish government campaigns. Hence associating certain ideas with such individuals undermines the credibility of these ideas in the eyes of many Turks.

The Turkish authorities will not accept the list of measures recommended by DeConcini as a whole package. Parts of it may be followed up in due course but some of the points are especially awkward to implement. What is meant by a 'high-profile conference'? Who would organize and participate in such a conference? Turkish officials could perceive this as an interference in the country's internal affairs if the conference were prepared or attended by leading international figures. A government-sponsored Institute of Kurdish Studies would also probably create controversy. Kurdish groups could claim that the Institute should function independently from the government. However, a non-government-sponsored Kurdish Institute had been established in Turkey in 1992. The dismantling of the village-guard system and the repealing of the state of emergency would most likely occur only after the conclusion of a ceasefire agreed upon by all involved in the conflict or the termination of hostilities through the total defeat of the PKK. Both scenarios do not appear likely in the short or medium term.

The question of the establishment of Kurdish political parties has been briefly discussed earlier. Horowitz has extensively analysed the adoption of certain electoral arrangements to facilitate the resolution of an ethnic conflict.[54] Assuming that ethnically-based political parties are permitted to operate, Horowitz has emphasized the importance of devising a system which would allow all parties to secure representation and which would create incentives for inter-ethnic co-operation and intra-ethnic competition. These arrangements coincide to an extent with his stress on the importance of federalism. Proportional representation is recommended in order to ensure that smaller, minority groups are better represented and take more interest in affairs of state. An element of consociationalism may even be introduced with reserved seats in the legislature and cabinet for some parties. The chief concern would be to avoid winner-takes-all situations which would be bound to frustrate the political parties of minority ethnic groups. Intra-ethnic competition could be generated by having a fixed number of seats reserved in the legislature for a particular ethnic group. As in the case of certain federal schemes, inter-ethnic co-operation could be encouraged by drawing electoral boundaries to create heterogeneous constituencies where the majority ethnic group would be a minority in certain areas.

Horowitz would certainly not have approved of the electoral arrangements for the national elections held in December 1995. Although HADEP was able to obtain over one million votes and performed very well in some of the Kurdish-populated provinces, the party (with its leftist electoral partners) fell well short of the ten per cent national threshold, securing only just over four per cent of the total national vote. Thus HADEP failed to secure any representation in Parliament. HADEP would have probably obtained considerably more votes if the unreasonably high electoral barrage had been lowered to five per cent. Many politicians and journalists in Turkey have criticized the threshold figure. HADEP officials also complained of biased media reporting, manipulation of results, intimidation at the polls, inadequate facilities with which to conduct an effective campaign, and failure to be allowed to register the more than three million Kurds who, according to their estimates, had recently migrated to urban centres. There were reports that HADEP members were considering an appeal to the European Commission of Human Rights to press the case that the principle of just representation had been violated.[55]

Commentators have argued that owing to the strength of communal identification, it would be almost impossible to move from a situation where political parties are strictly based on ethnic lines to one where this would not be the case.[56] The advantages of the Turkish party system are not that disguised Kurdish parties such as HADEP are allowed to function, but that there are numerous Kurds active within the established political parties. Political pluralism has led to identifiable Kurdish groups within ANAP, the DYP, the

RP and what was then the SHP.[57] Political parties in Turkey are thus ethnically heterogeneous. More importantly, many of these Kurds are not totally assimilated but rather are still conscious of their Kurdish identity and yet are nevertheless prepared to work through these party channels. The example of Şerif Bedirhanoğlu of ANAP has been mentioned. From time to time there have been problems. For instance, as we have noted, some Kurdish deputies were expelled from the SHP and others resigned after attending an international conference in Paris which addressed Kurdish issues.

Within these established political parties there would still appear to be certain restrictions on the activities of Kurdish members. Nevertheless, there are positive signs here. In future the authorities could perhaps legalize Kurdish political parties in Turkey provided that these parties renounced the use of violence. These parties would then most probably struggle to compete for votes against the more established parties having Kurdish groupings in their ranks. The latter would perhaps become even more like catch-all parties concentrating more on 'Kurdish issues'. Parties competing for votes on single issues alone, such as the Kurdish issue, would probably struggle against the more established political parties. On the other hand, the legalization of Kurdish political parties could also lead to further polarization in Turkish society.

Multiculturalism

Acknowledging the Kurdish reality by granting additional rights to the Kurds, moving towards the further democratization of Turkish society, and beginning a dialogue with certain Kurdish political groups would help to lessen ethnic tensions in the country. In time, some form of autonomy could even be accorded to the Kurds. These measures could be implemented without threatening the territorial integrity of the state. Several of these points have been picked up in a package of recommendations produced by the *İktisadi Kalkınma Vakfı* (Economic Development Foundation) of Turkey in late 1994. This specified in particular the importance of education, television and radio in Kurdish and other cultural freedoms, and suggested that Kurdish Institutes should be opened in universities in Turkey.[58] The TOBB Report also made similar recommendations.

The ultimate goal could be the fostering of a genuine multicultural society. This objective is closely connected with the notion of 'political community' discussed earlier. Once in place, an ideology of multiculturalism would transcend any ethnic nationalist ideology. Real civic nationalism would be in evidence. In a multicultural society citizenship and full civil rights need not imply a particular cultural identity. No groups would be forcibly assimilated. Different cultural identities would be allowed to co-exist and even flourish.

At the same time all groups would share the same feeling of belonging to one state.[59]

Examining in particular the case of Mauritius, Eriksen has indicated that multiculturalism requires certain conditions.[60] These include: equal access to the educational system, labour market and shared facilities for ethnic groups; the right to be different and 'the right not to participate in national society' in certain respects; the availability of national identity to all citizens regardless of their cultural differences; the decentralization of political power and the acceptance of different principles for local party organization; and the taking of measures to ensure that the state should not be identified with a set of symbols exclusively representing one or a few components of the population.

Admittedly, these conditions are not easily fulfilled. However, if properly implemented there would be an end to discrimination and voluntary assimilation, socio-economic disparities would in time be eliminated, groups would be able to preserve their separate identities and, indeed, dual identities would be encouraged by an allegiance to one's own group and also to the state. However, the central state authorities would have to be flexible. Autonomy or federation schemes could play a beneficial role. Tolerance, compromise and trust would be crucial features of a multicultural society. Like consociationalism, the aim would be to manage and not do away with differences between groups. Unlike consociationalism, a multicultural society would be much more adaptable and open to change.

Could Turkey become a genuine multicultural society? This could only be achieved gradually by adopting a cautious, step-by-step approach. The sheer size and traditional dominance of the Turkish ethnic group would pose a serious obstacle. In order to fulfill the conditions of multilateralism the leaders of the Turkish ethnic core may feel that they have to concede too much and that 'the Kurds' in return would receive disproportionate rewards. On the other hand, some individuals in Turkey do feel themselves to be both Turk and Kurd as indicated earlier. This notion of multiple identity could help in the development of multiculturalism. There is also the Ottoman experience to fall back on. A new form of a modern day *millet* system could be introduced with the emphasis this time on extending considerable autonomy to ethnic (cultural) as opposed to religious communities. This variant of neo-Ottomanism could apply to the Kurds and, in theory, in the future to other groups such as the Arabs, Circassians and Laz – recent developments related to Chechnya have resulted in a rise of ethnic consciousness among Circassian groups in Turkey. This arrangement is therefore also able to accommodate various forms of internal self-determination. The international community could lend its support and encouragement. The beginning of a dialogue with certain Kurdish groups and the granting of specific 'minority rights' could initiate a step-by-step approach toward the eventual creation of a multicultural society.

The problems are nevertheless immense. Multiculturalism in Turkey may succeed only in a stable and peaceful regional environment. The Kurdish question after all constitutes only part of a broader, trans-state, regional, ethnic conflict. The security-conscious Turkish government will not embrace the idea of multiculturalism as long as the PKK continues to organize its operations from bases across the border in neighbouring states.

It is far from clear how regional stability will be achieved given the complicated network of rivalries between Turkey, Iran, Iraq and Syria and given the nature of the regimes in Tehran, Baghdad and Damascus. The Kurds in the region may be destined to remain the pawns of states in the region and of interested outside actors such as the United States. The jurisdiction of the OSCE and the Council of Europe does not extend beyond the boundaries of Turkey. The series of tripartite discussions between Turkey, Iran and Syria are more an exercise in damage-control rather than conflict resolution. Certainly Western officials are conscious of the potentially highly destabilizing consequences for the region if their governments decided to recognize an independent Kurdish state in northern Iraq.

The international community should be aware of Turkey's legitimate security concerns and be mindful of the wider dimensions of the Kurdish question in the region. In contrast to Iran, Iraq and Syria, Turkey is an easier target for Western governments to criticize because of its democratic credentials. Ironically, therefore, Western officials' condemnations of the policies of the Turkish government are also in effect a demonstration of indirect praise for the workings of Turkish democracy. At least there is the possibility that these criticisms if couched in diplomatic language could be taken up by politicians in Turkey. Criticisms directed against Syria, Iran and Iraq are much more likely to fall on deaf ears.

Regional tensions should not be used as a pretext by Turkish officials to forestall moves towards the encouragement of a multicultural society. However, the success of multiculturalism in Turkey is undeniably dependent on considerable progress being made toward resolving the Kurdish question at the regional level.

Notes

1. I.W. Zartman, *Ripe for Resolution: Conflict and Intervention in Africa* (New York: Oxford University Press, 1985).
2. M. Kleiboer, 'Ripeness of Conflict: a Fruitful Notion', *Journal of Peace Research*, 31, 1 (Feb. 1994) pp.110–11, 115.
3. *Yeni Yüzyıl*, 21 Nov. 1995.
4. A. Heraclides, *The Self-Determination of Minorities in International Politics* (London: Frank Cass, 1991) pp.30–2.
5. A. Buchanan, *Secession: the Morality of Political Divorce from Fort Sumter to Lithuania and*

Quebec (Boulder CO: Westview, 1991) p.75.

6. J. Mayall, *Nationalism and International Society* (Cambridge: Cambridge University Press, 1990) pp.58, 61.

7. N. Chazan, 'Approaches to the Study of Irredentism', in N. Chazan (ed.), *Irredentism and International Politics* (Boulder CO: Lynne Rienner, 1991) p.2.

8. Chazan created problems by defining irredentism rather broadly as encompassing 'any political effort to unite ethnically, historically, or geographically related segments of a population in adjacent territories within a common political framework'. See ibid., p.1.

9. A. Buchanan, op. cit., pp.38–45.

10. Ibid., pp.110–11.

11. A. Heraclides, op. cit., pp.27–30; and H. Beran, 'A Liberal Theory of Secession', *Political Studies*, 32, 1 (March 1984) pp.21–31.

12. D.L. Horowitz, *Ethnic Groups in Conflict* (Berkeley, Los Angeles and London: University of California Press, 1985) pp.229–81.

13. See A. Lijphart, *Democracy in Plural Societies* (New Haven and London: Yale University Press, 1977); *Power-Sharing in South Africa* (Berkeley, Institute of International Studies: University of California Press, 1985); and 'The Power-Sharing Approach', in J.V. Montville (ed.), *Conflict and Peacemaking in Multiethnic Societies* (Lexington MA and Toronto: Lexington Books and D.C. Heath, 1991) pp.491–509.

14. For these criticisms see K.S. Shehadi, *Ethnic Self-Determination and the Breakup of States* (London: Adelphi Paper 283, International Institute for Strategic Studies, Brassey's, 1993) p.69; and K.D. McRae, 'Theories of Power-Sharing and Conflict Management', in J.V. Montville (ed.), op. cit., p.96.

15. B. Barry, 'Review Article: Political Accommodation and Consociational Democracy', *British Journal of Political Science*, 5, 4 (Oct. 1975), pp.502, 505.

16. J. McGarry and B. O'Leary, 'Introduction: the Macro-Political Regulation of Ethnic Conflict', in J. McGarry and B. O'Leary (eds.), *The Politics of Ethnic Conflict Regulation: Case Studies of Protracted Ethnic Conflict* (London and New York: Routledge, 1993) p.37.

17. P.R. Brass, *Ethnicity and Nationalism: Theory and Comparison* (Newbury Park, London and New Delhi: Sage, 1991) p.245.

18. B. Barry, op. cit., p.502.

19. P.R. Brass, op. cit., pp.333–48.

20. K.D. McRae in J.V. Montville (ed.), op. cit., pp.97–8; J. McGarry and B. O'Leary in J. McGarry and B. O'Leary (eds.), op. cit., p.37; and D.L. Horowitz, op. cit., pp.571–2.

21. W. Connor, 'Ethnonationalism', in W. Connor, *Ethnonationalism: the Quest for Understanding* (Princeton NJ: Princeton University Press, 1994) p.83.

22. H. Hannum, *Autonomy, Sovereignty and Self-Determination: the Accommodation of Conflicting Rights* (Philadelphia: University of Pennsylvania Press, 1990) pp.467–8.

23. T.R. Gurr, *Minorities at Risk: a Global View of Ethnopolitical Conflicts* (Washington DC: US Institute of Peace, 1993) pp.301–2.

24. J. Coakley, 'The Resolution of Ethnic Conflict: Towards a Typology', *International Political Science Review*, 13,4 (Oct. 1992) p. 348.

25. A. Lijphart in J.V. Montville (ed.), op. cit., p.502.

26. G. Gottlieb, 'Nations without States', *Foreign Affairs*, 73, 3 (May–June 1994) pp.100–12.

27. Türkiye Odalar ve Borsalar Birliği (TOBB) *Doğu Sorunu – Teşhisler ve Tespitler* (hereafter cited as *TOBB Report*) (Ankara: TOBB, 1995) p.38.

28. H. Hannum, op. cit., p.474.

29. I.W. Zartman, 'Negotiations and Prenegotiations in Ethnic Conflict: The Beginning, the Middle and the Ends', in J.V. Montville (ed.), op. cit., p.529.
30. D.L. Horowitz, op. cit., pp.601–28.
31. V. Stanovcic, 'Problems and Options in Institutionalizing Ethnic Relations', *International Political Science Review*, 13, 4, (Oct. 1992) p.366.
32. D.L. Horowitz, op. cit., p.622.
33. J. McGarry and B. O'Leary in J. McGarry and B. O'Leary (eds.), op. cit., pp.31–2.
34. H.J. Barkey, 'Turkey's Kurdish Dilemma', *Survival*, 35, 4 (Winter 1993–94) p.67.
35. *Yeni Yüzyıl*, 24 Dec. 1994.
36. *TOBB Report* op. cit., pp.38–9.
37. *Turkish Daily News (TDN)*, 11 March 1995.
38. *Aydınlık*, 3 April 1994.
39. The text of Öcalan's letter dated 10 March 1994, was provided by the Kurdistan Human Rights Project, London.
40. Interview with Lord Avebury, London, 22 July 1994.
41. *TOBB Report* op. cit., p.33.
42. *International Conference on North West Kurdistan (South East Turkey), March 12–13 1994, Brussels. Final Resolution*, organized by Medico International (Frankfurt/Berlin) and the Kurdistan Human Rights Project (London).
43. Information gathered by the authors in interviews conducted in south-eastern and eastern Turkey. The authors were also told that once music cassettes in Kurdish became widely available and were played publicly many of the local population soon lost interest in playing the music.
44. See *TDN*, 26 July 1995 for details of the constitutional amendments; and ibid., 13 Sept. 1995 for the ruling of the Constitutional Court.
45. Ibid., 14 Jan. 1996.
46. Note 40.
47. Interview with a representative of the Kurdistan Human Rights Project, London, 27 July 1995.
48. Note 42.
49. *Özgür Ülke*, 26 Nov. 1994.
50. *Sabah*, 24 Nov. 1994.
51. *TDN*, 30 Nov. 1994.
52. Ibid., 11 March 1995 – with reference to the ending of the state of emergency; the dismantling of the village-guard system, the toleration of freedom of expression for parties and organizations of Kurdish identity, and the recognition and guarantee of rights and liberties for the people of Kurdish identity in Turkey.
53. Ibid., 8 July 1995.
54. D.L. Horowitz, op. cit., pp. 628–52.
55. *Cumhuriyet*, 18 Dec. 1995.
56. J. McGarry and B. O'Leary in J. McGarry and B. O'Leary (eds.), op. cit., pp.212–21.
57. H. Bozarslan, 'Political Aspects of the Kurdish Problem in Contemporary Turkey', in P.G. Kreyenbroek and S. Sperl (eds.), *The Kurds: a Contemporary Overview* (New York and London: Routledge, 1992) p. 110.
58. *Sabah*, 7 Nov. 1994.
59. T.H. Eriksen, *Ethnicity and Nationalism: Anthropological Perspectives* (Boulder CO and London: Pluto, 1993) p.123.
60. T.H. Eriksen, 'Ethnicity versus Nationalism', *Journal of Peace Research*, 28, 3 (Aug. 1991) p.276.

8

Conclusion

THE KURDISH question in Turkey is a highly complex, controversial and extremely politically sensitive issue. And because of its trans-state nature, developments in northern Iraq in particular are also causing additional complications for Turkish decision-makers. At the time of writing the situation in Turkey is in a state of flux. In these circumstances, scholars, commentators and politicians alike within and outside Turkey should be particularly mindful of the use of such terms as 'nation', 'minority' and 'people'. The limitations of the conceptual tools at our disposal concerning how one may analyse issues related to nationalism and ethnicity have been noted. The term 'nation' especially is a politically loaded one. Labelling a certain group a nation could have wide-ranging and destabilizing consequences. Similarly, outside pressure for Turkey, for example, to grant territorial autonomy to the Kurds could provoke adverse reactions within the country. Such appeals or demands could incite Turkish nationalist extremists to resort to violence in order to pre-empt what they might fear to be the first steps toward the breakup of the unity of the state.

However, ultimately the political process is more affected by government actions rather than the 'other-labelling', as it were, of scholars and commentators. Hence, for instance, this study has drawn attention to the importance of the official recognition of a 'nation', 'minority group' or 'people'. Nevertheless, academics and other political analysts may also have an impact on the political process by at least initially drawing attention to the existence – real or otherwise – of a nation, minority or people.

The international community should therefore tread warily and not stoke up the fires of nationalist feeling in Turkey. Already there have been strong reactions at perceived outside interference in Turkey's internal affairs. Thus by late spring 1995 President Demirel was publicly referring to the existence of a supposed Western 'conspiracy' against Turkey. He also asserted that Western appeals for Turkey to grant minority rights and open up a dialogue with the Kurds could lead to a situation worse than that envisaged by the much-despised Treaty of Sèvres. The President remarked that the population of Turkey did not want a democracy which aimed to divide their country. According to Demirel, making such concessions to the Kurds could make

Turkey no longer manageable. He warned of the danger of Turkey's slipping towards a situation which would resemble that of a bloodbath.[1]

The importance of the Sèvres syndrome, given much more pointed emphasis with the public remarks of President Demirel, should not be under-estimated. Arguably Demirel was reacting to the increased debate and discussion within Turkey concerning the recognition of a 'Kurdish reality'. There is a danger here that further stress on the linkage between Sèvres, con-cessions to the Kurds, and the views of the West, could lead to a polarization within Turkish society between supposed compatriots and traitors. The term 'traitor' would then be employed to refer to those within the country prepared to give certain 'rights' to the Kurdish population. The prospects for polarization along these lines are real given that many of the deputies of the Turkish legislature – excluding the CHP and the RP Parliamentary groups – have adopted a hardline position on the Kurdish question.

There is no need for such polarization. One important observation of this study is that an individual may consider himself or herself to be both a Turk and a Kurd. Individuals may hold dual or several identities, choosing to emphasize one or another depending on the context. This multiple identification could actually facilitate the development of multiculturalism in a united and democratic Turkey in the longer term. It is crucial to com-prehend how individuals perceive themselves, although the limitations of self-definition and the importance of other-definition and other-determination have been raised here.

One should remember to bear in mind that identities themselves may change in time and that individuals may shift their allegiance across ethnic boundaries for personal interests. The impact of modernization on ethnic-identity formation should also be considered. These factors must be taken into account when one endeavours to understand the dynamics behind the assimilation of the several ethnic groups within Turkey. Why, in comparison with other ethnic groups, have 'the Kurds' been much more difficult to assimilate? The large numbers within the population who are aware of their Kurdish ethnic background obviously is one explanation. The tribal nature of Kurdish society also has an important bearing. Some Kurds, following the example of their tribal chiefs, have refused to be fully co-opted by the Turkish authorities. Other tribes, however, have been prepared to co-operate with Ankara. The fact that most of the Kurdish population originally lived in geographically-remote parts of the country which were difficult for the state authorities to penetrate must be taken into account too. Furthermore, the economically backward nature of these territories should not be overlooked. Perhaps one could develop an argument that the more prosperous and thus the more influential individuals or groups are better integrated in a society.

With regard to the general development of Kurdish consciousness in Turkey, almost all Kurds at one time considered themselves to be part of the

Moslem population of the Ottoman Empire. Most of these Kurds were not aware of a separate ethnic let alone a separate national identity. In spite of the lobbying and campaigning of a handful of educated activists who had become conscious of a separate Kurdish identity, the first rebellions against the newly-formed Turkish Republic were mostly tribal and regional in nature. The attempted forced assimilation by the dominant Turkish ethnic core of the population of the Republic in the 1930s led to an increased awareness among the Kurds of their separate ethnicity. After the Second World War some of the Kurds in Turkey would also perceive themselves to be a separate nation entitled to their own independent state. But in spite of the pressures of modernization, and in the face of further attempts at assimilation by the authorities in Ankara, many Kurds, whether or not conscious of a separate ethnic or national identity, remained attached to their tribal and regional allegiances. It was not surprising, therefore, that immediately before the 1995 elections Çiller was campaigning for electoral support from particular Kurdish tribes.[2]

Difficulties with the term 'assimilation' have been extensively discussed. In practice, it is not simply a matter of an individual from a different ethnic group being either totally assimilated or not at all. In line with the notion of dual and multiple identity, an individual may thus perceive him or herself in the political sense as a 'Turk', or at least as a Turkish citizen given the controversy over what exactly is meant by a 'Turk', and culturally as a 'Kurd'. Accordingly, therefore, many Kurds have no problem in identifying themselves personally with the famous phrase *'Ne mutlu Türküm diyene'* – 'Happy is one who can say he is a Turk'.[3]

Interestingly, the process of assimilation is not one way. Although it is undoubtedly true that many Kurds became in time assimilated in varying degrees and perceive themselves now as Turks and possibly even deny their original Kurdish ethnic background, there are also cases of Turks becoming, as it were, 'assimilated Kurds' – that is, regarding themselves as Kurds and no longer as Turks. For example, the Turkish tribes of Karakeçili, Turkan and Beğdili have in time become assimilated by the Kurds to the extent that they have become Kurdish speakers.[4] Van Bruinessen has noted that members of the Karakeçili tribe were 'Kurdophone but according to local tradition they were originally Turkmen from Western Anatolia and had been settled in the region by Sultan Selim I after the Ottoman Conquest'.[5] However, the grandson of the famous Simko (Ismail Agha) – Simko was the Kurdish tribal leader who had been active in territory which today lies in northern Iran – has claimed that his grandfather was a descendent of the Karakeçili tribe.[6]

With regard to the formation of a Turkish ethnic and then national identity, until the end of the nineteenth century the term 'Turk' in general referred to what in effect amounted to an 'ethnic category'. Many so-called 'Turks', like the Kurds, looked upon themselves as Moslem inhabitants of the Ottoman Empire. Moreover, unlike most Kurds the Turks at the time had no separate network of tribal structures with which they could also identify. The original Ottoman tribal confederation had long ago established itself as the dominant force in Ottoman politics. But at the turn of the twentieth century only a small number of the Ottoman elite, and some outside scholars and political thinkers, were interested in Turkish ethnicity and language. The task of Mustafa Kemal and his followers to build simultaneously a Turkish nation and state after the collapse of the Ottoman Empire was thus an immense one. Initially, a resistance movement of Turks, Kurds and other parts of the population of different ethnic backgrounds was organized to oust the occupying forces from Anatolia. With the founding of the Republic, Mustafa Kemal and his supporters attempted to transform this resistance movement into a national movement based on Turkish nationalism. Opposition from certain Kurdish tribes in particular, the fears of possible outside intervention, a lack of experience with the workings of democracy, and a general feeling of insecurity among many officials in Ankara, resulted in this nationalism rapidly taking the form of an ethnic rather than a civic nationalism. The dominant Turkish ethnic core sought to consolidate the Turkish state and nation through a policy of forced assimilation.

It will be exceedingly difficult to make significant progress in resolving the Kurdish question owing to the terrorist activities of the PKK and the reluctance of key Turkish officials to implement a political as opposed to a military solution. Arguably there is a lack of firm leadership at present in the corridors of power in Ankara. It seems that there is no key political leader who may follow in the footsteps of the late President Özal and be prepared at least to challenge longstanding taboos with regard to the Kurdish question by seriously considering the possibility of a 'political solution'. It appears that current Turkish politicians are more concerned with short-term interests and vote-catching policies.

In May 1995 President Demirel remarked that if the Kurds were given additional rights these would be equivalent to privileges which would make other Turkish citizens 'second-class citizens'.[7] This obviously struck a chord in the feelings of many in Turkey. The problem in part, though, is again one of terminology. Undoubtedly there are a number of sufficiently politicized and self-aware 'Kurds' in Turkey who are demanding additional 'rights' in order to protect their identity. Instead of addressing these demands by referring to so-called 'minority rights', the Turkish authorities could still make the necessary amendments to the Constitution in order to allow the use of the Kurdish language on radio, television and in education. These concessions need not be openly referred to as 'minority rights'. A Kurdish 'minority' need not be officially recognized *de jure*, although *de facto* this would be the case. Ironically, as noted earlier, the granting of such concessions would actually be in line with the provisions of the Treaty of Lausanne, an agreement much praised in Turkey. Of course, many political scientists would argue that granting 'minority rights' does not suddenly make another group second-class citizens. Such notions would be perceptions in the eye of the beholder. However, political sensitivities do need to be addressed, and certainly at the time of writing it seems extremely unlikely that leading Turkish officials are about to reverse their traditional policy and openly countenance the existence of an ethnic minority in Turkey. However, on the other hand, these officials should be mindful of the danger that the denial of 'minority rights' for a particular group could lead to serious minority discontent and could create a 'surge to self-determination' – in this case secession – about which the government is so much concerned.

The picture may not be quite so bleak though. What is meant by the term 'Turk' has come under increasing question in recent years. For many the term had come to refer to a 'Turk' in the ethnic sense. Now there are serious efforts to reformulate this meaning in order to stress that a Turk is in effect anyone who is a 'Turkish citizen' irrespective of his or her ethnic background. There has also been discussion about the relevance of the meaning 'Türkiye Vatandasığı' – that is, referring to the notion that a Turk is a person who lives in Turkey and whose roots lie there, again regardless of ethnic background. One of the main conclusions of the TOBB Report was that the phrase 'The people of Turkey' should be employed instead of the term 'The Turkish people'.[8]

Returning from a trip to Tajikistan and Mongolia in September 1995, President Demirel was quoted as saying: 'I would consider any person who chooses to call himself a "Turk" a Turk. However, if a person insists on saying "I am a Kurd", then I would consider him a Kurd but as a Turkish citizen and hence a part of the Turks.'[9] Even Ecevit, who has earned a reputation for his opinion that the Kurdish question was solely related to economic underdevelopment, has also lent his support to the notion of 'constitutional citizenship'.[10] A political solution to the Kurdish question would certainly need to embrace wholeheartedly a genuine civic nationalism. This could be achieved within a democratic and united multicultural Turkey.

One should always bear in mind that the Kurdish question is not confined to Turkey alone, and that it is an example of a trans-state ethnic conflict. The extent of co-operation among Kurds in the region has been examined. Although some tribes straddle the Turkish–Iraqi border, the lack of ethnic affinity links between Kurds in the area has contributed in part to tensions between the PKK and the KDP and between the KDP and the PUK in northern Iraq. Personal rivalries and ambitions have also resulted in increased tensions between these groups. Undoubtedly, Turkish officials are concerned that the PKK should not establish a dominant influence in northern Iraq and thereby perhaps form a genuine Pan-Kurdish nationalist movement. The government is able to take some consolation from the fact that the regimes in Iran, Iraq and Syria would also be bitterly opposed to the formation of such a Pan-Kurdish movement controlled by the PKK. The insecure regional environment, however, does pose grave problems for the Turkish government. The Kurdish issue will not be fully resolved unless the PKK is deprived of the use of its bases in neighbouring states. Entessar has noted: 'recognition of the legitimate rights of the Kurds that do not threaten the territorial integrity and political viability of Iran, Iraq and Turkey must be promoted by these states and by other regional states and the international community.'[11] What so-called 'legitimate rights' may entail with regard to the Kurdish question in Turkey has been discussed here in detail. But, in spite of their common fears and concerns, given the nature of the current regimes in Iran, Iraq and Syria, it would seem that for the foreseeable future Turkey will not be able to co-ordinate a concerted regional initiative with regard to the Kurdish question.

Within Turkey itself, hopes for further democratization and devolution of decision-making powers, the development of a dialogue, and the possible emergence of multiculturalism based on a real and genuine civic nationalism still remain at present only hopes. Not all Turkish officials and political parties are willing to accommodate moves toward further democratization and pluralism in Turkish society. At the same time, there is a tendency among many Kurdish radicals to pursue a policy based on what amounts to exclusive ethnic nationalism. Ironically, this appears to complement the type of nationalism which has prevailed throughout much of the history of the Republic of Turkey.

The lack of respect for established democratic norms among some of the ex-DEP deputies has been previously noted. Given its past track record it does not seem likely that the PKK, if given the opportunity to exercise power, would suddenly transform itself into a party which would be prepared to tolerate opposition and criticism from other Kurdish groups. The PKK's emphasis on violence and its lack of a democratic, pluralist tradition makes its participation in the political process very unlikely. In September 1995 at a conference convened in Oslo to discuss the Kurdish question, some of the participants harshly criticized the PKK for being a 'non-democratic and intolerant organization which is trying to monopolize debates, and, due to its violent actions, is obstructing the creation of a dialogue with Turkey on a possible solution.'[12] Speaking at the same conference, Van Bruinessen – an expert on the Kurds whose works the authors of this study have often cited – demanded that the PKK should cease violating human rights and learn to tolerate and respect ideas different from those of its own.[13]

Moderate Kurdish nationalists such as Kemal Burkay, head of the KSP, have often criticized the PKK for its use of violence and its tendency to interfere in the internal affairs of other Kurdish groups and organizations. At the time of writing it was unclear whether in the near future the PKK would choose to moderate its behaviour. One must bear in mind that the PKK is not a monolithic organization and that there are bound to be competing factions within its membership. Some of these may prefer to eschew the path of violence.

Would a government in Ankara ever agree to sit down at the same negotiating table with the PKK 'terrorists'? Perhaps the question is a redundant one. According to the TOBB Report, only 9.4 per cent of those Kurds surveyed wanted to include the PKK in talks to find a solution to the Kurdish question.[14] Significantly, Murat Bozlak, the leader of HADEP, has argued that the PKK should not be involved in negotiations with the Turkish government.[15] It would seem that the PKK is not that representative of the Kurdish population in Turkey. Many Kurds apparently believe that a peaceful solution to the Kurdish question is possible through a dialogue with the authorities from which the PKK could be excluded. There is an emerging opinion though that a comprehensive settlement without the inclusion of the PKK in some form in any talks will be difficult. Undoubtedly the PKK has played an important role in putting the Kurdish question firmly on the political agenda in Turkey, in the region and beyond.

Officials and commentators outside Turkey appealing for increased democratization within the country should be more aware of the lack of respect for democratic traditions among many radical Kurdish nationalists. Several key Turkish politicians have referred to the need to reach a political solution to the Kurdish question. As noted previously, shortly after assuming office in March 1996, Prime Minister Yılmaz emphasized that such a policy should be pursued. But words must be translated into deeds. Given the complicated nature of the Kurdish question, with its regional backdrop, only time will show whether officials and the public could move toward a more democratic and multicultural society in which 'the Kurds' in particular are able to express openly their identity without undermining the territorial integrity and stability of the Turkish state.

Notes

1. *Turkish Daily News (TDN)*, 10 and 22 May 1995.
2. *Yeni Yüzyıl*, 29 Nov. 1995.
3. Gathered from interviews the authors conducted with a number of Kurds while travelling between Van and Hakkari in eastern Turkey in June 1995.
4. S. Mutlu, 'Population of Turkey by Ethnic Groups and Provinces', *New Perspectives on Turkey*, 12 (Spring 1995) p.35.
5. M. Van Bruinessen, 'The Ethnic Identity of the Kurds', in P. Andrews (ed.), *Ethnic Groups in the Republic of Turkey* (Wiesbaden: Ludwig Reichert, 1989) p.618.
6. Interview with the authors, June 1995.
7. *TDN*, 8 May 1995.
8. Türkiye Odalar ve Borsalar Birliği (TOBB), *Doğu Sorunu: Teşhisler ve Tespitler*

(hereafter cited as TOBB Report) (Ankara: TOBB, 1995) p.63–4.

9.   *Yeni Yüzyıl*, 14 Sep. 1995.
10. Ibid., 18 Sep. 1995.
11. N. Entessar, *Kurdish Ethnonationalism* (Boulder CO: Lynne Rienner, 1992) p.10.
12. Quoted in *TDN*, 26 Sep. 1995.
13. Ibid..
14. TOBB Report, op. cit., p.25.
15. *TDN*, 9 Feb. 1996.

Bibliography

Books and Chapters in Books in English

M.Akehurst, *A Modern Introduction to International Law* (London: Allen & Unwin, 1987)

G.A. Almond and B.G. Powell, *Comparative Politics: a Developmental Approach* (Boston, MA: Little, Brown, 1966)

B. Anderson, *Imagined Communities* (New York and London: Verso, 1991)

M.S. Anderson, *The Eastern Question 1774–1923* (London: Macmillan, 1966)

P. Andrews (ed.), *Ethnic Groups in the Republic of Turkey* (Wiesbaden: Ludwig Reichert, 1989)

H. Arfa, *The Kurds: a Historical and Political Study* (London: Oxford University Press, 1968)

Asylum Under Attack (a Report of the Lawyers' Committee for Human Rights, 1992)

C. Balım, E. Kalaycıoğlu, C. Karataş, G. Winrow and F. Yasamee (eds.), *Turkey: Economic, Social and Foreign Policy Challenges for the 1990s* (Leiden: Brill, 1995)

F. Barth (ed.), *Ethnic Groups and Boundaries. The Social Organization of Culture Difference* (Oslo: Universitetsforlaget, Scandinavian University Press, 1969)

W. Bell and W.E. Freeman (eds.), *Ethnicity and Nation-Building: Comparative, International and Historical Perspectives* (Beverly Hills, CA and London: Sage, 1974)

W. Bell and W.E. Freeman, 'Introduction', in Bell and Freeman (eds.)

N. Berkes (ed.), *Turkish Nationalism and Western Civilization* (London: Allen & Unwin, 1959)

H. Bozarslan, 'Political Aspects of the Kurdish Problem in Contemporary Turkey', in Kreyenbroek and Sperl (eds.)

P.R. Brass (ed.), *Ethnic Groups and the State* (New York: Barnes & Noble, 1985)

P.R. Brass, *Ethnicity and Nationalism: Theory and Comparison* (New Delhi and Newbury Park, London: Sage, 1991)

P.R. Brass, 'Ethnic Groups and the State', in Brass (ed.)

J. Breuilly, *Nationalism and the State* (Chicago and Manchester: University of Chicago Press and Manchester University Press, 1982)

M.E. Brown (ed.), *Ethnic Conflict and International Security* (Princeton, NJ: Princeton University Press, 1993)

M.E. Brown, 'Causes and Implications of Ethnic Conflict', in Brown (ed.)

I. Brownlie, 'The Rights of Peoples in Modern International Law', in Crawford (ed.)

A. Buchanan, *Secession: the Morality of Political Divorce from Fort Sumter to Lithuania and Quebec* (Boulder, CO: Westview, 1991)

J.W. Burton, 'Conflict Resolution as a Political Philosophy', in Sandole and Van der Merwe (eds.)

J. Calleja, H. Wiberg and S. Busuttil (eds.), *The Search for Peace in the Mediterranean Region* (Malta: Mireva Publications, 1994)

S.C. Caton, 'Anthropological Theories of Tribe and State Formation in the Middle East: Ideology and Semiotics of Power', in Khoury and Kostiner (eds.)

G. Chaliand (ed.), *People Without a Country: the Kurds and Kurdistan* (London: Zed, 1980)

G. Chaliand (ed.), *Minority Peoples in the Age of Nation-States* (London: Pluto, 1989)

N. Chazan (ed.), *Irredentism and International Politics* (Boulder, CO: Lynne Rienner, 1991)

N. Chazan, 'Approaches to the Study of Irredentism', in Chazan (ed.)

I. Claude, *National Minorities: an International Problem* (Cambridge, MA: Harvard University Press, 1955)

W. Connor, *Ethnonationalism: the Quest for Understanding* (Princeton, NJ: Princeton University Press, 1994)

W. Connor, 'Nation-Building or Nation-Destroying', in Connor

W. Connor, 'A Nation is a Nation, Is a State, Is an Ethnic Group, Is a ...', in Connor

W. Connor, 'Eco- or Ethno-Nationalism', in Connor

W. Connor, 'Self-Determination: The New Phase', in Connor

W. Connor, 'Ethnonationalism', in Connor

L.A. Coser, *The Functions of Social Conflict* (New York and London: Free Press and Collier Macmillan, 1956)

J. Crawford (ed.), *The Rights of Peoples* (Oxford: Clarendon Press, 1988)

J. Crawford, 'The Rights of Peoples: "Peoples"or "Governments"?' in Crawford (ed.)

J. Crawford, 'The Rights of Peoples: Some Conclusions', in Crawford (ed.)

F. Cuny, *Northern Iraq: One Year Later* (Washington, DC: The Carnegie Endowment, 1992)

I.M. Cuthbertson and J. Leibowitz (eds.), *Minorities: the New Europe's Old Issue* (Prague: Institute for East West Studies, 1993)

R. Dalton, 'The Role of the CSCE', in Miall (ed.)

K.M. De Silva and R.J. May (eds.) *Internationalization of Ethnic Conflict* (London: Pinter, 1991)

K.W. Deutsch, *Nationalism and Social Communication – an Inquiry into the Foundations of Nationality* (Cambridge, MA and London: MIT Press, 2nd ed., 1966)

G. De Vos, 'Ethnic Pluralism: Conflict and Accommodation', in De Vos and Romannucci-Ross (eds.)

G. De Vos and L. Romannucci-Ross (eds.), *Ethnic Identity: Cultural Continuities and Change* (Palo Alto, CA: Mayfield, 1975)

D.F. Eickelman (ed.), *Russia's Muslim Frontiers – New Directions in Cross-Cultural Analysis* (Bloomington and Indianapolis, IN: Indiana University Press, 1993)

A. Eide, *New Approaches to Minority Protection* (London: Minority Rights Group, 1995)

N. Entessar, *Kurdish Ethnonationalism* (Boulder, CO: Lynne Rienner, 1992)

T.H. Eriksen, *Ethnicity and Nationalism: Anthropological Perspectives* (Boulder, CO and London: Pluto, 1993)

A. Fenet, 'The Question of Minorities in the Order of Law', in Chaliand (ed.) (1989)

A. Finkel and N. Sırman (eds.), *Turkish State and Turkish Society* (New York and London: Routledge, 1990)

F. Fonval, 'Ethnocide and Acculturation', in Chaliand (ed.) (1989)

F. Frey, *The Turkish Political Elite* (Cambridge, MA: MIT Press, 1965)

G. Fuller, *Iraq in the Next Decade: Will Iraq Survive until 2002?* (Santa Monica, CA: RAND Corporation, 1992)

G.R. Garthwaite, 'Reimagined Internal Frontiers: Tribes and Nationalism – Bakhtiyari and Kurds', in Eickelman (ed.)

E. Gellner, *Nations and Nationalism* (Oxford: Blackwell, 1983)

Ö.F. Gençkaya, 'The Kurdish Issue in Turkish Politics', in Calleja *et al.* (eds.)

Z. Gökalp, 'Historical Materialism and Sociological Idealism', in Berkes (ed.)

Z. Gökalp, 'What is a Nation?', in Berkes (ed.)

L. Greenfield, *Nationalism: Five Roads to Modernity* (Cambridge, MA and London: Harvard University Press, 1992)

J. Grugel, 'The Basques', in Watson (ed.)

M. Gunter, *The Kurds in Turkey: a Political Dilemma* (Boulder, CO: Westview, 1990)

T.R. Gurr, *Minorities at Risk: a Global View of Ethnopolitical Conflicts* (Washington, DC: US Institute of Peace, 1993)

T.R. Gurr and B. Harff, *Ethnic Conflict in World Politics* (Boulder, CO, San Francisco and Oxford: Westview, 1994)

I. Gyurcsik, 'New Legal Ramifications on the Question of National Minorities', in Cuthbertson and Leibowitz (eds.)

W. Hale, *Turkish Politics and the Military* (London: Routledge, 1994)

M.H. Halperin, D.J. Scheffer, with P. Small, *Self-Determination in the New World Order* (Washington, DC: Carnegie Endowment for International Peace, 1992)

H. Hannum, *Autonomy, Sovereignty and Self-Determination: the Accommodation of Conflicting Rights* (Philadelphia PA: University of Pennsylvania Press, 1990)

H. Hannum (ed.), *Guide to International Human Rights Practice* (Philadelphia, PA: University of Pennsylvania Press, 1992)

G. Harris, *Turkey: Coping with Crisis* (Boulder, CO: Westview, 1985)

M. Hechter, *Internal Colonialism. The Celtic Fringe in British National Development 1536–1966* (London: Routledge, 1975)

M. Heiberg, *The Making of the Basque Nation* (Cambridge: Cambridge University Press, 1989)

A. Heraclides, *The Self-Determination of Minorities in International Politics* (London: Frank Cass, 1991)

U. Heyd, *Foundations of Turkish Nationalism* (London: Luzac, Harvill Press, 1950)

A.O. Hirschman, *Exit, Voice and Loyalty: Responses to Decline in Firms, Organizations and States* (Cambridge, MA: Harvard University Press, 1970)

E.J. Hobsbawm, *Nations and Nationalism since 1780 – Programme, Myth, Reality* (Cambridge: Cambridge University Press, 1990)

E.J. Hobsbawm, and T. Ranger (eds.), *The Invention of Tradition* (Cambridge: Cambridge University Press, 1983)

D.L. Horowitz, *Ethnic Groups in Conflict* (Berkeley, Los Angeles and London: University of California Press, 1985)

D.L. Horowitz, 'Ethnic Conflict Management for Policymakers', in Montville (ed.)

D.L. Horowitz, 'Irredentas and Secessions: Adjacent Phenomena, Neglected Connections', in Chazan (ed.)

H. Howard, *The Partition of Turkey: a Diplomatic History, 1913–1923* (Norman, OK: University of Oklahoma, 1931)

S.P. Huntington and C. H. Moore (eds.), *Authoritarian Politics in Modern Society* (New York: Basic Books, 1970)

International Institute for Strategic Studies, *The Military Balance 1994–1995* (London: IISS, 1995)

H.R. Isaacs, *Idols of the Tribe: Group Identity and Political Change* (New York and London: Harper & Row, 1975)

M. Izady, *A Concise Handbook: the Kurds* (Washington, DC and London: Taylor & Francis, 1992)

I. İmset, *The PKK: a Report on Separatist Violence in Turkey* (Ankara: Turkish Daily News Publication, 1, 1992)

A. Kazamias, *Education and the Quest for Modernity in Turkey* (Chicago: University of Chicago Press, 1966)

M. Keating, 'Spain: Peripheral Nationalism and State Response', in McGarry and O'Leary (eds.)

E. Kedourie, *Nationalism* (Oxford: Blackwell, 4th ed., 1993)

J.G. Kellas, *The Politics of Nationalism and Ethnicity* (Basingstoke: Macmillan, 1991)

N. Kendal, 'Kurdistan in Turkey', in Chaliand (ed.) (1980)

R.O. Keohane and J.S. Nye (eds.), *Transnational Relations and World Politics* (Cambridge, MA: Harvard University Press, 1971)

R.O. Keohane and J.S. Nye, 'Transnational Relations and World Politics: an Introduction', in Keohane and Nye (eds.)

P.S. Khoury and J. Kostiner (eds.), *Tribes and State Formation in the Middle East* (Berkley, Los Angeles and Oxford: University of California Press, 1990)

P.S. Khoury and J. Kostiner, 'Introduction: Tribes and the Complexes of State Formation in the Middle East' in Khoury and Kostiner (eds.)

K. Kirişci, *The PLO and World Politics: a Study of the Mobilization of Support for the Palestinian Cause* (London: Pinter, 1986)

K. Kirişci, 'New Patterns of Turkish Foreign Policy Behaviour', in Balım *et al.* (eds.)

K. Koch, 'The International Community and Forms of Intervention in the Field of Minority Rights Protection', in Cuthbertson and Leibowitz (eds.)

J. Kolars and W. Mitchell, *The Euphrates and the Southeast Anatolian Development Project* (Carbondale, IL: Southern Illinois Press, 1991)

D. Korn, *The Men who Put the Kurds into Iraq: Percy Cox and Arnold Wilson* (Silver Spring, MD: KNC Publications, 1993)

P.G. Kreyenbroek and S. Sperl (eds.), *The Kurds: a Contemporary Overview* (New York and London: Routledge, 1992)

J. Landau, *Radical Politics in Modern Turkey* (Leiden: Brill, 1974)

J. Landau (ed.), *Atatürk and Modernization of Turkey* (Boulder, CO: Westview, 1984)

J. Landau, 'The Ups and Downs of Irredentism: the Case of Turkey', in Chazan (ed.)

B. Lewis, *The Emergence of Modern Turkey* (London: Oxford University Press, 1962)

G.L. Lewis, 'Ataturk's Language Reform as an Aspect of Modernization in the Republic of Turkey', in Landau (ed.)

A. Lijphart, *Democracy in Plural Societies* (New Haven and London: Yale University Press, 1977)

A. Lijphart, *Power-Sharing in South Africa* (Berkley: University of California Press, Institute of International Studies, 1985)

A. Lijphart, 'The Power-Sharing Approach', in Montville (ed.)

C.A. Macartney, *National States and National Minorities* (London: Oxford University Press, for the Royal Institute of International Affairs, 1934)

C.G. MacDonald, 'The Kurds', in Schechterman and Slann (eds.)

J. Mayall, *Nationalism and International Society* (Cambridge: Cambridge University Press, 1990)

J. Mayall, 'Sovereignty and Self-Determination in the New Europe', in Miall (ed.)

J. McGarry and B. O'Leary (eds.), *The Politics of Ethnic Conflict Regulation: Case Studies of Protracted Ethnic Conflicts* (New York and London: Routledge, 1993)

J. McGarry and B. O'Leary, 'Introduction: the Macro-Political Regulation of Ethnic Conflict', in McGarry and O'Leary (eds.)

K.D. McRae, 'Theories of Power-Sharing and Conflict Management', in Montville (ed.)

H. Miall (ed.), *Minority Rights: the Scope for a Transnational Regime* (London: Pinter, for the Royal Institute of International Affairs, 1994)

J.V. Montville (ed.), *Conflict and Peacemaking in Multiethnic Societies* (Lexington, MA and Toronto: Lexington Books and D.C. Heath, 1991)

T. Nairn, *The Break-up of Britain: Crisis and Neo-Nationalism* (London: New Left Books, 2nd ed., 1977)

R. Olson, *The Emergence of Kurdish Nationalism 1880–1925* (Austin: University of Texas Press, 1991)

E. Özbudun, 'Established Revolution versus Unfinished Revolution: Contrasting Patterns of Democratization in Mexico and Turkey', in Huntington and Moore (eds.)

A. Powell, *The Struggle for Power in Moslem Asia* (New York: Century, 1923)

R.R. Premdas, 'The Internationalization of Ethnic Conflict: Some Theoretical Explanations', in De Silva and May (eds.)

N.S. Rodley, 'United Nations Non-Treaty Procedures for Dealing with Human Rights Violations', in Hannum (ed.)

J.S. Roucek, *The Working of the Minorities System under the League of Nations* (Prague: Orbis, 1929)

K. Rupesinghe (ed.), *Internal Conflict and Governance* (New York and Basingstoke: St. Martin's Press and Macmillan, 1992)

D.J.D. Sandole and H. Van der Merwe (eds.), *Conflict Resolution Theory and Practice: Integration and Application* (New York and Manchester: Manchester University Press, 1993)

B. Schechterman and M. Slann (eds.) *The Ethnic Dimension in International Relations* (Westport, CT and London: Praeger, 1993)

H. Seton-Watson, *Nations and States: an Enquiry into the Origins of Nations and the Politics of Nationalism* (Boulder, CO: Westview, 1977)

K.S. Shehadi, *Ethnic Self-Determination and the Breakup of States* (London: Adelphi Paper 283, International Institute for Strategic Studies, Brassey's, 1993)

O. Sheikhmous, 'The Kurdish Question in Regional Politics: Possible Peaceful Solutions', in Rupesinghe (ed.)

A.D. Smith, *The Ethnic Revival in the Modern World* (Cambridge: Cambridge University Press, 1981)

A.D. Smith, *The Ethnic Origins of Nations* (New York and Oxford: Blackwell, 1986)

A.D. Smith, *National Identity* (Harmondsworth, Middlesex: Penguin, 1991)

A.D. Smith, 'The Ethnic Sources of Nationalism', in Brown (ed.)

J. Snyder, 'Nationalism and the Crisis of the Post-Soviet State', in Brown (ed.)

R. Tapper, 'Anthropologists, Historians and Tribespeople on Tribe and State Formation in the Middle East', in Khoury and Kostiner (eds.)

P. Thornberry, *International Law and the Rights of Minorities* (Oxford: Clarendon, 1991)

P. Thornberry, 'International and European Standards on Minority Rights', in Miall (ed.)

B. Toprak, *Islam and Political Development in Turkey* (Leiden: Brill, 1981)

A.J. Toynbee, *The Western Question in Greece and Turkey* (Boston: Houghton Mifflin, 1922)

A.J. Toynbee and K. Kirkwood, *Turkey* (London: Benn, 1926)

US Department of State. *Country Reports on Human Rights Practices for 1991* (Washington, DC: 1992)

US Department of State, *Patterns of Global Terrorism, 1993* (Washington, DC: 1994)

US Department of State, *Patterns of Global Terrorism, 1994* (Washington, DC: 1995)

UNHCR Report on Northern Iraq: April 1991–May 1992 (Geneva: UN High Commissioner for Refugees, 1992)

M. Van Bruinessen, *Agha, Shaikh and State* (London: Zed, 1992)

M. Van Bruinessen, 'The Ethnic Identity of the Kurds', in Andrews (ed.)

M. Van Bruinessen, 'Kurdish Society, Ethnicity, Nationalism and Refugee Problems', in Kreyenbroek and Sperl (eds.)

P.L. Van den Berghe, 'Protection of Ethnic Minorities: a Critical Appraisal', in Wirsing (ed.)

M. Watson, (ed.) *Contemporary Minority Nationalism* (New York and London: Routledge, 1992)

D. Welsh, 'Domestic Politics and Ethnic Conflict', in Brown (ed.)

M. Winter, 'The Modernization of Education in Kemalist Turkey', in Landau (ed.)

R.G. Wirsing (ed.) *Protection of Ethnic Minorities: Comparative Perspectives* (New York and Oxford: Pergamon, 1981)

R.G. Wirsing, 'Dimensions of Minority Protection', in Wirsing (ed.)

World Refugee Survey 1992 (Washington, DC: US Committee for Refugees, 1992)

Yalçın-Heckmann, L. 'Kurdish Tribal Organization and Local Political Processes' in Finkel and Sırman (eds.)

M.E. Yapp, *The Making of the Modern Near East, 1792–1923* (London: Longman, 1987)

M.C. Young, 'The National and Colonial Question and Marxism: a View from the South', in Motyl (ed.)

I.W. Zartman, *Ripe for Resolution: Conflict and Intervention in Africa* (New York: Oxford University Press, 1985)

I.W. Zartman, 'Negotiations and Prenegotiations in Ethnic Conflict: the Beginning, the Middle and the Ends', in Montville (ed.)

S. Zenkovsky, *Pan-Turkism and Islam in Russia* (Cambridge, MA: Harvard University Press, 1960)

E.J. Zürcher, *The Unionist Factor* (Leiden: Brill, 1984)

Articles in English

Y. Alexander, 'Narco-Terrorism: Future Threats', *Intersec*, 10, 11/12, (Nov.–Dec. 1995)

H.J. Barkey, 'Turkey's Kurdish Dilemma', *Survival*, 35, 4 (Winter 1993–94)

B. Barry, 'Review Article: Political Accommodation and Consociational Democracy', *British Journal of Political Science*, 5, 4, (Oct. 1975)

O. Bengio, 'The Challenge to the Territorial Integrity of Iraq' *Survival*, 37, 2 (Summer 1995)

H. Beran, 'A Liberal Theory of Secession', *Political Studies*, 32, 1 (March 1984)

J. Brown, 'The Turkish Imbroglio: Its Kurds' *Annals AAPSS*, 541 (Sep. 1995)

J. Coakley, 'The Resolution of Ethnic Conflict: Towards a Typology', *International Political Science Review*, 13, 4, (Oct. 1992)

N.B. Criss, 'The Nature of PKK Terrorism in Turkey', *Studies in Conflict and Terrorism*, 18, (1995)

S. Deringil, 'The Ottoman Origins of Kemalist Nationalism: Namık Kemal to Mustafa Kemal', *European History Quarterly*, 23, (1993)

Ü. Ergüder, 'Changing Patterns of Electoral Behavior in Turkey', *Boğaziçi University Journal*, 8–9, (1980–81)

T.H. Eriksen, 'Ethnicity versus Nationalism', *Journal of Peace Research*, 28, 3, (Aug. 1991)

A. Etzioni, 'The Evils of Self-Determination', *Foreign Policy*, 89, (Winter 1992/93)

F.W. Frey, 'Socialization to National Identification among Turkish Peasants', *Journal of Politics*, 30, 4, (Nov. 1968)

G. Fuller, 'The Fate of the Kurds', *Foreign Affairs*, 72, 2, (Spring 1993)

G. Gottlieb, 'Nations without States', *Foreign Affairs*, 73, 3, (May–June 1994)

M. Gunter, 'A *de facto* Kurdish State in Northern Iraq', *Third World Quarterly*, 14,2 (1993)

W. Hale, 'Turkey's Time: Turkey, the Middle East and the Gulf Crisis', *International Affairs*, 68, 4, (Oct. 1992)

M. Hroch, 'From National Movement to the Fully-Formed Nation – the Nation-Building Process in Europe', *New Left Review*, 198, (March–April 1993)

H. Hyman, A. Payaslıoğlu, and F.W. Frey, 'The Values of Turkish College Youth', *Public Opinion Quarterly*, (Fall, 1958)

K. İnan, 'The South-East Anatolia Project: "A Perspective for Future Investors"', *Turkish Review Quarterly Digest*, Spring 1989.

R. Jalali and S.M. Lipset, 'Racial and Ethnic Conflicts: a Global Perspective', *Political Science Quarterly*, 107, 4, (1992–93)

M.M. Kampelman, 'Secession and the Right of Self-Determination: an Urgent Need to Harmonize Principle with Pragmatism', *Washington Quarterly*, 16, 3, (Summer 1993)

K. Kirişci, 'Refugee Movements and Turkey', *International Migration*, 29, 4, (Dec. 1991)

K. Kirişci, '"Provide Comfort" and Turkey: Decision Making for Refugee Assistance', *Low Intensity Conflict and Law Enforcement*, 2, 2, (Autumn 1993)

K. Kirişci, 'Post Second World War Immigration from Balkan Countries to Turkey', *New Perspectives on Turkey*, 12, (Spring 1995)

M. Kleiboer, 'Ripeness of Conflict: a Fruitful Notion?', *Journal of Peace Research*, 31, 1, (Feb. 1994)

G. Kut, 'Burning Waters: the Hydropolitics of the Euphrates and Tigris', *New Perspectives on Turkey*, 9, (Fall 1993)

R. Lapidoth, 'Sovereignty in Transition', *Journal of International Affairs*, 45, 2, (Winter 1992)

Ş. Mardin, 'Ideology and Religion in the Turkish Revolution', *International Journal of Middle East Studies*, 2, (1971)

S. Mutlu, 'Population of Turkey by Ethnic Groups and Provinces', *New Perspectives on Turkey*, 12, (Spring 1995)

A. Roberts, 'Humanitarian War: Military Intervention and Human Rights', *International Affairs*, 69, 3, (July 1993)

P. Robins, 'The Overlord State: Turkish Policy and the Kurdish Issue', *International Affairs*, 69, 4, (Oct. 1993)

A.B. Prados, 'The Kurds: Stalemate in Iraq', *Congressional Research Service Report for Congress*, 95-397F, (Nov. 1995).

F. Shorter, 'The Crisis of Population Knowledge in Turkey', *New Perspectives on Turkey*, 12, (Spring 1995)

A.D. Smith, 'The Nation: Invented, Imagined, Reconstructed?', *Millenium–Journal of International Studies*, 20, 3, (Winter 1991)

V. Stanovcic, 'Problems and Options in Institutionalizing Ethnic Relations', *International Political Science Review*, 13, 4, (Oct. 1992)

C. Tilly, 'A Bridge Halfway: Responding to Brubaker', *Contention*, 4, 1, (Fall 1994)

Official Documents, Statistics, Texts and Collections of Documents in English

Collection of International Instruments Concerning Refugees, (Geneva: Office of the UN High Commissioner for Refugees, 1988)

Conference on Security and Cooperation in Europe Final Act, (Helsinki, 1975)

Document of the Copenhagen Meeting of the Conference on the Human Dimension of the CSCE, 5–29 June 1990, Copenhagen

Document of the Moscow Meeting of the Conference on the Human Dimension of the CSCE, 10 Sept.–4 Oct. 1991, Moscow

Eastern Mediterranean, Report submitted on behalf of the Defence Committee of the WEU, Rapporteur Mr Cuco, Doc. 1465, 24 May 1995

Framework Convention for the Protection of National Minorities and Explanatory Report, Council of Europe, Feb. 1995, (Strasbourg: Council of Europe Press, 1995)

J.C. Hurewitz, *Diplomacy in the Near and Middle East. A Documentary Record: 1914–1956, Vol.2* (Princeton, NJ, New York, Toronto and London: van Nostrand, 1956)

International Conference on North West Kurdistan (South East Turkey), March 12–13, 1994, Brussels, Final Resolution

Parliamentary Assembly Council of Europe Documents

Report of the CSCE Meeting of Experts on National Minorities, 19 July 1991, Geneva

The Constitution of the Republic of Turkey (Ankara: 1990)

UN General Assembly Declaration on the Granting of Independence to Colonial Countries and Peoples, UN GA Res. 1514 (XV), 14 Dec. 1960

UN General Assembly Declaration on Principles of International Law Concerning Friendly Relations and Co-operation among States in Accordance with the Charter of the UN, UN GA Res. 2625 (XXV), 14 Oct. 1970

UN General Assembly Declaration on the Rights of Persons Belonging to National or Ethnic, Religious and Linguistic Minorities, UN GA Res. 47/135, 18 Dec. 1992

UN General Assembly Resolution 1541, 15 Dec. 1960

UNHCR Report on Northern Iraq: April 1991–May 1992 (Geneva: UN High Commissioner for Refugees, 1992)

UN Security Council Document S/22435, 3 April 1991

UN Security Council Resolution 688, 5 April 1991

Conference Papers in English

E. Avebury, 'Not a mere Phrase' paper presented at Evangelischen Akademie, Kamburg-Dammtor, 21 Jan. 1994.

Theses in English

A. Demirel, *Government and Opposition in the First Grand National Assembly* (Istanbul: PhD thesis, Department of Political Science and International Relations, Boğaziçi University, 1993)

D. Mersin-Alıcı, *The Impact of Turkey's Nationalistic Culture on Turkish Foreign Policy Making as Observed in Turkey's Relations with the Central Asian Turkic Republics* (Istanbul: MA thesis, Department of Political Science and International Relations, 1995)

U. Sipahioğlu, *The Mosul Question and Anglo-Turkish Relations, 1922–1926* (Cambridge: PhD thesis, University of Cambridge, 1995)

Newspapers, News Services, Magazines and Digests in English

Courrier International
Dispatch
International Herald Tribune
Middle East Intelligence Report
Newsweek
New York Times
Reuters
The Economist
Time
Turkish Daily News
Turkish Probe

Books and Chapters in Books in Other Languages

N. Abadan, *Anayasa Hukuku ve Siyasi Bilimler Açısından 1965 Seçimlerinin Tahlili* (Ankara: Siyasi Bilimler Fakültesi Yayınları, 1967)

T. Alp, *Türk Ruhu* (Ankara: Remzi Kitabevi, 1944)

V. C. Aşkun, *Sivas Kongresi* (Istanbul: Inkilap ve Aka, 1963)

Atatürk'ün Söylev ve Demeçleri (1906–1938) (Ankara: Türk Tarih Kurumu Basımevi, 1959)

S. Ayata, *GAP Bölgesi Nüfus Hareketleri Araştırması* (Ankara: T.C. Başbakanlık GAP Bölge Kalkınma İdaresi Başkanlığı, 1994)

E. Aybars, *İstiklal Mahkemeleri* (Izmir: İleri Kitabevi, 1995)

R. Ballı, *Kürt Dosyası* (Istanbul: Cem Yayınevi, 1992)

İ. Beşikçi, *Doğu Anadolu'nun Düzeni: Sosyo/Ekonomik ve Etnik Temeller* (Ankara: E. Yayınları, 1969)

İ. Beşikçi, *Kürtlerin Mecburi İskanı* (Ankara: Yurt Kitap Yayın, Ankara, 1991)

S. Beysanoğlu, *Kürt Aşiretleri Hakkında Sosyolojik Tetkikler* (Istanbul: Sosyal Yayınları, 1992)

M.A. Birand, *Apo ve PKK* (Istanbul: Milliyet Yayınları, 1992)

A.A. Candar, *Türklüğün Kökleri ve Yayılışı* (Istanbul: Necmi İstikbal Matbaası, 1934)

N. Dersimi, *Kürdistan Tarihinde Dersim* (Istanbul: Zel Yayıncılık, 1994)

B. Ersanlı-Behar, *İktidar ve Tarih: Türkiye'de 'Resmi Tarih' Tezinin Oluşumu (1929–1937)* (Istanbul: Afa Yayınları, 1992)

M.S. Fırat, *Doğu İlleri Varto Tarihi* (Ankara: Milli Eğitim Basımevi, 1961)

I. Giritli, *Kürt Türklerinin Gerçeği* (Istanbul: Yeni Forum Yayıncılık, 1989)

J. Glasneck, *Türkiye'de Faşist Alman Propagandası* (Ankara: Onur Yayınları, Ankara)

M. Goloğlu, *Erzurum Kongresi* (Ankara: Nüve Matbaası, 1968)

Z. Gökalp, *Türkçülüğün Esasları* (Istanbul: Arkadaş Basımevi, 1939)

I. Göldaş, *Kürdistan Teali Cemiyeti* (Istanbul: Doz Yayınları, 1991)

Ş. Gözübüyük and Z. Zengin, *1924 Anayasası Hakkındaki Meclis Görüşmeleri* (Ankara: Balkanoğlu Matbaacılık, 1957)

Ş. Gözübüyük and S. Kili, *Türk Anayasa Metinleri* (Ankara: Ajans-Türk Matbaası, 1957)

I. İmset, *PKK, Ayrılıkçı Şiddetin 20 Yılı (1973–1993)* (Ankara: Turkish Daily News Yayınları, 1993)

N. Kutlay, *İttihat Terakki ve Kürtler* (Ankara: Beybun, 1992)

S. Kili, *Türk Devrim Tarihi* (Istanbul: Tekin Yayınevi, Istanbul, 1982)

M. Kocaoğlu, *Uluslararası İlişkiler Işığında Ortadoğu* (Ankara: Gnkur. Basımevi, 1995)

C. Kutschera, *Le Mouvement National Kurde* (Paris: Flammarion, 1979)

U. Mumcu, *Kürt Dosyası* (Istanbul: Tekin Yayınevi, 1993)

U. Mumcu, *Kürt-İslam Ayaklanması 1919–1925* (Istanbul: Tekin Yayınevi, 1992)

K. Öke, *Musul ve Kürdistan Sorunu 1918–1926* (Ankara: Türk Kültürü Araştırma Enstitüsü, 1992)

B. Oran, *Atatürk Milliyetçiliği: Resmi İdeoloji Dışı Bir İnceleme* (Ankara: Bilgi Yayınevi, 1990)

B. Oran, *'Kalkık Horoz': Çekiç Güç ve Kürt Devleti* (Ankara: Bilgi Yayınevi, 1996)

A. Öcalan, *Kürdistan Halk Savaşı ve Gerilla* (Köln: Wesanen Serxwebun Publications, 1991)

E. Özbudun, *Türkiye'de Sosyal Değişme ve Siyasal Katılma* (Ankara:Ankara Üniversitesi Hukuk Fakültesi Yayınları No. 363, 1975)

T. Parla, *Türkiye'de Siyasal Kültürün Resmi Kaynakları Cilt 3: Kemalist Tek-Parti İdeolojisi ve CHP'nin Altı Ok'u* (Istanbul: İletişim Yayınları, 1995)

PKK, Kürdistan Devriminin Yolu, Program (Köln: Serxwebun Yayınları, 1983)

S. Sonyel, *Türk Kurtuluş Savaşı ve Dış Politika I* (Ankara: Türk Tarih Kurumu Basımevi, 1973)

B.N. Şimşir (ed.), *İngiliz Belgeleriyle Türkiye'de 'Kürt Sorunu' (1924–1938)* (Ankara: Türk Tarih Kurumu, 1981)

T. Z. Tunaya, *Türkiye'de Siyasi Partiler* (Istanbul: Doğan Kardeş, 1952)

M. Tunçay, *Türkiye Cumhuriyeti'nde Tek Parti Yönetimi'nin Kurulması* (Ankara: Yurt Yayınları, 1981)

G.D. Tüfekçi, *Atatürk'ün Okuduğu Kitaplar* (Ankara: Türkiye İş Bankası Kültür Yayınları, 1983)

Türk İstiklal Harbi, IV ncu Cilt, Güney Cephesi (Ankara: Gnkur. Basımevi, 1966)

Türk İstiklal Tarihi VI ncı Cilt: İstiklal Harbinde Ayaklanmalar (1919–1921) (Ankara: Gnkur. Basımevi, 1974)

Türkiye Cumhuriyeti'nde Ayaklanamalar (1924–1938) (Ankara: Gnkur. Basımevi, 1972)

Türkiye İnsan Hakları Vakfı, *Olağanüstü Hal Bölgesi'nde Eğitim Raporu* (Ankara: 1994)

Türkiye Odalar ve Borsalar Birliği, *Doğu Sorunu: Teşhisler ve Tespitler* (Ankara: TOBB, 1995)

M. Van Bruinessen, *Kürdistan üzerine Yazılar* (Istanbul: Iletişim Yayınları, 1993)

H. Yıldız, *Fransız Belgelerinde Sevre-Lozan-Musul üçgeninde Kürdistan* (Istanbul: Koral, 1992)

20 Yüzyıl Ansiklopedisi, Vol.4 (Istanbul: Tercüman Gazetesi, 1990)

Articles in Other Languages

Y. Akçura, 'Üç Tarz-ı Siyaset', *Türkiye Günlüğü*, 31, Nov.–Dec. 1994

A. Aygan 'PKK Yapısı İdeolojisi ve İşleyiş', *Yeni Forum*, 190, (Aug. 1987)

M. Belge, 'Türkiye Işçi Partisi', *Cumhuriyet Dönemi Türkiye Asiklopedisi, Vol.8* (Istanbul: İletişim Yayınları, 1983)

A. E. Özsoy, I. Koç and A. Toros, 'Türkiye'nin Etnik Yapısının Ana Dil Sorularına Göre Analizi', *Nüfusbilim Dergisi/Turkish Journal of Population Studies*, 14, (1992)

Official Documents, Statistics, Texts and Collections of Official Documents in Other Languages

Doğruyol Partisi ile Sosyaldemokrat Halkçı Parti Arasında İmzalanan Ortak Hükümet Protokolü ve Ekleri, 19 Nov. 1991

İller İtibariyle Çeşitli Göstergeler (Ankara: Devlet Planlama Teşkilatı Yayınları, 1993)

İl ve Bölge İstatistikleri (Ankara: Devlet İstatistik Enstitüsü, 1993)

Milletvekili: Genel ve Cumhuriyet Senatosu üyeleri Yenileme Seçimi Sonuçları. 5 Haziran 1977 (Ankara: Başbakanlık, DIE, 1977)

Türkiye Büyük Millet Meclisi (TBMM) Gizli Celse Zabıtları 3, 4 (Ankara: Türkiye Iş Bankası Kültür Yayınları, 1985)

TBMM Tutanak Dergisi

Türkiye Büyük Millet Meclisi Zabıt Ceridesi

T.C. Anayasa Halkoylaması Sonuçları (Ankara: Devlet İstatistik Enstitüsü, 1983)
T.C. Resmi Gazete
Türkiye Gayri Safi Yurt İçi Hasılasının İller İtibariyle Dağılımı (Istanbul: Istanbul
   Sanayi Odası, 1988)
Türkiye İstatistik Yıllığı 1994 (Ankara: Devlet İstatistik Enstitüsü, 1995)
*Yürürlükteki Kanunlar Külliyatı, Başbakanlık Mevzuatı Geliştirme ve Yayın Genel
   Müdürlüğü* (Ankara: Başbakanlık Basımevi)
1965 Genel Nüfus Sayımı (Ankara: Devlet İstatistik Enstitüsü, 1969)

Conference Papers in Other Languages

A. Özer, 'Güneydoğu Anadolu Bölgesinde Göç; Sorunlar ve Çözümler' Paper
   presented at the Conference, *Düşünce Özgürlüğü ve Göç Sempozyumu*, 10–
   12 Dec., Ankara, 1994

Newspapers and Magazines in Other Languages

Aktüel
Aydınlık
Cumhuriyet
Evrensel Ekonomi
Hürriyet
Le Monde Diplomatique
Milliyet
Nokta
Özgür Ülke
Sabah
Ulus
Yeni Yüzyıl
2000'e Doğru

Index